Mediating the Nation:

News, Audiences and the Politics of Identity

UCL
PRESS

Mediating the Nation:

News, Audiences and the Politics of Identity

Mirca Madianou

UCL

PRESS

First published in Great Britain 2005 by UCL Press
An imprint of Cavendish Publishing Limited, The Glass House,
Wharton Street, London WC1X 9PX, United Kingdom
Telephone: + 44 (0)20 7278 8000 Facsimile: + 44 (0)20 7278 8080
Email: info@cavendishpublishing.com
Website: www.cavendishpublishing.com

Published in the United States by Cavendish Publishing
c/o International Specialized Book Services,
5824 NE Hassalo Street, Portland,
Oregon 97213-3644, USA

Published in Australia by Cavendish Publishing (Australia) Pty Ltd
45 Beach Street, Coogee, NSW 2034, Australia
Telephone: + 61 (2)9664 0909 Facsimile: + 61 (2)9664 5420
Email: info@cavendishpublishing.com.au
Website: www.cavendishpublishing.com.au

British Library Cataloguing in Publication Data
Madianou, Mirca
Mediating the Nation
1. Mass media – Social aspects
2. Consumption (Economics) – Social aspects
3. Identity (Psychology) and mass media
4. Mass media and anthropology
I. Title   302.2'3

Library of Congress Cataloguing in Publication Data
Data available
Hardback ISBN-10: 1-84472-029-2
Hardback ISBN-13: 978-1-844-72029-3
Paperback ISBN-10: 1-84472-028-4
Paperback ISBN-13: 978-1-844-72028-6

1 3 5 7 9 10 8 6 4 2

Typeset by Phoenix Photosetting, Chatham, Kent
Printed and bound in Great Britain

Cover illustration: Zafos Xagoraris, Building with Periscopes, 1999, Private Collection

Acknowledgments

During my research and writing of this book I have been privileged to have received support from a number of people and institutions. My first debt is to all those who participated in this study but who cannot be named for obvious reasons. I want to thank them for sharing their stories and parts of their everyday lives with me. I hope that what follows does justice to their experiences and realities.

Sonia Livingstone has followed the research reported in the book from its early stages and I am extremely grateful for her encouragement and constructive criticism. Daniel Miller has been a source of inspiration with his generosity and enthusiasm. I am very thankful to Michael Worton for generous support during my Mellon fellowship at UCL, which allowed me to write the book. I would also like to thank John Thompson at the Faculty of Social and Political Sciences and the fellows of Lucy Cavendish College at the University of Cambridge who have made me feel very welcome at my new intellectual home.

Discussions with Allen Abramson, Georgie Born, Richard Collins, Nick Couldry, Nicos Demertzis, Peter Lunt, Stelios Papathanassopoulos, Andreas Onoufriou, Maggie Scammell, Eugenia Siapera, Charles Stewart and the participants of the Media@LSE research seminar in the period 1998–2002 have helped me shape the ideas presented in the book. I am particularly thankful to Roger Silverstone for initiating and continuing a thought provoking dialogue and to Kevin Robins and Annabelle Sreberny who provided valuable feedback as examiners of the thesis on which this book is based.

My family and friends in Athens and London have made this project possible with their emotional support and intellectual stimulation. Many thanks to Bariş Celiloğlu for Turkish lessons and Zafos Xagoraris for providing the book cover. My brother George Madianos and my parents Dimitra Gefou-Madianou and Michael Madianos have been a source of invaluable support in this process – to them I dedicate the book. This book is also dedicated to the memory of my friend Serafim Petrakis.

Parts of chapters 5 and 7 have appeared in the *Journal of Ethnic and Migration Studies*, vol 31(3).

Contents

Contents

CHAPTER 1

INTRODUCTION

On 26 April 1999, thousands of people gathered in the central square of Athens for a concert, albeit a rather unusual one. People were holding flags of all sorts: Greek flags were prominent, often tied together with Serbian ones; there were also flags symbolising the Byzantine Empire, as well as flags of the Communist Party. Some people were also holding candles and posters with anti-military and anti-American slogans. On stage paraded over sixty of Greece's artists, mainly musicians, singers and actors. In the end they all sang together under the direction of Mikis Theodorakis, a famous Greek composer and public figure. The concert, which lasted five hours, was a peace concert against the NATO bombings in Kosovo and Serbia. It was co-organised by one of the private television channels and was broadcast through live links by almost all terrestrial channels.

Images like this were common in Greece throughout the 1990s during protest marches and rallies in defence of 'national rights'. The reader may be familiar with the large, well-attended rallies that took place during the Macedonia controversy in 1993.[1] Television was omnipresent in these events, sometimes not only broadcasting, but also co-organising them (as happened in the case of the peace concert mentioned above). It was through the observation of such events in Greek public life that the idea for this book was born. What role did the media play in the gathering of one million people in the centres of Athens and Thessaloniki in 1993?

This book investigates the relationship between media and identities in Greece. My interest in this topic stemmed from my observations of the resurgence of nationalism in Greece in the 1990s, and the deregulation and commercialisation of the Greek broadcasting system. These two issues are related as private television channels played a central role in orchestrating and broadcasting public events, as well as adding a sensationalist touch to the reporting of national issues during that period. Moreover, the chaotic broadcasting landscape, which caused deregulation and the proliferation of channels, led to the dominance of television in Greek public life. The Greek media system is characterised by what Papathanassopoulos has described as an excess of supply over demand:

> By the mid 1990s there were about 160 local, regional and national daily newspapers, as well as 800 popular and special interest magazine titles, 150 national and local television channels and 1,200 radio stations for a market of 11 million inhabitants. (1999: 381)

---

1   In the 1993 Athens rally 'For Macedonia', around one million people gathered. For a discussion of the Macedonian Conflict, see Danforth (1995) and Mouzelis (1994).

Television news featured prominently in the programme mix and created the phenomenon of wall to wall news. It was common for news broadcasts to last two – and in exceptional circumstances up to three – hours and one wonders what impact this might have had on public and everyday life.

My initial research question was whether the media, and television in particular, is a catalyst for belonging to the nation. How do viewers interpret what they see on their screens? What does it mean for their sense of nationhood? Does television provide some kind of 'social glue', binding people together, as the relevant literature suggests?

Popular perceptions about the relationship between media and identities often take media power for granted. I was confronted with such views during my fieldwork when, for example, the satellite dishes in the Turkish-speaking neighbourhood of Gazi were considered as the 'umbilical cord' that links the minority with the 'home' country, Turkey. Such views have gained prominence across Europe, particularly in relation to the use of satellite television by Muslim populations. In academia, theories about the relationship between media and culture have generally oscillated between two assumptions: on the one hand, there are theories that assume that the media play a powerful role in shaping cultures and identities, while on the other, there are those that contend that it is national, ethnic, or local cultures that shape media and their consumption.

In the above paradigms, identity seems to be taken for granted while culture is left under-theorised. Moreover, the problem with a media-centric approach is that foregrounding the role of the media from the start inevitably influences the conclusions of a study. In order to understand the relationship between media and identity it became increasingly clear that I had to start with identity. A historical perspective on identities in Greece revealed their changing and dynamic character through time. The awareness of the constructedness and changing character of identities in the Greek context emerged in stark contrast to the official discourses about the nation, which are found in the media and school textbooks. To ignore these historical trajectories and the diversity within the nation would be to start with a false assumption. Moreover, focusing on an isolated national case and its media emerged as problematic. Greek audiences do not rely solely on national news sources to become informed; they have access to a variety of resources, from global channels and the foreign press to the internet and their personal experiences through travelling, working or studying abroad. A wider – global – media structure needs to be taken into account.

Taking the constructedness and dynamism of identities as a starting point, I became increasingly interested in the different ways in which identities become reified and naturalised. Recognising that such constructions are ongoing, I decided to focus on the ways in which people articulate their identities and how they shift from open to closed discourses. In this context I became particularly interested in whether the media have any role to play in these shifts, from openness to closure and vice versa. Instead of asking whether the media catalyse a sense of belonging, I decided to ask what impact, if any, the media have on the ways people talk about themselves and the nation.

Thus, the initial research question – 'Is television a catalyst for belonging to the nation?' – needs to be rephrased to emphasise the interplay between identity and the media. The theoretical framework of mediation that is proposed in the book allows the dynamism and diversity, which the concept of culture contains, to emerge. Mediation involves following the circulation of meanings about culture and the nation in different media and non-media related contexts. This book argues that there is a need for a bottom-up perspective that will examine identities as lived and as performed. The juxtaposition of the bottom-up and the top-down approaches is part of the effort to point to the power of the media. In other words, to reply to the question: whether, and in what ways and contexts do the media influence identity discourses? What role do the media play in relation to inclusion and exclusion from public life?

This book explores how people of different cultural or ethnic backgrounds who live in Athens, namely the Greeks, the Greek Cypriots, the Turks, the Pomaks and the Roma,[2] articulate their identities, both in the context of media consumption and in relation to the news. Fieldwork took place from October 1998 to May 2001 and involved participant observation and interviews with seventy-two informants. The inclusion of minorities in this study was driven by the recognition that it is problematic to examine an increasingly multicultural society without taking into account its diversity.

The book also examines the news by focusing on the reporting of two events; the first involves the reporting of a relatively frequent incident between Greece and Turkey, which was reported as 'the violation of Greek airspace by Turkish planes during a joint military exercise of Greece and Cyprus' in October 1998. Such incidents have been common (even despite the recent rapprochement), and in that respect may be considered routine.

The second case study focuses on the reporting of an international crisis, the NATO offensive in Kosovo[3] and Serbia in the spring of 1999. The main reason that led me to consider the 'Kosovo crisis'– apart from its significant impact at a public level (for example, demonstrations and protests against the bombings became an everyday routine) – was that it introduced a local/global dimension in the analysis, allowing me to explore the ways in which viewers living in Greece articulate their identities, both in relation to the Greek and global media.

---

2   The Turkish, Roma and Pomak populations of Greece are officially recognized as the 'Muslim minority'. For a number of complex reasons detailed in Chapter 3 they are referred to here as Turkish-speaking.

3   Kosovo and Kosova are the respective Serbian and Albanian names of the province. The choice of name used is politically charged (as well as the choice between Kosovars or Kosovans, the names of the people of the province). In Greece, only the Serbian name was used. In the book I use the name Kosovo on the grounds that this has been the name most commonly used to refer to the conflict in the relevant literature (see, among others, Ignatieff 2000; European Journal of Communication, Special Issue on the reporting of the Kosovo conflict, September 2000).

DESCRIPTION OF THE BOOK

Chapter 2, after reviewing the dominant approaches for the study of the media/ identity relationship, proposes a bottom-up perspective that sees identities as lived and as performed. The perspective from below is then juxtaposed to a top-down approach, in order to establish whether the media influence any shifts in identity articulations, from openness to closure.

Chapter 3 provides a historical account of identities in the Greek context. Instead of a singular and homogenous Greek identity, this chapter highlights the diversity within the nation state and the different layers and experiences of identities that co-exist giving rise to different sets of discourses of identity and belonging. By focusing on some particular instances of recent Greek history, this chapter performs the additional function of introducing the *dramatis personae* of this book, namely the Greeks, Cypriots and the Turkish speakers who live in Athens, thus providing the context for the study.

Following the emphasis on a bottom-up perspective, Chapter 4 theorises audiences and media power. In particular, Chapter 4 aims to develop a working approach toward a theory of mediation (Couldry, 2000b; Silverstone, in press), drawing on developments in audience research and the emerging field of media anthropology. Media are understood as a process and media power is diffuse, extending beyond the point of contact between texts and audiences. The chapter proposes a holistic, ethnographic approach that takes into account not only consumption and reception, but also issues of access and availability, and personal experiences with journalists. At the same time the chapter also argues for the retaining of the notion of the text in the analysis of media and identity. Representation is still important in relation to identity articulations and in the investigation of processes of inclusion and exclusion, especially when ethnic minorities are concerned.

Chapter 5 maps out the media used by the informants. This chapter, however, is not only descriptive, but provides an empirically informed answer to the question of whether the media have an impact to the informants' identity discourses. Are identities shaped by technologies? Are technologies shaped by identities? Also, of course, how do all these relate to existing material and power structures? The focus of Chapter 5 is on the media as technologies, not as texts. As there are separate chapters on the news and its reception, this chapter can be seen to complement what follows as it provides the context in which the reception and the interpretation of the news takes place; but it also stands on its own as an exploration of the relationship between identities and the media as objects and technologies. In Chapter 5 I challenge the dominant view that media and identities are linked in a causal way. However, it emerges that the media create a common point of reference for some, which is experienced as exclusive by others. In interpreting these processes I draw on Barth's theory in *Ethnic Groups and Boundaries* (1969a) to argue that the media, through a number of practices, often raise symbolic boundaries or reinforce existing ones, thus playing an important role in the ways that people talk about themselves and the nation.

The fluidity of identities (albeit grounded in material conditions and limitations) explored in Chapter 5 is in sharp contrast to the news discourse about the nation discussed in Chapter 6. Drawing on the analysis of 473 news reports during two different periods, one period being during the routine reporting of Greek-Turkish relations and the other during the Kosovo conflict, the chapter discusses how the nation, the common 'we', is continually invoked both through the text and the form of the news. The analysis also takes into account the televisation of public rituals in the context of the news. By way of the Kosovo reports, Chapter 6 explores the global dimension of identity articulations. The Kosovo conflict, being an international crisis, inevitably introduces concerns about how Greece positions itself in the world and how it defines itself in relation to its others. The analysis shows how the conflict was nationalised and internalised and points out that the essentialism in the anti-American reports during the Kosovo crisis was also a reaction to the essentialist representation of the Balkans as a volatile and flammable area where 'anything can happen'.

Chapter 7 focuses on the viewers' reactions to, and interpretations of, the news reports analysed in Chapter 6. This chapter brings together the theoretical framework on identity discussed in Chapter 2 and the research on audiences (Chapter 4), in order to examine whether the news influences the ways people talk about the nation and their position within it. In particular, what happens to the rather open identity discourses identified in Chapter 5, when they come into contact with the dominant discourse about the nation analysed in Chapter 6. Do critical viewers contest the 'banal nationalism' (Billig, 1995) and the essentialist projection of the nation in the news? When do people become more essentialist about their own identities and those of others?

Discourses about the nation (through the news media) are not homogenous and uniform, but rather dynamic and relational. This does not mean that people become Greek and then Turkish; it rather implies that in some contexts people contest discourses about the nation and its representation in the media, while in some other contexts, especially when challenged externally, people rely on a more emotional framework that essentialises themselves and their others. This chapter is about competing definitions of the nation and in this context I draw on Herzfeld's concept of cultural intimacy (1996) to account for my informants' discursive shifts. Chapter 7, as well as Chapter 5, points to the power of the media to raise the boundaries for inclusion in, and exclusion from, public life. This is particularly relevant in the case of the Turkish speakers who, in other everyday contexts, express a more open discourse about their position in Athenian society.

The book argues that the media/identity relationship is not a causal one. Media consumption is a complex process that involves a number of parameters, material, social and individual. Although the media do not shape identities, they do contribute, through a number of practices, to the creation of symbolic communicative spaces. Such spaces are experienced as exclusive by some informants, suggesting the power of the media to determine the boundaries that affect practices and discourses about 'home' and 'belonging'. The book argues that essentialism produces essentialism. When informants reflected on their identities and place in society there was openness in their discourses. Conversely, when they were confronted with closure they often reverted to an 'us and them' binary scheme of thought. Such closure can have far reaching effects, taking identity politics into a vicious circle.

The book points to the pervasiveness of media power that is not only found at one level (the text, or the institutions), but rather at various interconnected levels. This has important theoretical and methodological consequences that media studies need to address. Here, we consider the media as a text and as a technology, people's direct experiences with the journalists and the media, and news reception. The book is a contribution to the theoretical developments towards a theory of mediation (Couldry 2000b; Silverstone in press) and media anthropology. What an anthropological perspective on the media can offer is insight to the subtlety and unpredictability that is involved in the processes of mediation.

RETHINKING IDENTITIES IN A MEDIATED WORLD

This chapter argues for a new direction in the theorisation of the relationship between media and identity in order to understand what role – if any – the media play in the articulation of identities. Existing theories on media and identity, regardless of whether they are situated in the nationalism or media literatures, seem to be divided according to the dichotomy between powerful media and weak identities, or alternatively, strong identities and weak media. Such dichotomies echo the oscillations in media theory between theories that privilege powerful media and those that argue for powerful audiences (Katz 1980; Morley 1992). Another common theme running through a number of theories concerned with the media/identity relationship is that they either privilege a top-down or a bottom-up approach. Theories that argue for powerful media most often adopt a top-down perspective; that is, they do not investigate empirically the nature of audiences and their identities as lived and as performed. On the other hand, theories that argue for powerful audiences and identities are grounded on audience research. In this chapter I argue that both these approaches are inadequate for they essentialise identities, culture and in some cases the media themselves. What is needed is a new way to think about these processes.

What have remained largely undertheorised in these approaches are the concepts of culture and identity themselves, which are often objectified. Underlying many theories concerned with the relationship between media and identities is the assumption that cultures are distinct and homogenous entities. Consequently, the world is seen as a collection of such entities, like exhibits in a museum or billiard balls on a global pool table, to paraphrase Wolf (1982: 6). Such an approach fails to conceptualise the fact that cultures – and identities – are processes rather than naturally occurring objects. The idea of a pristine culture, not only today, in the era of mobility and global transformations, but always, has been deeply flawed. To see culture in such a historical perspective means that the openness of cultures and their inherent syncretism as well as the existence of cultures within cultures is recognised, an approach that has gained increasing prominence in recent years (Carrithers 1992; Gupta and Ferguson 1992; Hall, S 1996 and 2000; Hannerz 1992; Said 1993; Wolf 1982).

In this context, a theoretical framework is needed that will allow the dynamism and diversity that the concept of identity contains to emerge. This chapter draws on anthropological theory of ethnicity and culture to argue for an approach that understands identities and cultures as performed and experienced, thus resisting reification. This entails the inclusion of a bottom-up perspective. The starting point is the diversity within the nation state and not an assumption about its – often fictive – unity and homogeneity. The juxtaposition of the bottom-up and the top-down approaches, or else, the vertical and the horizontal dimensions of communication, is part of the effort to point to the power of the media. In other words, to reply to the questions: whether, and in what ways do the media influence identity articulations? What role do the media play in relation to inclusion and exclusion from public life?

This chapter will begin with a discussion about the two dominant traditions for theorising identity and nationalism and then will move to a consideration of the media and how they affect these processes. By starting with identity, as Schlesinger (1987) has recommended, I aim to avoid the media-centrism found in a number of media studies. Indeed, identity is the starting and final point in this chapter: I will return to it after reviewing the theories concerned with the media/identity relationship, in order to make a case against the existing theoretical dichotomies and develop an approach that will capture the dynamism of the media/identity relationship.

DOMINANT PARADIGMS IN THEORISING IDENTITY AND THE NATION: PRIMORDIALISM AND MODERISM

Unsurprisingly, there is no such thing as a single theory of nationalism, for, as Calhoun has remarked, '[n]ationalism is a rhetoric for speaking about too many different things for a single theory to explain it' (1997: 21). Different disciplines and theories provide divergent definitions for identity, the nation and its origins and nationalism. There is a large distance between the work of Kedourie (1960), who considered nationalism as an inherently evil doctrine, and the writings of Smith (1986; 1991; 1995), who has argued that nations are the result of persisting ethnic identities. There are three interrelated concepts here – identity, nation and nationalism – all of which are understood and defined differently, depending on the perspective and the discipline of each author. In general, identity refers to the cultural realm, whereas nationalism refers to the political realm. I will resist a detailed definition of nation, nationalism and identity in this introductory remark, as the different approaches to be discussed understand these concepts in very different ways.

In general, two major traditions can be distinguished in theorising identity and nationalism, namely primordialism and modernism. Primordialists emphasise the ancient roots of nations and the fixity of identity as a quality given by birth. Conversely, modernist theories, also referred to as constructionist, situationalist or contextualist, emphasise the modern character of the nation state and the constructedness of identity. Of course, there are differences within these traditions, which have led some authors to identify more than two major approaches.

Primordialist theories

Primordialism is not a single theory, but rather an 'umbrella term' that contains a number of theories. According to Geertz primordial attachments stem as follows:

... from the 'givens' – or more precisely, as culture is inevitably involved in such matters, the assumed 'givens' – of social existence: immediate contiguity and kin connection mainly, but beyond them the givenness that stems from being born into a particular religious community, speaking a particular language, or even a dialect of a language, and following particular social practices. These congruities of blood, speech, custom, and so on, are seen to have an ineffable and at times overpowering, coerciveness in and of themselves ... (1973: 259)

The fact that Geertz stresses in his definition the 'assumed givens' has led authors to argue that he is in fact a constructionist rather than a primordialist (Goldmann *et al* 2000: 13; Ozkirimli 2000: 72–73). Nonetheless, what needs to be retained from Geertz's definition is the emphasis on 'the congruities of blood, speech and custom', which constitute the basic tenet of primordialist theories. Identity, ethnicity and culture are given prominent status in primordialist approaches as they legitimate the political existence of nations and their claims to territory and autonomy. For the primordialists, nations and ethnic identities precede the nation state. The nation is seen as a cultural community that has survived from time immemorial and finds its political recognition in its 'historical homeland' (Smith 1998: 22–23). Needless to say, such views are shared by nationalists themselves.

There are different theories that can be grouped under the primordialist category. The socio-biological approach examines the links between biological ties, kinship and ethnicity (see van den Berghe 1981). Perennialists emphasise the continuity of ethnic groups through time, but they differentiate themselves from primordialists in that they do not assert that ethnic differences are natural and given (see Armstrong 1982; Llobera 1994). For perennialists, like primordialists, nations are 'seamless wholes, with a single will and character' (Smith 1998: 23). Under the primordialist 'umbrella term', I also include the ethnosymbolist approach. Ethnosymbolists adopt a milder approach than the perennialists, while accepting one of the fundamental principles of modernism, that nations are modern phenomena. Nations are modern, ethnosymbolists argue, but they have their roots in primordial attachments from time immemorial. Smith, together with Hutchinson, the other main proponent of this approach, makes a point of distinguishing ethnosymbolism as a distinct school.[1] Although their approaches are synthetic, they are placed here within the broader primordial tradition as most of the research in ethnosymbolism focuses on the survival of primordial attachments and symbols[2] (see Smith 1986; 1999). Summing up, primordialists see ethnic differences and identities as natural and given; perennialists accept that there is continuity through time although differences are not necessarily given. Finally, ethnosymbolists accept the continuity of ethnic traits, but recognise their transformation through modernity.

---

1   Taxonomy is not clear-cut in this literature. For Smith and Hutchinson, Armstrong is a perennialist, while for Hutchinson, both Smith and Armstrong are 'ethnicists' (see Ozkirimli 2000: 168). Armstrong does not use the term ethnosymbolism himself (although his arguments are strikingly similar to those of Smith).

2   Breuilly, a modernist theorist himself, has described ethnosymbolism as a less radical version of primordialism (1996: 150).

Criticisms

The ethnic origins of nations rooted in antiquity and the primordial attachments that they entail are the only way for Smith to explain the readiness of people to sacrifice in the name of the nation (1986: 11; 1995: 7). This argument has been criticised for stealthily re-introducing an ahistorical, hitherto abandoned, perspective (Lekkas 1992: 103). In an article of his translated into Greek, Smith argues that the roots of the Greek nation and nationalism are located 'in elements from previous centuries that go back to the Ancient Greeks and their anti-Persian Panhellenism' (Smith 1993: 9). This approach, as some commentators have remarked, 'invalidates any sense of historicity and serious historical analysis' and for the contemporary Greek researcher 'it would mean a retreat to the Paparreghopoulos[3] era and the acceptance of the most extreme ideological manipulation of Greek history' (Kitromilides 1993: 15–16; for similar comments, see Aggelopoulos 1997: 43). As Eley and Suny have remarked:

> An ethnoreligious formation (such as the ancient Jews or the medieval Armenians) was not yet (nor could be) a modern nationality with its self-conscious sense of the value of ethnic, or secular cultural (as opposed to religious) traditions and with consequent political claims to territory, autonomy, or independence ... (1996: 11)

In short, as the same authors note, 'earlier histories of classes and nations should be read not simply as prehistories, but as varied historical developments whose trajectories remained open' (1996: 11).[4] In this context, to speak of a historic homeland to which nations are entitled to becomes problematic both historically and politically.

Such arguments are often the result of a terminological chaos that one encounters in the ethnosymbolist camp, as a number of authors have remarked (see Ozkirimli 2000: 183). Ethnicity and nation are sometimes used interchangeably. O'Leary has remarked that:

> It is not too surprising to find nationalism in the 1500s if one grants the term such empirical range. Most of those who discuss nations before nationalism are in fact establishing the existence of cultural precedents [...] which are subsequently shaped and re-shaped by nationalists in pursuit of nation-building. (1996: 90)

The strongest objection, however, to all primordialist approaches to identity is their adverse political consequences. This becomes obvious in the context of recent conflicts and wars that are labelled as 'ethnic conflicts'. Underlying the term ethnic conflict is the assumption that the causes of the conflict are based on

---

3   Constantine Paparreghopoulos is the 19th century historian credited with the writing of the official history of the Greek nation that argued for an undisrupted continuity from Ancient Greece, through Byzantium, to modern times.

4   Greeks in the classical period were not – and could not be – a nation in the modern sense of the term. Whatever their degree of linguistic cohesion, Greeks did not constitute a political entity making claims to self-administration and statehood. In fact, ancient Greek cities were fighting against each other as vehemently as they did against the Persians.

ethnic differences. Consequently, conflicts are seen as inevitable since their causes lie in what are considered 'natural', and thus insurmountable, ethnic differences. Another consequence of such an ahistorical approach is that 'by reducing the social and economic realities and the complex historical causes that underlie and prolong these conflicts to "ethnicity" de-politicises them' (Seaton 1999: 43). Such explanations collude with the protagonists' nationalistic interpretations of history and often make their authors complicit in the human suffering they legitimate. Such views, which seem to be gaining prominence,[5] have been expressed by Huntington and his controversial theory in the *Clash of Civilisations* (1996), Kaplan (1994) and Moynihan (1993). Kaplan, who in his book *Balkan Ghosts* (1994) described the wars in former Yugoslavia as the result of innate hatreds, is thought to have dissuaded the Clinton administration from its initial interventionist line in Bosnia (Allen 1999: 27). Huntington (1996) argued that the world is made up of seven inherently different civilisations,[6] with rigid ethnic and cultural divisions that produce unavoidable and insoluble conflicts. According to Huntington, democracy is the creation of Western civilisation and cannot be transplanted into other civilisations.

The problem with such approaches is that they have direct political and material consequences for the lives of the people that they describe. At a more abstract level, primordialist approaches fail to capture the changing and often contradictory character of identities through time. By stressing the given and fixed nature of identity they sit uncomfortably close to theories that have privileged race and biological differences. The school of thought that developed partly as a response to these limitations was that of modernism, or constructionism.

Modernism

Modernism is not a homogenous tradition. The common denominator in modernist theories is that, contrary to the beliefs of primordialists, the assertion that nations are modern phenomena. If, for primordialists, identity precedes the nation state, for the modernists it is the other way round. Modernists make this argument in varying degrees, as will be discussed below. In general, however, it can be argued that in modernist theory emphasis is placed on the nation as a political entity and not on the cultural traits that primordialists focus on. Moreover, underlying the work of many modernists (and this is another significant difference with the primordialists) is the assumption that there will be an inevitable decline of the nation state and national identities. As Hobsbawm graphically put it, 'the owl of Minerva which brings wisdom, said Hegel, flies out at dusk. It is a good sign that it is now circling round nations and nationalism' (1992: 192).

---

5   Primordialist discourses about identity have proliferated in the media and public life in recent years. Their use has been heightened after 11 September 2001, and in the context of the ongoing conflict between Israelis and Palestinians. The popularity of such discourses is explained because they provide a simple explanation for conflicts and other complex social problems, such as crime.

6   Namely, the Sinic, Japanese, Hindu, Islamic, Orthodox, Western and Latin American.

Different theories emphasise different aspects in accounting for the emergence of nations and nationalism. In general, three broad approaches can be discerned in the modernist tradition (although this is not an exhaustive categorisation), namely the economic, the political and the socio-cultural. Some authors have linked the rise of nationalism and national identities to economic factors and the economic interests of individuals (Hechter 1975). Others have emphasised the role of power (through processes involving the state and its institutions, the role of the elites and war) for the emergence and maintenance of nationalism (Giddens 1985; Mann 1993). The socio-cultural perspective is exemplified in the work of Gellner (1983), who argued that nations and nationalism are the result of a 'high culture', which in turn is linked to modernisation and industrialisation.

Gellner understood nationalism as the political ideology resulting from the advent of industrialisation and the complex division of labour it entailed (Gellner 1983). Industrialised societies called for a more sophisticated division of labour provided by a homogenised education system. Education was the major conveyor of collective identity, or nationhood. According to Gellner, nationalism is primarily a political principle, which holds that the political and the national unit should be congruent (1983: 1). Importantly, the political principles of nationalism appear as if they were natural.

Two other influential authors, who draw upon a Marxist perspective as well, can be included in the broader socio-cultural category. Hobsbawm holds that nationalism is an invented ideology that, as a false consciousness, legitimates the capitalist order (1992; see, also, Hobsbawm and Ranger 1983). Cultural traditions are not given, but are invented and manipulated in order to legitimate the political dimension of nationalism (claims to autonomy and territory). According to Hobsbawm, 'nations do not make states and nationalism, but the other way around' (1992:10).[7]

Anderson sees nationalism largely as the consequence of the convergence of capitalism and print technology (1991). In his seminal book, *Imagined Communities* (1991 [1983]), Anderson understood the nation state as a modern construct, an imagined community, and nationalism as a cultural artefact (1991: 4). According to Anderson, nations are imagined political communities because '... the members of even the smallest nation will never know most of their fellow members, meet them, or even hear of them, yet in the minds of each lives the image of their communion' (1991: 6). Moreover, Anderson says that:

> The nation is imagined as limited because even the largest of them ... have finite boundaries, beyond which lie other nations. It is imagined as sovereign, ... as well as a community, or a fraternity, which masks the actual inequality and exploitation that may prevail in each. (1991: 6–7)

---

7   Of course, the nation/state relationship is a complex one. Calhoun has argued for a dialectical process and remarked that 'it would be a mistake to imagine that either state formation or ethnicity could provide a master variable accounting for the whole rise and character of modern nationalism'. (1997: 66)

Criticisms

Different modernist theories have invited different criticisms. Overall, modernist theories have been criticised of being reductionist as they often emphasise one aspect, over many others, in the explanation of the emergence of nations. Gellner (1983) has been criticised for placing too much emphasis on industrialism. Mouzelis and O'Leary have pointed out that in some cases, such as the Balkan states, nationalism emerged before industrialisation (Mouzelis 1998: 158; O'Leary 1998: 73). Another criticism on which many authors converge is Gellner's functionalism: 'it very often seemed as if he means to say that industrial society's need for social and linguistic homogeneity was the cause of nationalism' (Hall J 1998:8; and for a detailed discussion of this point, see Hall J 1998a; O'Leary 1998; Laitin 1998).

Another weak point of modernist theories is that they fail to explain the spell of nationalism, or else, the appeal of nationalism to the extent that people are prepared to sacrifice their lives for the nation. This is the criticism commonly repeated by ethnosymbolists (Smith 1998). This limitation is explained by the fact that modernists have ignored the perspective from below, the ways identities are experienced and performed. By ignoring the perspective from below they cannot confirm any assumption about the spell of nationalism, nor about the contestation of nationalism.

The emphasis on a top-down perspective also implies that all nationalisms and identities are the same, 'cut from the same European cloth' (Herzfeld 1996: 10), thereby underestimating the complexity and historical specificity of the different empirical cases. Nationalism appears as a monolithic force that has homogenised populations in a uniform way, regardless of historical, economic and social conditions. The relationship between the top-down and bottom-up perspectives is central to this study and will be discussed later in this chapter, together with the issue of essentialism.

Primordialists and modernists understand the role of the media in very different ways. It has to be noted, however, that there is a striking absence, even in the recent proliferation of writings on nationalism and identities, of analysis concerned with the role of the media. This is not surprising in the case of primordialists (or perennialists, or ethnosymbolists for that matter); if identities are given by birth and the nations are rooted in an ancient past, what role can the media possibly play? This absence is more conspicuous in the case of modernist writers who, apart from a few notable exceptions, have failed to address the media as possible actors in the processes of identity and nation building. Thus, the following section will focus on those few modernist theories and authors who have considered the media in their analysis. Such examples are Deutsch (1966 [1953]), Gellner (1983), Anderson (1991 [1983]) and Hobsbawm (1992). This approach is also known as the 'social communication approach', drawing its name from Deutsch's theory (1966 [1953]). Along with nationalism theories, the contributions of media theorists will be discussed as there are many similarities among them.

MEDIA AND IDENTITY: STRONG MEDIA/WEAK IDENTITIES

The approach that privileges powerful media is so prevalent that it is almost enjoying a consensus.[8] The majority of media theories of identity seem to fall in this category, although there are differences of degree to the power granted to the media. Nationalism theorists in the modernist vein are also discussed in this section. This choice perhaps requires some explanation as none of the authors involved have argued that the media, print or electronic, are solely responsible for the spread of nationalism. Gellner (1983) and Hobsbawm (1992) only make short references to the power of the media, which they consider, among other forces, as disseminators of a common culture and language. Anderson (1991 [1983]) is a case on his own as he does pay considerable attention to the media, although he still sees them as part of a wider process.

Nationalism theory and the media

Deutsch is the first author who took the role of communication into account in his theory of nationalism. He developed what is known as social communication theory; for Deutsch, it is social communication, the shared cultural and communicative practices, that strengthens the identity of a group, creates boundaries and thus makes the nation state possible (Deutsch 1966 [1953]). As Schlesinger has remarked, 'Deutsch's underlying concept of social communication … lives on strongly, mostly half-recognised at best, in … Gellner's *Nations and Nationalism*' (Schlesinger 2000b: 21). As discussed previously, Gellner attributed central importance to the role of culture in the spread of nationalism. Through the education system an elite, high culture became available to the masses, who started recognising themselves as part of the same nation. In this context, Gellner makes a fleeting argument about the role of the media which, interestingly, echoes McLuhan (1964) as he writes that media matter in nationalism not for what they say, but for what they are. This is perhaps surprising given that Gellner lived through the Second World War and its consequences and one would expect to find in his writings a concern with propaganda.

> The media do not transmit an idea that happens to have been fed into them. … it is the media themselves, the pervasiveness and importance of abstract, centralised one to many communication, which itself automatically engenders the core idea of nationalism quite irrespective of what in particular is being put into the specific messages transmitted. The most important and persistent message is generated by the medium itself, by the role which such media have acquired in modern life. The core message is that the language and style of the transmissions is important … what is actually said matters little. (Gellner 1983: 127)

---

8   The various approaches that address the relationship between media and identity are summarised in Table 1:1 at the end of this chapter. As inevitably happens with all summaries, this mapping cannot do justice to all the nuances present in the theoretical approaches. It is meant as an attempt to compare the two dominant paradigms in the relationship between the media and identity with the approach that this book adopts, which is discussed in the two final sections of this chapter.

A similar argument is made by Anderson (1991 [1983]). Anderson is one of the writers who elaborated the role of the print media and their contribution to the emergence of nationalism. He saw 'the convergence of capitalism and print technology' as the catalyst for the emergence and consolidation of imagined community, which 'in its basic morphology set the stage for the modern nation' (Anderson 1991: 46). For Anderson the print media provided the social 'glue' that made the nation possible. Print capitalism allowed for a simultaneous mediated communication across the nation state. People all over the country would read the same newspapers or novels and recognise themselves as part of an imagined community. This simultaneity, made possible by the media, gave 'a hypnotic confirmation of the solidity of a single community, embracing characters, authors and readers ...' (1991: 27). Print capitalism is also closely linked to the standardisation of languages and the formalisation of education. People have to speak and read the same language in order to read the same paper and novel.

It is easy to misinterpret Anderson's argument as a technological determinist one. However, this would not do justice to his position as Anderson emphasises print capitalism, that is the mass production of books and newspapers, as industrial commodities (1991: 34, 46), and not just print technology, in the spread of nationalism. Moreover, in his most recent work, Anderson (1998 and 2001) sees the development of new technologies as enabling what he calls 'long distance nationalism' (2001: 42). New technologies do not undermine nationalism in favour of a global, homogenous society, as a technological determinist approach would argue, but rather rework and redefine nationalistic politics and attachments in a global context.

Anderson's theory is speculative. Indeed, most theories in the modernist vein do not focus on empirical research from below. By adopting a top-down perspective, they assume a common identity for all the people that they investigate. In a somewhat ironic way, modernist theory, which started as a reaction to the essentialism of primordial theories, ends up reifying identity itself. Nations are the products of a top-down process whereby an elite discourse is taken up by people at a local level. Such a perspective ignores that people might contest the nation and its official ideology and leaves open the question of how people come to embrace the official discourse.

Hobsbawm (1992), a modernist himself, has criticised other writers in the same vein, particularly Gellner, for ignoring a bottom-up approach. Although he does not develop one himself, his understanding of the role of the media is indicative of his interest in the lived experience of the nation. Like Gellner, Hobsbawm does not elaborate the role of the media. but he does consider them as one of the significant forces that have shaped nationalism and identity in the 20th century. Hobsbawm observed that what the media achieved, apart from disseminating and in some extreme cases exploiting political ideologies, is to link the public and private worlds by making national symbols part of people's everyday lives. Media have thus managed to break down the traditional divisions between the national public sphere and the private lives of citizens (Hobsbawm 1992: 142). It is because of the media and their rituals, such as the royal broadcast instituted in 1932, that the British royal family evolved into 'a domestic as well as a public icon of national identification' (Hobsbawm 1992: 142).

Media studies: strong media/weak identities

As noted earlier, theories developed within media studies that have been concerned with the relationship between media and identities seem to follow the swings of the powerful media/weak media pendulum. There are two main assumptions that underlie most theories: either that powerful media shape weak identities, or that weak media are shaped by powerful identities. It should be noted, however, that the former assumption has been more prominent while the latter was often developed as a reaction to the former.

The research that argues that the media plays a catalytic role in forming and maintaining national, ethnic and cultural identities is not homogenous. There are, in fact, many differences among the various studies, which will be unpacked in this section. There are theories that focus on the role of media in the processes of nation formation (Eisenstein 1979; Innis 1951; McLuhan 1964; Martin-Barbero 1993) and globalisation (McLuhan 1964; Meyrowitz 1985), while others focus on nation maintenance and reproduction (Billig 1995; Morley and Brunsdon 1999; Scannell 1989). The former theories tend to focus on the media as technologies, while the latter focus more on the form or content of the media. Of course, these distinctions are not clear-cut and often theories draw on more than one tradition. Thus, for instance, the proponents of the cultural imperialism thesis examine both the sheer presence and quantity of (North American) media and the content of these particular media when arguing about the emergence and sustenance of cultural homogenisation. These arguments also have political and practical implications as they are often associated with official policies about culture, media and representation.

Strong technologies/weak identities: technological determinism

For medium theorists, language has been a focal point linking identity and the media. Eisenstein saw national consciousness and culture as a result of the standardisation of vernaculars through printing (1979: 117). She even considered the media more pivotal than religion to the rise of nationalism. McLuhan (1987 [1964]), Innis (1951) and Ong (1967) have considered nationalism as related to print media mainly through the standardisation of language. McLuhan has famously characterised typography as the architect of nationalism (1987 [1964]: 172).

For McLuhan the media shape the forms of communities that people have. If typography was the architect of nationalism, then electronic media would create a 'global village' (1987 [1964]). Similar arguments have been made by a second generation media theorist, Meyrowitz, who has argued that electronic media have altered the significance of time and space for social interaction. Physical presence is not a prerequisite for social experience as information can travel instantly across great distances. 'As a result', Meyrowitz notes, 'where one is has less and less to do with what one knows and experiences.' (1985: viii).

The advent of new technologies has been considered by a number of authors to be the driving force which creates infinite possibilities for people's identities (inter alia see Turkle 1996; Poster 1995). Although the arguments here are not about homogenisation, technology is granted an omnipotent status, driving social and personal changes in a relentless manner. Such arguments are part of what Robins and Webster have termed technological utopianism (1999: 67) and the 'ideology of technoculture' (1999).

Strong technologies/weak identities: phenomenology

In a similar vein, although more grounded in media history and phenomenology and less technological determinist, Martin-Barbero has stressed the key role of the mass media in the emergence of collective identities in Latin America (1988; 1993). He has argued that 'film in many countries and radio in virtually all countries gave the people of the different regions and provinces their first taste of the nation' (1993: 164). It was only through mass culture that the political idea of the nation could be transformed into the daily experience and feeling of nationhood. Mexican films in the 1930s to the 1950s formed Mexicans into a 'national body', 'not in the sense of giving them a nationality but in the way they experienced being a single nation', by seeing 'themselves' on screen (1993: 166).

In the British context, Scannell and Cardiff have advanced similar arguments in their social history of the British Broadcasting Corporation (BBC) (1991). Scannell has even argued that public service broadcasting provides the space for a contemporary public sphere (1989). According to Scannell, public service broadcasting has contributed unobtrusively to the democratisation of everyday life. By placing political, religious, civic, cultural events and entertainments in a common domain, public life was equalised in a way that had never been possible before (1989: 136).

> ... Consider the FA Cup Final, the Grand National or Wimbledon. All these existed before broadcasting, but whereas previously they existed only for their particular sporting publics they became, through radio and television, something more. Millions now heard or saw them who had direct interest in the sports themselves. The events became, and have remained, punctual moments in a shared national life. Broadcasting created, in effect, a new national calendar of public events (Scannell 1989: 140–41).

Yet one might ask how 'public' or, in the case of the BBC, how British the public sphere that Scannell describes is. It seems that, in his example, 'British' is conflated with 'English', overlooking the other nations, or ethnic minorities who are citizens of the UK. Such a perspective implies a national homogeneity, the 'inclusive and extensive sociability' as Scannell calls it (1989: 136), which may not exist. As Morley (2000) has observed, to think of broadcasting as a common and singular public sphere, as Scannell does, ignores the fact that all public spheres are inevitably exclusive. 'By the very way ... a programme signals to members of some groups that it is designed for them and functions as an effective invitation to their participation in social life, it will necessarily signal to members of other groups that it is not for them.' (Morley 2000: 111)[9]

---

9   These criticisms echo the criticisms that Habermas' theory of the public sphere (1989) has received, pointing to the fact that all public spheres, starting from the ideal type, are inevitably exclusive (see chapters in Calhoun (1992)).

Textual determinism, national reproduction and identity maintenance

An influential study on the relationship between nationalism and the media was developed by Billig, who put forward an argument for what he calls *banal nationalism* and which focuses on the reproduction of nationalism in the established nations, that is 'the states which have confidence in their own continuity, and that, particularly, are part of what is conventionally described as the West' (1995: 8). Through his analysis of the national press, Billig identifies the routine and familiar forms of nationalism – banal nationalism – which contribute to identity maintenance.

> In the established nations there is a continual flagging, or reminding, of nationhood.
> … However, this reminding is so familiar, so continual, that it is not consciously
> registered as reminding. The metonymic image of banal nationalism is not a flag
> which is being consciously waved with fervent passion; it is the flag hanging
> unnoticed on the public building. (1995)

This ideological reproduction of nationalism 'can still call for ultimate sacrifices' (1995), and most importantly can construct the way 'we' perceive the 'others'. Perhaps the ultimate power of nationalism is that it is naturalised to the extent that it becomes invisible.

Arguments about the daily reproduction of nationalism have been made by Morley and Brunsdon in their *Nationwide Television* study (1999). In the introduction to a recent re-publication of the 1978 study, the authors, drawing on Anderson, argue that *Nationwide* and other programmes that succeeded it in the same vein (such as *This Morning*), are one of the sites in which the '"horizontal camaraderie" that is national identity is constructed and reconstituted daily' (1999: 12). They describe how, in *This Morning*, a map of England's outline fills the screen, with little illuminated points showing where the viewers call from, thereby enabling the imagining of the nation as a collection of different regions and cities (1999: 12–13).

The work by Dayan and Katz in *Media Events* (1992) is another important contribution to our understanding of how television can perform rituals that enhance a sense of belonging to a nation. In contrast to Billig's 'banal reminding of nationhood', Katz and Dayan argue that it is through the broadcasting of special occasions, what they call the 'high holidays of mass communication' (1992: 1), that the sense of collective identity is heightened. The banal reproduction of nationalism (Billig 1995) and the celebration of the nation through the festive viewing of media events (Dayan and Katz 1992) are not contradictory, but can occur in parallel. One of the aims of this study is to examine their interrelationship and, more importantly, to ground this in empirical evidence with audiences.

Criticisms

The main criticism of the aforementioned studies is that they do not ground their assumptions on empirical research at a local level, thus leaving their assumptions largely unsubstantiated. Some of the above theories, particularly medium theories, are speculative and have no empirical confirmation. When they are tested, they have favoured a top-down perspective, focusing mainly on textual or formal analysis (Billig 1995; Morley and Brunsdon 1999; Dayan and Katz 1992). Scannell's phenomenological approach falls in the same category (1989; 1996). The lack of empirical confirmation about the effects of these processes on audiences explains why the theories' assumptions about homogeneity are often contradicted by empirical realities; as Waisbord has noted, 'the distribution of media throughout large territories has not always fostered cultural homogeneity.' (1998: 382) Moreover, culture and identity are treated as complete entities. When global forces are taken into account they are, in turn, homogenising and monolithic. However, such a perspective ignores the fact cultures have always been based on exchanges and fusions.

Another criticism of media theories is that they imply a transmission model of communication, taking us back to contested models, such as the hypodermic needle models. Media are powerful, identities are weak. This happens, paradoxically, as questions about culture and identity fall, almost by definition, in the ritual or cultural model of communication (cf Carey 1989). Indeed, many authors explicitly identify themselves with the ritual or cultural model of communication, only to offer conclusions that are based upon a transmission model. Such cases are the writings of medium theorists who write within a historical perspective. The determinism in their approach, however, is openly suggesting a linear model that is not far from the hypodermic needle models of media effects. Perhaps conclusions are predetermined from the onset as the research questions foreground the role of the media.

Such criticisms, however, should not lead us to jettison these theories altogether. Although the approaches that favour strong media may not capture identity in its complexity, they offer a number of important insights that need to be investigated empirically. One element that is common to most of the above approaches, whether they favour technologies or texts, is that the media enabled the merging of the hitherto distinct public and private spheres. Media may have made a language available to people enabling them to think and talk about the nation. This, of course, can only be investigated empirically from a bottom-up perspective. This assumption will be incorporated in the synthetic approach proposed here. Moreover, the modernist perspective in which they are grounded is the prerequisite for all current developments in the identity literature. In this chapter I argue that the assumptions suggested by the modernist tradition should be investigated by focusing on empirical research with audiences, and answers to questions such as: is banal nationalism actually reproduced as Billig claims it to be? and, do media events bring the nation together?

WEAK MEDIA/STRONG IDENTITIES

The study at the centre of the 'strong identity' paradigm is the *Export of Meaning*, which was intended as a response to the media imperialism thesis and concomitant fears of cultural homogenisation. Liebes and Katz studied the reception of *Dallas* among different ethnic groups in Israel, as well as with

American and Japanese audiences (1993). *Dallas* was widely considered *par excellence* the product of American cultural imperialism in the 1980s. The study showed that audiences appropriated the programme in different ways according to their ethnic and cultural background. For example, Israeli Arabs and Moroccan Jews emphasised kinship relations, while Russian émigrés saw characters as manipulated by the writers and producers of the programme. Kibbutz members and American viewers took a critical view – but interpreted the programme in psychological terms, as an ongoing saga of interpersonal relations and intrigue. Conversely, the Japanese audiences found it difficult to deal with *Dallas'* inconsistencies. This was, according to the authors, a reason why *Dallas* failed in Japan.

Despite the importance of this study in raising doubts about the homogenising forces of Western popular culture, one issue needs to be considered. It seems that the authors argue that people interpret *Dallas* in particular ways *because* they are Israelis, Californians or Japanese. Such an approach glosses over other parameters that also shape media reception, such as gender, age, class and the text itself. By attributing explanatory power to cultural difference, culture is reified and taken for granted, instead of being something that needs to be explained itself. A quote from the book illustrates these points:

> The two more traditional groups – Arab and Moroccan Jews – prefer linearity. They retell the story in a modified Proppian form. They select the action-oriented subplot for attention, defining a hero's goals and his adventures in trying to achieve them. … The Russians … ignore the story line in favour of exposing the overall principles which they perceive as repeated relentlessly, and which in their opinion, have a manipulative intent. Like the Arab Moroccans, their retellings are closed and deterministic, but the ideological force is ideological rather than referential. … Americans and kibbutzniks tell the story psychoanalytically. … Their retellings are open, future oriented, and take into account the never-ending character of the soap opera. (Liebes and Katz 1993: 80–81)

It seems that in the *Export of Meaning* differences in interpretations are grounded in ethnicity and culture, with no further analysis of how they themselves are shaped and determined by other factors. This might be an unintentional consequence of the study, but the problem with such arguments becomes salient in the context of identity politics. Is the suspicion that Russian viewers express about the meaning of *Dallas*, an inherent Russian quality? Are Arab and Moroccan Jews inherently 'traditional'? Note that the term 'traditional' often carries a negative meaning associated with backward. As Harindranath has noted, 'the modern-traditional dichotomy was intrinsic to the values system which … supported the creation of a hierarchy of cultures and races during colonialism' (2000: 151). This criticism is not to deny that there *were* differences among the groups in question, but rather to question the way these differences are accounted for. Explanations that rely solely on culture or ethnicity sometimes sit uncomfortably close to perspectives that favour race or biological differences. In other words, by attributing explanatory power to culture, a term that is not thoroughly theorised in *The Export of Meaning*, other numerous (political, social and economic) factors that shape the experience of being an Arab, a Jew or an American are neglected. Although the *Export of Meaning* has assumed a paradigmatic status as a response to the limitations of the theories that favour a top-down perspective, it in fact reproduces some of the same shortcomings.

GLOBAL – LOCAL DIALECTIC AND TRANSNATIONAL MEDIA

The way culture and identity have been theorised in the previous examples confirms Schlesinger's comment that in media studies identity often functions as a residual category (1987: 233). However, a new generation of studies drawing on recent theories of globalisation has stressed the dialectic relationship between local (cultures) and the global (media), without privileging either of the two. Examples include the studies by Abu-Lughod (1989 and 1993), Miller (1992) and Sreberny-Mohammadi and Mohammadi (1994). Studies on diasporic and transnational audiences also fall into this category (Gillespie 1995; Hargreaves and Mahjoub 1997; Aksoy and Robins 2000; Robins and Aksoy 2001). In these studies globalisation is understood not as homogenisation, but as the intensification of the relationship between the global and the local (Thompson 1995), or as the intensification of global interconnectedness (McGrew 1992: 62).[10] These studies echo Stuart Hall's writings on identity as an ongoing process that always remains incomplete (1992: 287).

In her fieldwork among the Bedouins of Western Egypt, Abu-Lughod observed that the advent of media technologies, namely tape recorders, radio and television, did not cause social relations to atrophy as had been feared, but rather enhanced sociability as people gathered to listen to the radio or watch television (1989: 8). The impact of media technologies on social relations was that they brought about 'the mixing of the sexes and the muting of age hierarchies' as people watched programmes together (1989). Apart from this 'democratising effect' of television, tape recorders enhanced cultural creativity, as they revitalised the fading poetry reciting tradition, when Bedouins discovered that they could tape themselves, a practice that eventually led one of them to pop stardom (1989: 10). Finally, for many Bedouin women Egyptian soap operas were emancipatory as they gave them access to 'stories of other worlds', hence coming into dialogue with the local culture (1989; 1993). Television's central importance is that it brings a variety of vivid non-local experiences into the most local of situations, the home. Similarly, Miller observed the local appropriation of a US soap opera, the *Young and the Restless*, in Trinidad. Trinidadians interpreted the soap opera through the key for Trinidadian culture, the term 'bacchanal', which connotes scandal, confusion and truth (Miller 1992: 170–76).

Sreberny-Mohammadi and Mohammadi (1994) observed, in the context of the Iranian revolution, that it was small media[11] that led to the big revolution in the

---

10   Similarly, Tomlinson defines globalisation as the rapidly developing and ever-densening network of interconnections and interdependences that characterise modern social life (1999: 2). Giddens defines globalisation as the dialectic between the global and the local, that is the oppositional tendencies between local involvements and globalising tendencies (1991: 22, 242).

11   The authors define small media as alternative, participatory media (1994: 20–21).

late 1970s. Small media promoted an indigenous identity and created opportunities for participation, which were oppositional to the autocratic state and its mass media (1994: 193). As the authors note, 'the greatest irony was that the theocratic state then imposed religious identity against the expression of all other identities, and severely limited political and communications participation.' (1994) This work exposes the complex negotiation of identities by showing how religion and religious media were invested with one set of ideological connotations in one moment of political struggle and 'reinvested with completely the opposite connotations at a subsequent, but differently defined, political moment' (Sreberny 2000a: 109). Thus, as Sreberny observed, while the veil was a sign of resistance under the Shah's regime, it became a sign of oppression at another point in time (2000a: 109). Such observations suggest that identities and their symbols need to be understood in a dynamic way that takes into account their historical and political context.

In a similar vein, a number of studies on diasporic or ethnic minority media have managed to overcome some of the aforementioned problems of linearity and determinism. Of course, studies on media and migration do not form a homogenous literature. For instance, Ogan (2001) has argued that satellite television from Turkey is impeding the assimilation of Turks in Amsterdam, directly reverting to the strong media-weak identities paradigm, this time with political consequences as she confirms the fears of conservative politicians and thinkers about the non-assimilation of immigrants (cf Hutmeiyer cited in Aksoy and Robins 2000).

There are a number of helpful insights in this literature that can be applied to the present study. Several studies have argued against the homogeneity of immigrant communities and their monolithic consumption and use of the media. Gillespie (1995) and Hargreaves and Mahjoub (1997) have observed significant differences among different generations of immigrants. Similarly, in her study of Iranians living in London, Sreberny has observed not only generational and gender divisions, but also those relating to political factionalism, waves of migration, and internal linguistic and ethnic differentiation (2000b: 195).

Robins and Aksoy have argued convincingly against the fictive unity through which immigrant groups are often understood (2000 and 2001). Drawing from their fieldwork among Turkish-speaking groups in London, they have stressed that media consumption is not determined ethnically, but, rather, socially. Turkish television culture is ordinary, they argue, thus countering fears about the growth of Islamic fundamentalism through Turkish media that some authors have advocated (cf Hutmeiyer, cited in Aksoy and Robins, 2000). Turkish-speaking viewers move across cultures and are more cosmopolitan than the sedentary autochthonous audiences (Robins, 2000: 294). Given their findings, they argue for a shift of focus from 'identity' and 'community', to 'experience' and 'resources' in an attempt to find a new and more pertinent language to describe processes of migration, belonging and media consumption (Robins and Aksoy 2001: 705).

Recent studies on media consumption in the context of diasporas and immigrant communities have contributed to overcoming a number of the previously mentioned limitations. First of all, these studies are grounded in much-needed empirical work that takes a bottom-up perspective into account. Secondly, most of these studies have emphasised the changing and dynamic nature of identities. The term often used to describe the multiple identifications of the diasporic experience is that of hybridity, which has proved to be a useful term as it has moved the discussion about identity away from static and essentialist assumptions.

Nonetheless, a number of points need to be considered here. First, despite its advantages, hybridity is a problematic term as it often implies the existence of two pristine cultures that have contributed in producing the hybrid (Sreberny 2002: 219). Secondly, hybridity can be reified as well. Once hybrid identities are formed out of the 'parent' cultures, they are often considered as static and fixed. In this sense, hybridity does not help us overcome the objectification of identities as is apparent in the context of romanticisation of hybrid identities. Moreover, hybridity, like ethnicity, emphasises culture while glossing over other parameters and inequalities that are in play, such as social class, age and gender. Culture is understood as an explanation, and not something that needs to be explained. Such observations have led Anthias argue that hybridity is in fact an 'old' concept (2001: 619). Finally, research on diasporas and hybridity often imply a national centre, a pristine home culture of which diasporas are satellites. This is problematic for it implies that the nation is a natural, given and homogenous entity and that immigration is the exception, the deviation from the rule.

This book argues that the fluidity of identities needs to be recognised and studied within the nation state. Diversity, rather than homogeneity, needs to be the starting point (cf Robins 2001). However, before examining what role, if any, the media play in enhancing diversity or homogenisation we need to return to the concepts of identity and culture.

FROM IDENTITIES TO IDENTITY DISCOURSES AND PERFORMANCES

The existing dichotomies that have prevailed in theorising identity and culture are not adequate. As Comaroff has remarked, what is surprising is the sheer tenacity of these binary schemes (modernism versus primordialism) pointing to the poverty of theory (Comaroff 1996: 164). Modernist theories may stress the constructedness of identity, but by favouring a top-down approach reify identity and culture. Once identity is 'made', it remains fixed. This thesis has acquired dominant status as is evident in a number of areas: policymaking, media, minority rights organisations, academia, and in people themselves. Cultures seem frozen in time as distinct entities, whereas in fact, as research has forcefully demonstrated, they are always the result of a 'mish-mash, borrowings, mixtures that have occurred, though at different rates, ever since the beginning of time' (Levi-Strauss and Pouillon 1961 cited in Kuper 1999: 243).

Perhaps then the problem lies with the term 'culture' itself, as it implies a homogenous, coherent, timeless and discrete whole (Abu-Lughod 1991: 147). The greatest advantage of the concept of culture was that it shifted the explanation of difference away from the notions of race and nature and the biological connotations they entail. Yet, as Abu-Lughod has remarked, despite its anti-essentialist intent, culture 'tends to freeze difference' in a similar way such as the concept of race has done (1991: 144). In short, there is a paradox lying at the heart of the multiculturalism literature. By adhering to the concept of difference, one reproduces the same ideology one purports to question. As Kuper has noted, 'the insistence that radical differences can be observed between people serves to sustain them' (1999: 239).

Furthermore, there is another issue related to the above debates, that of cultural determinism, where 'culture shifts from something to be described, interpreted, even perhaps explained, and is treated instead as a source of explanation in itself' (Kuper 1999: xi). By reducing everything to cultural differences the researcher falls prey to the same mistakes she has set out to criticise. The problem of essentialism, of 'imputing a fundamental, basic, absolutely necessary constitutive of quality to a person, social category, ethnic group, religious community, or nation' (Werbner 1997: 228), becomes of central importance.

The threat of essentialism has led, however, to a series of conundrums as Werbner has observed (1997: 228). 'If to name is to represent, to imply a continuity in time and place, then it follows that all collective namings or labellings are essentialist and all discursive constructions of social collectivities are essentialising' (1997), thus making any research enterprise obsolete. Moreover, the acknowledgement that difference can be (and has been) manipulated should not make us deny difference altogether. This runs the danger of colluding with a strand of conservative thinking and politics that promotes assimilation and refuses to grant minority rights to people who feel differently.

It is a problem as well, then, to 'essentialise essentialism'. As Herzfeld has remarked: 'distrust about essentialism in social theory should not blur our awareness of its equally pervasive presence in social life' (1996: 26). Indeed, both majorities and minorities use essentialist categories as much as the media and the official discourse do. To address essentialist discourse is not the same as endorsing essentialism. As Eagleton reminds us, the fact that a social category is 'ontologically empty' does not mean that it cannot 'exert an implacable political force' (1990: 24). It becomes then the task of the social scientist to investigate how identities become essentialised and how their qualities become objectified (Comaroff and Stern 1995: 250).

In order to find a way out of this impasse, I draw on two interrelated lines of thought. First, I draw on the work of Barth who, in his seminal work in *Ethnic Groups and Boundaries*, argued that ethnicity is a form of social organisation that results from the interaction between group and environment (1969b). This meant that 'the critical focus for investigation [becomes] the ethnic boundary that defines the group rather than the cultural stuff that it encloses' (1969b: 15). Barth argued that ethnic group membership must depend on ascription and self-ascription, rather than in possessing a certain cultural inventory. In this context, identities are understood as relations rather than objects. It is in relation to something or someone else that the boundary is drawn.

This book benefits from Barth's theory in that instead of focusing on difference, and thus taking it for granted, the focus will be on the processes that create boundaries and thus difference. Do the media play any role in creating boundaries?

The second line of thought follows what has become a recent trend among some anthropologists. Instead of focusing on groups and identities as complete wholes, research should focus on the process of objectification itself and the ways in which people describe, re-describe and argue who they are (Dominguez 1989: 38). This description and re-description is performative, including discursive, but also material, practices. Thus, a shift is proposed; instead of focusing on identity in the singular, this book will focus on discourses[12] and practices about identity and belonging.

This is the strategy followed by Baumann in his ethnography of Southall, a multicultural London neighbourhood (1996). Baumann identified two discourses about culture and identity: a dominant discourse that reifies culture and identity and a demotic discourse that challenges and works against existing reifications. Although these are separate discourses, they co-exist as people fluctuate between the two according to context. Baumann describes how the same people, who contest the rigid boundaries of the official discourse, will revert to it when it suits their interests (1996).

This discursive oscillation in relation to identity is well-documented in anthropology. Wallman (1979) has argued that people articulate their ethnicity differently at home and at the workplace. Malkki (1995), in her fieldwork with two groups of Hutu refugees in Eastern Tanzania who had fled the mass killings of 1972 in Burundi, observed radical differences in the way identity, history and exile were experienced. The group of people living in a segregated refugee camp developed an 'overarching historical trajectory' that rendered themselves as 'the rightful natives' of Burundi (1995: 3). They mythologised their collective identity in such a way that it could hardly be separated from a personal, individual identity. Conversely, the group of people living in the more cosmopolitan town of Kigoma did not construct such a categorically distinct collective identity, but rather sought ways of assimilating and inhabiting multiple identities. As Malkki writes:

> The identities managed in Kigoma were situational identities embedded in pragmatic concerns and in shifting relations with a very rich variety of different social actors. Sometimes fictional, sometimes not, these adoptive identities were cloaks of protective coloration that lent their bearers security and a range of options in complex social arenas. Hence these identities involved elements of individual choice and calculation. ... In Kigoma, the play of identities operated on a more individual basis and was thought of as responding to the practical needs of the immediate, lived present (1995: 169).

Malkki's study echoes Barth's theory (1969b), as the articulation of identities among the refugees did not depend on some inherent quality, but rather was

---

12 Discourse here is understood in the broadest sense as any form of spoken interaction, formal and informal (Gilbert and Mulkay 1984; Potter and Wetherell 1987: 7).

situational. The city provided the space for personal identities to be expressed. Such practices, however, should not be interpreted as free-floating; they are partly determined by the demands and competitiveness of a complex social environment thus echoing Stuart Hall's writings on identities as a discursive practice that 'emerge within the play of specific modalities of power, and thus are more the product of the marking of difference and exclusion, than they are the sign of an identical, naturally-constructed unity' (1996: 4).

In order to make sense of the paradoxes, ambiguities and perplexity of the identities in Greece today – and in order to find a way to deal with the tension between essentialism and particularism – I borrow the term 'cultural intimacy' from the work of the anthropologist Herzfeld (1996). Cultural intimacy refers to the tensions between collective self-knowledge and collective self-representation. In other words, cultural intimacy refers to 'the aspects of cultural identity that are considered a source of external embarrassment, but that nevertheless provide insiders with the assurance of their common sociality' (Herzfeld 1996: 3). The distinction between the public and the private is of paramount importance here. Although cultural intimacy is not particular to Greece (but rather present in most cultures in various guises and degrees), there are some particular features that shape the Greek version. An expression that casts light on this is a popular Greek saying *ta en oiko mi en dhimo*, which means that 'the affairs of the house should not be brought into the public sphere'. Domesticity is commonly used as a metaphor for the nation in the Greek context. It is within the confines of the nation state, 'at home' as it were, that dissent and rebelliousness are accepted as long as they are not brought into public display, to the attention of the outside world. In this context Greek people may refuse to pay their taxes, criticise the army and the government's handling of the relationship with Turkey, but will present (or will be expected to do so by fellow Greeks) a homogenous and harmonious identity to the outside world.[13]

Cultural intimacy allows for a dynamic conceptualisation of identity that accommodates contradiction and ambiguity. Perhaps the most appealing element of the concept is that it cannot be understood without taking the other (be it the West, Europe, Turkey) into account as identity is performed differently at home, 'internally' and 'externally', in relation to the other. Thus, identity has to be understood in a comparative context and not in isolation. Cultural intimacy also allows us to deal with essentialism, which is recognised as a basic discursive strategy. As noted previously, identity politics are all about essentialising and counter-essentialising. This is particularly relevant in the case of Greece as the essentialist self-identity pronounced by the Greeks is often a reaction to equally essentialising stereotypes about Greece and the Balkans by the West. The

---

13 Cultural intimacy is similar to what Mouzelis has termed 'reactive nationalism' (Mouzelis 1994: 41) when referring to the Greek case. This type of nationalism is characterised by an almost paradoxical national identity that oscillates between the glorification of an ancient past, to feelings of inferiority towards the 'modern'. The result is a contradictory attitude toward the nation state; patriotic sentiments are not linked with actual practices at an everyday level. In other words, there is a discrepancy between how 'Greek' Greeks claim to be, and are proud to be, and the extent to which they fulfil their duties as Greek citizens (eg pay taxes).

challenge for the researcher is to identify the meaning and the shifts in these essentialisms rather than to dismiss the term altogether.

CONCLUSIONS: MEDIATING IDENTITIES?

This chapter has argued that in order to understand the relationship between identities and the media a new approach is needed. This means to rethink radically both the concept of identity and the media. This chapter has mainly dealt with identity, while the media and the theory of mediation will be discussed in Chapter 4. Chapter 3, which follows, complements this chapter as it discusses identities in Greece, grounding the theories discussed here in the Greek context.

This chapter has argued that identities are inherently relational and thus can only be investigated as performed. Given the difficulty of the empirical task, the challenge is to theorise identity while respecting its diversity and dynamism. In order to do so, the emphasis will be on the symbolic and material performance of identities. The point is to investigate when people express a relatively open discourse about their identities (a 'demotic discourse'), and when they articulate a

	strong media / weak identities	*weak media / powerful identities*	*media and identities in context*
emphasis	top-down often speculative	bottom-up empirical	top-down and bottom-up empirical
communication	technologies or texts	audiences	texts, audiences and context
model of communication	transmission and culture	transmission and culture	mediation
identity	essentialising identities and often the media	essentialising identities	discourses and practices about identity
culture	timeless, discrete, coherent, homogenous culture	reifying culture	culture as lived and as performed
driving force	technological or textual determinism	ethnic or cultural determinism	processual
keywords	ideology nationalism cultural imperialism power	empowerment localisation	transnational diversity boundaries power
key theories/ authors	medium theory phenomenology 'banal nationalism'	*Export of Meaning*	media anthropology

Table 1.1 Synopsis of the theoretical approaches regarding the relationship between media and identity

closed and essentialist discourse, what Baumann has termed a 'dominant discourse' (1996 and 1997). Finally, the challenge for this study becomes to explore whether the media have any influence in these discursive shifts. In order to do so, the study will follow the circulation of discourses about the nation, both at a local level and in the media, as an attempt to investigate the power of the media.

CHAPTER 3

CHANGING IDENTITIES: GREECE AND ITS MINORITIES IN CONTEXT

This chapter complements Chapter 2 by providing a historical account of identities in the Greek context. The aim here is to discuss the changing and dynamic character of identities and the historical contexts in which they were shaped. This is why this admittedly brief account will start from the origins of Greek nationalism and the nation state in the Ottoman past. Such an approach denaturalises the concept of the nation and allows the situatedness and syncretism of identities to emerge. It should be noted however, that the constructedness of identities does not imply that identities are false or spurious. Once constructed, identities can become forceful. This, in turn, does not mean that they will remain so forever. In other contexts they will be reconstructed thus making cultural change possible.

This chapter aims to reveal how different layers and experiences of identities co-exist giving rise to different sets of discourses and practices of identity and belonging. These discourses can be 'dominant' or 'demotic' as discussed in Chapter 2. Three aspects of Greek history will be highlighted. These are the arrival of refugees in Greece in 1923 as a result of the population exchange with Turkey, the 'Muslim' minority and, finally, the issue of Cyprus. Each of these sheds light on the actual research questions, particularly as people from the Muslim minority and Cyprus are included as informants in the study. In this sense this chapter performs the additional function of introducing the *dramatis personae* of this book, namely the Greeks, the Greek Cypriots and the Turkish speakers who live in Greece.

THE OTTOMAN LEGACY, THE NEW STATE AND THE 'GREAT IDEA'

The Ottoman Empire succeeded the Byzantine Empire after the fall of Constantinople (now Istanbul) in 1453. Yet, it would be mistaken to think of Byzantium as a 'Greek' empire. Although Greek language and Christianity were dominant, other languages and religions were present. Byzantium was by no means a homogenous empire, neither across its vast territory nor through time. After the fall of the Byzantine Empire, what is today known as Greece became part of the Ottoman Empire for almost four centuries.

In the Ottoman Empire there were no ethnic or national identities, although there was linguistic and religious diversity. Religion and language, however, did not correspond to ethnic differences. The Ottoman administrative system organised populations through the *millet* system, which classified inhabitants on the basis of religion; the Orthodox 'Rum' millet, the Jewish millet and the Muslim millet were some of the dominant groups. 'Rum', meaning Orthodox Christian, included all Orthodox Christians regardless of their language, and thus included Albanian, Bulgarian, Romanian, Turkish and Greek speakers (Danforth 1995: 59). Thus to assume that 'Rum' equalled Greek, as reinterpreted by Greek nationalists, is flawed (Clogg 1992; Danforth 1995). Similarly, it would be equally flawed to assume that language corresponded to ethnicity; for example, Greek was the language of trade and would be spoken by all those involved in commerce or holding administrative positions. During the Ottoman period, therefore, terms like 'Greek' or 'Bulgarian' were not used to designate different ethnic or national groups, but rather broad socio-cultural categories (Danforth 1995: 59). *Millets* were administrative rather than territorial jurisdictions (Karakasidou 1997: 78–79). Recent studies now point to the fact that there was a wide degree of autonomy in the different *millets* (Clogg 1992).

What is interesting is to observe how these socio-cultural categories came to acquire political significance. This is explained by the development of Greek nationalism in the late 18th and early 19th centuries, initially by Greek speakers living in Europe, which eventually led to the war of independence in 1821. Greek and Turkish nationalisms developed asynchronously. The Muslim *millets* of the Ottoman Empire, being the dominant ones, developed their nationalisms later than the rest. On the contrary, the Christian *millets*, which included Greek speakers, developed their nationalisms earlier, partly due to the awareness of their subordinate position.

Given the multicultural environment of the Ottoman Empire, it is not surprising that the first Greek state, which was comprised of the Peloponnese (the southern part of mainland Greece), was not exclusively Greek-speaking Orthodox Christian. Hobsbawm notes that Albanian speakers were some of 'the most formidable fighters against the Turks' (1992: 65). A number of languages were juxtaposed, including Greek, Albanian, Slavic, Vlach (a Romanian dialect) and Turkish, suggesting that the Greek nation was made 'by a sum of minorities' (Tsoucalas 1977: 50), by no account a Greek phenomenon. Massimo d'Azeglio famously remarked after the Risorgimento, the political unification of Italy: 'We have made Italy; now we have to make Italians.' (quoted in Hobsbawm 1992: 44) Minorities emerged synchronously with the nation state because the borders of the state hardly corresponded with those of the nation. This is why for every expansion of the borders of the Greek state, the Guarantor powers[1] demanded the guarantee of the protection of minority rights.[2]

The ideology that provided the *raison d'être* for the young Greek kingdom was that of the 'Great Idea', literally an irredentist ideology that aspired to the annexation of Greek speaking territories that previously made up the Byzantine Empire (Kitromilides 1990; Skopetea 1988). This was part of the nation-building process and was justified by the fact that only a small proportion of the Christian

---

1   Guarantor powers were Britain, Russia and France, ie the states that signed the Treaty of London in 1827 (Clogg 1992: 42).
2   For a discussion of the legal framework of the minority protection in Greece, see Divani (1995).

Orthodox Greek speakers were included within the borders of the new state. However, as Kitromilides notes, the ideology of the Great Idea '… was motivated by concerns about social and ideological cohesion, at least as much as, if not to a considerably greater degree than, by aspirations of territorial aggrandisement' (1990: 59).

After its independence Greece embarked on a number of successive wars to 'liberate' the Greek-speaking lands from the Ottoman Empire, the last of which was the war between Greece and Turkey in Asia Minor after the end of the First World War.[3] Turkey emerged victorious and the war is still referred to in Greece as the 'Asia Minor catastrophe' of 1922. Greece and Turkey signed the Treaty of Lausanne in July 1923. This Treaty sealed the fate of the populations in Greece and Turkey as the peace deal comprised a forced population exchange between the two countries. It was the first time in the history of international law that such a forced population exchange took place (Troumbeta 2001), the purpose of which was to create two 'ethnically homogeneous' nation states. Approximately 1.4 million Orthodox Christian 'Greeks' came as refugees to Greece and 500,000 Muslim 'Turks' went to Turkey from Greece (Karakasidou 1995: 71).

CONTESTED IDENTITIES: ANATOLIAN REFUGEES

It is a myth that the population exchange ensured an uncontested and harmonious national homogeneity or that the refugees became integrated into Greek society in an unproblematic way. The criterion used for the population exchange was that of religion, in line with the tradition of the *millet* system. In many instances, the refugees could hardly speak Greek[4] and many had been reluctant to leave their lands and homes where they had lived for generations.

Although the refugees from Asia Minor are often collectively referred to as a single group, in fact they came from various cultural, linguistic, social and regional backgrounds. Karakasidou has noted that perhaps the only shared experience of all refugees was their Orthodox Christian religion (1997: 148). Herzfeld (1991), Hirschon (1989) and Karakasidou (1997) have documented how mainland Greeks would often call the refugees 'Turks', or 'Turkish seeds' (*Tourkosporous*). Among the refugees were the Pontic Greeks who came from the Black Sea area. Even today there are still numerous jokes in circulation about Pontic Greeks and have their roots in the 1920s. Other refugees came from a more cosmopolitan environment and were despised in Greece for bringing new mores and traditions with them.

---

3   The coasts of Asia Minor were populated by a significant number of Christians and Greek speakers making parts of Asia Minor more 'Greek' than the recently annexed parts of Northern Greece. For example, Thessaloniki, now the second largest city in Greece, was a predominantly Jewish city with a large Muslim community at the turn of the 19th century.

4   There is the case of Karamanlides, a predominantly Turkish-speaking Christian Orthodox people, who were forced to go to Greece although they did not necessarily identify 'ethnically' with the Greeks. At the time of the exchange they numbered as many as 400,000 (Clogg 1992: 55).

Herzfeld (1991) discusses the impact of the arrival of the Asia Minor (Greek-speaking Christian) refugees on the Greek population of the island of Crete. By 1924 all Cretan Muslim-Turks had left Crete as part of the population exchange. Drawing on personal history narratives and parallel research in the town archives, Herzfeld writes that the Muslims' departure was accompanied by immediate hostility toward the refugees who had taken their place.

> For the refugees, though suddenly destitute, were more cosmopolitan than the indigenous Cretan population, especially the villagers recently arrived in town. Unlike the departed Turks, they were, simply, not Cretan. Intense mutual dislike resulted. The refugees lamented a fate that placed them among rude peasants, while rural Cretans called the refugees 'Turks'– a clear acknowledgement that in some ways they were more alien than the Turkish Cretans (*Tourkokritiki*) who had departed (Herzfeld 1991: 64).[5]

Herzfeld quotes a Cretan historian, Prevelakis, who noted that the 'Turkish' flavour of the market street actually intensified when the refugees replaced the Muslims (1991: 64). Van Boeschoten, writing about the Macedonian context, Macedonia being where most refugees actually settled, points out that the local Slav speakers refer to the arrival of the refugees as the time when 'the unbaptised Turks left and the baptised Turks came' (2000: 37). I came across a story of a teenage girl who started dating a boy who came from the same island as her in the 1990s. When the relationship became known to her grandmother she expressed her disapproval by pointing out the fact that the young man was 'a refugee'. His grandparents had indeed come from Asia Minor as a result of the 1922 war and population exchange; three generations were not enough to erase the stigma of the refugee in the eyes the girl's grandmother. Today, three generations after the population exchange, there are no tensions between refugees and locals. Interestingly, patterns similar to those discussed above emerged in the 1990s upon the arrival of Pontic Greeks from the former Soviet Union republics who were 'repatriated' to Greece to search for better lives. These 'new refugees' are commonly called Russian Pontics (*Rossopontii*).

Another point to be considered is what Hirschon observed about refugees who settled in hostile neighbourhoods. In the Yerania neighbourhood in Piraeus, where Hirschon conducted fieldwork, refugees became particularly vocal about their Greek identity in order to legitimise their presence (1989). Karakasidou notes that 'in a dramatic twist of fate, these refugees were both the victims of nationalism as well as the unwitting agents of its legitimation.' (1997: 150)

Examples like these highlight the arbitrariness of the top-down definitions of who is Greek, or Turkish, and who is not. They also suggest that the idea of home and the sense of attachment to place are socially constructed and not dictated by blood or some primordial attachment to territory. People modify their strategies of belonging according to the context, echoing Malkki's work on Hutu identities in Tanzania (1995).

---

5   Herzfeld notes that a similar fate awaited the departing Muslim-Turks. Upon their arrival in Turkey, 'the local Turks called them "chattels", a term usually reserved for the infidel Christians' (Herzfeld 1991: 64).

Through processes of official top-down policies of nation building and through the education bureaucracy, the church and the army, people have constructed their identities as Greeks. Such processes are not unique to Greece. On the contrary, most modern nation states have undergone similar processes. What is interesting, however, is how these processes do not always succeed in incorporating everyone. This is what the next section will discuss by way of exploring the case of the Turkish, Pontic and Roma minorities in Greece, officially known as the 'Muslim minority'.

CONTESTED IDENTITIES: THE 'MUSLIM' MINORITY

The Muslim population of Western Thrace,[6] as well as the Greeks of Istanbul (and the islands of Imvros and Tenedos), were exempted from the population exchange. The Treaty of Lausanne designated the existence of a 'Muslim minority' in Western Thrace that set the framework for subsequent Greek policy. However, the name 'Muslim minority' implies one homogenous group of people, yet it contains three different minorities, namely the Turks, the Pomaks and the Roma.

The Turkish minority is a vestige of the Ottoman past (Karakasidou 1995). The Turkish speaking Muslims of Western Thrace are descendants of various Turkish groups who settled in the area after the Ottoman conquest in 1361 AD (Karakasidou 1995: 71). The Pomaks are a group of Slavic speakers who converted to Islam in the 17th century.[7] The Roma people of Thrace, known as Gypsies, are distinguished from the Roma of southern Greece in terms of religion and language. Most Muslim Roma speak Turkish and only a small group speak the Romani language (Karakasidou 1995: 71).

These minorities, having preceded the nation, are interesting because they challenge the artificiality of borders. The case resembles the Russian speakers living in post-Soviet republics, who Laitin calls a 'beached diaspora', in the sense that they never crossed any international borders. What happened rather is that the borders receded after the collapse of the Soviet Union (Laitin 1998). In a similar fashion, the Turkish minority in Thrace is a vestige of the Ottoman past, a beached Turkish diaspora that was the result of the making of a new nation state and the collapse of an empire. In other words, the Turks of Greece never left Turkey, they are Greek citizens born in Greece and this is one of the most significant differences between them and other Turkish communities living outside Turkey.

---

6   Thrace is the north-eastern region of Greece, bordering Turkey and Bulgaria.

7   The Pomak language, which is not a written language, is similar to Bulgarian. A large Pomak minority lives in Bulgaria. Until 1989, Pomaks remained isolated in the mountainous areas of Thrace as one needed a special permit from the police in order to enter or exit their designated area. They remain mainly an agricultural population although a large number have moved to the urban centres of Thrace. Being part of the Muslim minority they had their right to religious expression, but had to go to Turkish language schools.

In the absence of any official data,[8] there are competing figures about the size of the minorities. A sober estimate is that the 'Muslim' minority numbers around 110,000–120,000 people (Human Rights Watch 1998; MRG 1992). Figures available from 1970 (Siguan 1990) provide an indication of the ratio of the different groups within the Muslim minority: 49.1% were Turks, 32.5% were Pomaks and 18.3% were Roma.

Name trouble

Greece does not recognise any ethnic or national minorities apart from a religious minority, the 'Muslim minority' of Thrace. The Treaty of Lausanne referred to the minority as Muslim, and Greece always refers to the Treaty in defence of the official name policy. However, the name 'Muslim' has to be understood in the context of the *millet* system as a broad socio-cultural category, rather than simply connoting religion. This has led some commentators to suggest that the intention of the Treaty was not to connote a religious minority, but an ethnic one (on the basis of the *millet* system) (Herakleidis 1997: 32). It has to be noted, however, that the attitude toward naming this group has depended on the quality of Greek–Turkish relations. In the 1950s, the policy of the Greek government was to call the minority Turkish (Minority Rights Group 1992: 4; Human Rights Watch 1999: 2), providing yet another indication of how ethnic categories are shaped historically and politically.

In the context of non-recognition, the name of the minorities emerges as an urgent issue. The official name 'Muslim' is deeply problematic for a number of reasons. First, it implies a homogenous minority, which, as just argued, is a false assumption. To lump three groups under the same name is problematic as it conceals differences and the right to self-ascription. Moreover, the name 'Muslim' makes the religious dimension central even though some members of the minority might not be religious.

I refer to the minorities as Turkish, Pomak and Roma respectively. However, in the text, in line with the theoretical framework, I always use the definition(s) that people use, whether it is 'Turkish', 'Muslim', or 'Greek Muslim' (Greek usually connoting Greek citizenship). No informant described themselves as Romani or Gypsy. This is perhaps related to the negative connotations associated with the word gypsy (*çingene* in Turkish), especially in Thrace. I also use the term 'Gaziots' to refer to the people in the particular Athens neighbourhood where I did fieldwork, as well as the term 'Turkish-speaking' when referring to people across ethnic groups who use Turkish as their first language. I only use the term 'Muslim minority' (often in inverted commas) when referring to the official name.

However, it is a challenging question to examine how the Muslim identity of the past became the Turkish identity of the present. As Verdery has argued, ethnic identities develop from national identities, and not the other way round, because of the homogenising effects of nation building that heighten the visibility of the

---

8   The last Greek census to give data on religious affiliation and mother tongue was in 1951.

non-conforming other (1994: 47). The homogenising and assimilating melting pot that the state is, poses a threat to difference (and vice versa). According to Eriksen, threat, or perceived threat, can explain the emergence of ethnicity (1993: 68). In the case of the minorities in Thrace, threat is felt by all those involved; Greeks feel that the minorities pose threats to their homogeneity; the Muslims are threatened not only symbolically, but through a number of state-sponsored processes, the majority of which have now been eclipsed, but have nonetheless left a legacy of distrust.

The minorities were marginalised economically in a number of ways. This has to be seen in the context of Thrace being one of the poorest areas in the EU in terms of per capita income (Anagnostou 1999: 70), with agriculture being the major source of income. There are, however, some striking divisions within the region. The southern coastal part of Thrace, which is more fertile and prosperous, is mainly populated by Christians, while the northern, mountainous, arid and much poorer zone is almost exclusively populated by Muslims, who mainly cultivate tobacco (Anagnostou 1999: 73).

Moreover, until 1991,[9] the state directly curtailed some of the minority's economic and social rights. Muslims needed special permission in order to build or modify their property or to expand their business. A consequence of this policy of marginalisation was that people from the minority channelled a significant part of their activities toward Turkey, while some people migrated to Turkey permanently. Furthermore, for reasons related to the Greek educational system and its limited opportunities for the minorities, many students chose to study in Istanbul rather than in Greek universities.[10] In 1984, Greece's Supreme Court decreed that the adjective 'Turkish' should be banned as it created a false impression about the existence of foreign nationals within Greece.

The emergence of the 'independents' movement' in the 1980s was partly a response to these exclusions. The 'independents' movement consisted of politicians from the Turkish minority who were fighting for the lifting of discriminatory policies and the recognition of the name 'Turkish'. However, the independence of this movement was questionable as it is generally accepted that the independents were actually receiving financial support from Turkey and were actively promoting Turkish nationalism. The controversial local politician, the late MP Ahmet Sadik, referred to the then Turkish Prime Minister Özal as 'my Prime Minister', a comment that caused turmoil in the Greek political scene. In 1990, a law introduced the 3% threshold of the national vote in order to enter Greek parliament. This percentage was larger than the minority's proportion of the

---

9   In 1991, state-sponsored discrimination was denounced in the declaration of 'legal equality and equal citizenship' [isonomia-isopoliteia].

10   One also needs to take into account pragmatic choices that influence these decisions. Another reason given for the choice of university is the proximity of Istanbul to Thrace; one can get to Istanbul by taxi in 3 hours while a train journey to Athens takes around 10 hours and costs double the price.

population and meant that the 'independent' candidates could not be represented in parliament.[11]

The ways in which Turkish and Greek nationalism have reinforced each other is exemplified in the bilateral reciprocity clause (*kathestos amiveotitas*), dictated by the Lausanne Treaty. This obliges Greece and Turkey to institute state policies that protect the Muslim minority of Thrace and the Greek Orthodox minority of Istanbul respectively. The most serious drawback of this clause was that the minorities suffered when the relations between the two countries were tense. This clause was also interpreted to mean that any infringement of the Treaty by either one of the two countries would give the right to the other to intervene.[12] This resulted in the minorities being the object of political calculation and manipulation, a process that directly affected peoples' lives. In Thrace this is exemplified through the (nationalist) activities of both the Turkish Consulate in Komotini and the Orthodox archbishop, who are major players in this political game.

The Turkish, Pomak and Roma minorities in Athens

The Turkish-speaking minority in Athens is the result of internal migration from Thrace that started in the 1960s. In the 1980s the Greek government offered (mainly clerical) jobs in banks and public administration institutions in Athens to members of the Muslim minority, allegedly to weaken its presence in Thrace. Those who accepted the jobs were deprived of their minority rights when they came to Athens. This partly explains why there are no mosques or Turkish language schools in Athens. Moreover, the special quotas that apply to the minority students from Thrace, in relation to entering university, do not apply to their Athenian peers. Generally, the people who came to Athens from Thrace were the least affluent, and very often come from the Roma/Gypsy populations, which fit this demographic criterion, although Turks and Pomaks have migrated as well (Troumbeta 2001: 148).

People from Thrace have moved to various Athens neighbourhoods; usually those from the same town or village have moved to the same neighbourhood. My fieldwork focused on the neighbourhood of Gazi, close to the centre of Athens. People in Gazi are primarily from Komotini and to a lesser extent from Xanthi. There are different estimates about the number of people from Thrace who live in the Athens vicinity (Attica), which vary between 5,000 and 10,000 people, but there are no official data. A recent report estimated that there are around 2,500 people living in Gazi.[13] Unemployment among Gaziots is quite high (again there

---

11　The most vocal representative of the independents movement, Ahmet Sadik, appealed about this decision to the Council of Europe on the grounds that this decision infringed the minority's right to representation. The Council ruled that the 3% threshold intended to create more unified electoral formations representing larger sums of the electorate, which it considered a positive goal and thus dismissed Sadik's claim (Giakoumopoulos 1997).

12　Indicatively in Istanbul, of the 120,000 strong community only a few thousand have remained.

13　Published in the daily *Eleutherotypia* (10 April 2002). This number is also given by Avramopoulou and Karakatsanis (2002).

is no official data); this was the most common complaint heard in the coffee houses and clubs in the neighbourhood in which I conducted fieldwork. Apart from those who were given jobs by the government in the 1980s, the rest are finding it hard to make ends meet.

Interestingly, when I mentioned to someone from Komotini that I did fieldwork with Turks living in Gazi he said: 'Oh, there are no Turks in Gazi, only Gypsies.' I was surprised because this was coming from a Turk living in Komotini. I was used to similar comments coming from Greek people, echoing the official Greek policy on the issue, which is that there are no ethnic minorities, only religious ones. A typical phrase would be that there are no Turks in Greece, only Muslims; but why would a Turk make a similar comment? It is true that Roma, as well as Pomak people, have migrated to Attica from Thrace; but there are Turkish families too. Moreover, the majority in Gazi claim to be Turkish.

It seems, then, that the 'name problem' relates not only to the official Greek policy, but is also reflected in the discourses (official and unofficial) within the minorities. Both the Greek and the Turkish leaders have made claims on the minorities within the 'Muslim minority'; both Turks and Greeks have emphasised the Turkishness or Greekness of the Pomaks and Gypsies respectively. Such claims depend on the context and reasons, which have little to do with the people themselves, but often with the quality of Greek–Turkish relations (see Troumbeta 2001: 184). The Roma people of Thrace are a case in point. According to Troumbeta, some of the Roma people of Thrace have been self-ascribing themselves as Turkish since Ottoman times, while those settled in urban areas have been speaking Turkish for decades (2001: 205). Roma people are pursued by the officials of the Turkish minority (as potential minority votes, for example), and yet are derided by the Turks of Thrace at a local level as backward, dirty and dangerous (Demetriou 2002; Troumbeta 2001: 184). This immediately raises questions about who has the power to define who is what (including the power to define oneself). The strategy of following people's discourses proved useful here. Instead of trying to identify who is the 'real' Turk or the 'real' Gypsy (an impossible and undesirable task), I examined the shifts in people's discourses, that is, why they would identify themselves in certain ways in certain (mediated and unmediated) contexts.

It can be argued that the Athenian Turkish-speakers are a liminal category, to use the term employed by Turner (1967) and van Gennep (1960). By leaving Thrace and integrating in chaotic and diverse Athens, where there are no institutions to hold the community together, people are seen as impure and even dangerous (Douglas 1966). Athenian Turkish-speakers are seen as losing the traditional markers of ethnicity (the boundaries) that, according to some, hold the minority communities in Thrace together. By moving to Athens, they have symbolically 'betrayed' their community and transgressed its boundaries – in the eyes of some Thracian Turks at least. This interpretation indicates the fluidity and social construction of categories, such as ethnicity, and highlights the divisions within the minorities.

It becomes clear that ethnicity is not a given category, but that it is rather constructed and re-constructed according to context. The Greek speaking

Orthodox refugees in Piraeus or Crete were called 'Turkish seeds' after the population exchange. The Pontic Greeks are called 'Russians'. The Turks in Gazi, 'Gypsies' by fellow Thracian Turks. The Turks in Gazi often call themselves Greeks, while the Greeks call them Muslims. All these categories shift according to context and according to who is the other in relation to whom one defines oneself. In the following section these constructions of identity will be examined in relation to Cyprus.

CONTESTED IDENTITIES: CYPRUS

The Cyprus problem has been on the agenda for the past 50 years and has gained attention at different times of crisis. The recent accession of Cyprus to the European Union, in 2004, triggered a new round of negotiations for a solution, but negotiations ended in stalemate as the UN-backed peace plan aimed at reunifying the island was rejected by Greek Cypriots in a referendum on 24 April 2004. Although it is beyond the scope of this thesis to include a comprehensive account of the history of Cyprus, I will here present a brief history of the conflict and how it is linked to Greek nationalism.

Cyprus is an island in the eastern Mediterranean close to the coasts of southern Turkey and Syria and was part of the Ottoman Empire for more than 300 years. In 1878 it was handed over to Britain and became a British colony. Independence was gained in 1959. The London–Zurich agreements set up the Cyprus Republic in February 1959. In 1960, of an estimated population of 573,566, Greek Cypriots numbered 442,138 (77.1%), whereas 104,350 (18.2%) were Turkish Cypriots. The remainder, apart from around 17,000 Britons, were smaller minorities, such as Maronites and Armenians (MRG 1997: 5).

The Cyprus problem is a story of postcolonialism and competing nationalisms. Greek and Turkish nationalisms must be seen as they developed from the multicultural environment of the Ottoman Empire, which was based on the coexistence of different cultures and languages through the *millet* system. Evidence of this coexistence can be found in the human geography of Cyprus before the violent uprootings of 1967 and 1974. Before these events most villages were mixed and there was no concentration of a single ethnic group in any area of the island (Kitromilides 1977: 37).

In Cyprus the Christian *millet* was organised around the Church and, in particular, through the Archbishop, who was also the 'Ethnarch' (the leader of the nation). Greece played the role of the national centre. It is in this context, as a facet of Greek nationalism, that the ideology of *enosis* (of union with 'motherland' Greece) that has determined Greek Cypriot politics, should be understood. During the British rule Greek Cypriots strengthened their national consciousness and organised the struggle for independence. The Turkish Cypriots, who developed their national consciousness later on (Attalides 1979: 1), had a different relation to the British. As a numerical minority and as an opposition to the dominant ideology that demanded union of the island with Greece (*enosis*), they largely conformed to the colonial rule.

The struggle for independence from the British colonial rule was basically run by Greeks and, in particular, by two men, Makarios, the Archbishop since 1950, and Colonel Grivas, a Greek Cypriot known for his anti-communist actions in the Greek Civil War, who was head of the underground army EOKA (the National Organisation of Cypriot Fighters). In 1958, the Turkish Cypriots formed the TMT (Turkish Defence Organisation) and both guerrilla organisations focused on reciprocal violence.

Great Britain relinquished sovereignty over the island except for two bases in Akrotiri and Dekheleia. Setting up the new republic meant that the Greeks, who had fought for *enosis*, would give up their aspirations for union with Greece, and the Turkish Cypriots, subsequently, would give up *taksim* (partition) (Panteli 1984: 345). Moreover, the two ethnic groups would have to collaborate, something which was very difficult largely due to the enmity between EOKA and TMT. Hence, soon after the constitution of the new republic, leaders from both sides engaged in a power game demonstrating their adherence to their nationalisms (Panteli 1984: 345-6). The already complex situation was worsened by the problems caused by the new constitution (Polyviou 1980). The new republic was set up through a 'very elaborate and rigid' constitution and three Treaties, all of which were interrelated (MRG 1997: 9). It would require a detailed analysis to go through the constitutional and legal problems that impeded the survival of this bicommunal state. It is important to mention, however, the problems associated with the Treaty of Guarantee, which was signed by the three guarantor states, Britain, Turkey and Greece. Under this Treaty 'each of the three guaranteeing powers reserves the right to take action with the sole aim of re-establishing the state of affairs created by this present Treaty' (MRG 1997: 9). It was on the pretext of this Treaty that Turkey invaded Cyprus in 1974, after a coup inspired by the military junta in Greece took place on the island.

The major disputes between the two ethnic communities concerned issues such as the ratio in public services, taxes, the army, the administration of separate municipalities and the status of the vice president (MRG 1997: 10). President Makarios proposed thirteen amendments to the Constitution, which were rejected as they were perceived as demoting Turkish Cypriots to the status of a minority and subsequently preparing for *enosis*. The tension led to the eruption of violence in 1963 and 1964.[14] The UN ceasefire that followed only lasted until 1967, when, following the provocative moves of the colonels' *coup* in Greece, violence erupted again. On 15 July 1974, the Greek junta from Athens staged a *coup d'etat* against Makarios and Nicos Sampson was installed as a puppet president. On 20 July Turkey invaded Cyprus and on the same day the military junta in Athens collapsed and democracy was restored. On 13 August, after negotiations in Geneva broke down, a new Turkish attack occupied 36.5% of the land, which still remains under Turkish occupation.

---

14   At the end of 1963 and in the first half of 1964, 191 Turkish Cypriots and 133 Greek Cypriots were killed. Many Turkish villages were abandoned, in many cases as ordered by the Turkish paramilitaries (MRG 1997: 12). These 'moves', which appeared as spontaneous in the first instance, were the necessary territorial basis for partition.

The effects on the Cypriot populations were traumatic. There were around 180,000 Greek Cypriot refugees out of a population of 574,000. It has been estimated that 3,000 Greek Cypriots and 500 Turkish Cypriots were killed in a month. Moreover, to this list we should add 1,619 Greek Cypriots who went missing and whose fate has been ignored ever since (MRG 1997: 19). On 15 November 1983 Denktash proclaimed the independence of the 'Turkish Republic of North Cyprus' (TRNC), which has not been recognised by any state other than Turkey. Bilateral discussions under the aegis of the UN have been taking place since 1974.

Competing identities

One of the consequences, for the Greek Cypriot side, of the military defeat of 1974 was the temporary marginalisation of Greek Cypriot nationalism and the parallel rise of Cypriotism, an ideology that envisaged Cyprus as an independent and distinct political unit. The political priority in the post-1974 era became the independence of the island, and not unification with Greece. The ideology of *enosis* was held responsible for the events of 1974. Cypriotism stands in opposition to the nationalist ideologies, Greek Cypriot and Turkish Cypriot, which regard Cyprus as the extension of Greece and Turkey respectively. Consequently, Cypriotism and Greek Cypriot nationalism have opposing interpretations of the causes of the Cyprus problem and opposing perspectives on possible solutions. The contrast between Greek Cypriot nationalism and Cypriotism broadly corresponds to the political opposition between left and right (Mavratsas 2001: 152), the right being associated with Greek Cypriot nationalism and the left with Cypriotism. The two slogans that these competing ideologies employed are indicative of their underlying principles. While for the proponents of Greek nationalism, 'Cyprus belongs to Greece', for those adhering to Cypriotism, 'Cyprus belongs to its people' (Papadakis 1998: 149).

Mavratsas notes that the '… emphasis upon Cypriot independence led to significant shifts in Greek Cypriot official historiography and to the reinterpretation of certain aspects of the island's recent political past' (2001: 157). For example, after the events of 1974, the EOKA movement began to be interpreted as an anti-colonial independence struggle, rather than as a movement aiming at union with Greece. Perhaps most significantly, after 1974, the Cypriot flag began to be publicly displayed on a large scale and to displace – or at least, to be placed next to – the Greek flag, which had, until 1974, expressed the attachment of the Greek Cypriots to Greece and their ambivalence toward Cypriot independence (Mavratsas 2001: 157). Moreover, it was only after 1974 that the day of Cypriot independence began to be celebrated as, until then, the emphasis was on the national commemorations of the Greek state (Mavratsas 2001). However, Greek Cypriot nationalism has proven to be highly resilient and has gained prominence again in the 1990s and the early 21st century.

Greek-Cypriot nationalism in the late 1990s was expressed through the efforts to strengthen the ties between the Republic of Cyprus and Greece. It is in this context that the common defence dogma between Greece and Cyprus should be understood. According to Mavratsas, the common defence dogma must be seen

'... as the institutionalisation of the position that Greece constitutes the most genuine, or even the only ally and protector of the Greek Cypriots' (2001: 163). The *airspace incident*, which is the basis for the first case study of news analysis and viewers' decodings, took place in the context of a military exercise as part of the common defence dogma between Greece and Cyprus (see Chapters 6 and 7).

Greek Cypriots in Athens

Greek Cypriots are often regarded by the official discourse as belonging to the same nation (*ethnos*) as Greek people, although Cypriots living in Greece are not necessarily Greek citizens. There are around 55,000 Greek Cypriots living in Athens.[15] Nonetheless, despite the links with Greece (language and cultural traditions being the most obvious), as Loizos has remarked, '... to attempt to classify Cyprus sociologically as a "region of Greece" is to follow a line of thought that concludes that the Turkish minority had no rightful place in the 1960 independent republic.' (Loizos 1976: 361)

CONCLUDING REMARKS

This chapter offered a historical account of identities in Greece and an analysis of their changing and dynamic character. It also discussed the Cyprus problem and how it is linked to Greek nationalism. In so doing, it provided some concrete examples for the abstract concepts introduced in Chapter 2. Instead of showing a singular and homogenous Greek identity this chapter revealed different layers and experiences of identities that co-exist, thereby giving rise to different sets of discourses of identity and belonging.

The next chapter addresses media theory and identifies a possible way in which the media can be investigated in relation to the complex field of identity discourses and politics.

---

15   Number given by the Cypriot Embassy.

CHAPTER 4

TEXTS, AUDIENCES, CONTEXTS:
TOWARD A THEORY OF MEDIATION

To understand identity as lived and as performed, as suggested in Chapter 2, entails an investigation of the role of audiences. However, the focus here is not solely on audiences, but rather on the relationship between audiences and media technologies and texts. The aim is to understand the media as a process of mediation, a process that takes into account the viewers, the text, the technologies and the context.

The concept of mediation can be traced back to the work of Raymond Williams (1977) and has been developed in media studies by Martin-Barbero (1993), Thompson (1995) and Silverstone (1999; in press). All these authors emphasise that we should think of the media as a process. Silverstone defines mediation as a:

> ... fundamentally dialectical notion which requires us to understand how processes of communication change the social and cultural environments that support them as well as the relationships that participants, both individual and institutional, have to that environment and to each other. At the same time it requires a consideration of the social as in turn a mediator: institutions and technologies as well as the meanings that are delivered by them are mediated in the social processes of reception and consumption. (Silverstone in press: 3)

Such a holistic approach requires that the focus of research extends beyond the point of contact between texts and audiences and considers, instead, the 'circulation of meaning' (Silverstone 1999: 13). This book seeks to examine the circulation of discourses about the nation and identity in the media and in people's lives. The aim is to contrast these official and local, public and private discourses and make an argument about the mediation of the nation, the different ways in which the nation is experienced and talked about and how these discourses are interrelated. The attempt to see the media as a process of mediation is not without problems, both theoretical and methodological. How can the 'circulation of meaning' be examined empirically? Where is the meaning located? This chapter aims to identify a working approach towards a theory of mediation. It does so by drawing on existing work in media studies (Couldry 2000a; Livingstone 1998a and 1998c; Morley 1992; Silverstone 1994 and in press) and, in particular, the developments towards the field of media anthropology (Ginsburg *et al* 2002).

The seeds for a mediational approach to communication can be found in the early days of media studies. Lazarsfeld and Merton, as early as 1948, wrote about the need to examine the effects of the sheer presence of the media in social life.

Although they concluded that such a question is simply impossible to examine empirically, this chapter argues that such an investigation is possible. The challenge is still present and perhaps more urgent than ever, as media studies and its sub-disciplines face a number of criticisms, both internally and externally.

Arguments for a theory of mediation echo the cultural or ritual model of communication (Carey 1989). Perhaps the field that has come closer than any other to developing a mediational and ritual approach is that of audience studies. It was with audience studies that the two previously antagonistic research traditions, the critical and administrative, converged in an attempt to take into account both media power and the possibility for resistance on the part of the audiences. This is evident in Morley's suggestion, drawing from Hall (1988, cited in Morley 1996), to 'incorporate both the vertical and the horizontal dimension of the communication process', or else, '[the integration of] the analysis of questions of ideology and interpretation with the analysis of the uses and functions of television in everyday life' (Morley 1996: 323).

In the following paragraphs I will focus on some of the elements that constitute the mediation process, namely the audiences, the media as technologies and objects and the media as texts. Audiences are included in this study because identity is understood as lived and as performed. Texts are included as they contain a set of public (if not official) discourses about the nation that might be significant in generating discourses about identity at a local level. Technology and text are included because a number of theories point to their centrality in shaping identity (an assumption that will also be examined empirically). These distinctions are of analytical value, for the point is to see all these elements as part of the same process. The aim of this chapter is to examine how they are interrelated. First, it is useful to examine them separately as they are already laden with theories and meanings that need to be unpacked. Moreover, these are not the only constitutive moments in the mediation process, although arguably they are very central. Economics, institutional analysis or the production side of the mediation process are not included in the study, although there is an effort to provide some context about the development of news programmes after deregulation in Greece as a first step towards the inclusion of the political economy of the news media. This will be included in the section on texts, which incorporates the discussion of news that is part of the focus of this study. At the end of the chapter I turn to the emerging field of media anthropology (Askew and Wilk 2002; Ginsburg *et al* 2002) in order to identify a working model of mediation.

AUDIENCES AND MEDIA POWER

The 1980s saw the development of a new field of research, namely audience studies, which drew on cultural studies (Hall 1980), the social psychological research on uses and gratifications (Blumler and Katz 1974), and literary criticism (Iser 1978; Eco 1979), and brought together the critical tradition's concern with issues of power with a focus on audiences (which was the concern of the administrative tradition). The beginning of the 'new audience research' is often associated with Morley's empirical study *Nationwide* (published in 1980).

Influenced by Hall's 'encoding/decoding' model, which in turn drew on Parkin's political sociology, Morley examined the different interpretations of the popular current affairs programme, *Nationwide*, by different groups. The study demonstrated that the readings of the text were based on 'cultural differences embedded within the structure of society … which guide and limit the individual's interpretation of messages' (Morley 1992: 118). Thus the 'meaning' of a text or message was understood as being produced through the interaction of the codes embedded in the text, with the codes inhabited by the different sections of the audience (Morley 1992).

Audience research documented that audiences are not a homogenous, uncritical mass, but are, rather, plural and inventive in their decodings. The most significant achievement of audience studies is that they '… made visible an audience which has hitherto been devalued, marginalized and presumed about in policy and theory' (Livingstone 1998c: 240). As Livingstone remarks, this visibility matters theoretically, empirically and politically (1998a: 195). Such empirically grounded arguments have significant consequences, also for theories on nationalism and identity. If audiences are not passive recipients of media messages, but rather critically interpret and appropriate media products, do nationalist media texts have any effects? The next paragraphs address this question by examining the relationship between audiences and power.

The 'new and exciting phase in audience research' (Hall 1980: 131) has received a number of criticisms. Most critiques converge on the argument that audience studies have celebrated audience activity as exemplified in Fiske's phrase 'semiotic democracy' (1987). Critics have argued that audience research has ignored issues of power, neglecting questions concerning the economic, political and ideological aspects in the production and distribution of media texts, therefore signalling a return to the 'discredited' limited effects paradigm (Curran 1990: 153). In the same vein, Murdock observes that the position that argues for audience activity '… is simply another version of the market system's own claim that the ultimate power lies with the consumer [and] it conveniently ignores the ways in which demands, desires and identities are shaped by what is on offer' (1989a: 229).

Such criticisms have centred upon the extreme cases and do not do justice to the diversity within audience studies. The celebration of the popular and the neglect of power were certainly not the intention of most scholars working within the paradigm. As Morley points out, 'the power of viewers to reinterpret meanings is hardly equivalent to the discursive power of centralised media institutions to construct the texts which the viewer then interprets' (1992: 31). Or, as Ang puts it, 'it would be out of perspective to cheerfully equate "active" with "powerful", in the sense of "taking control" at an enduring structural or institutional level' (1996: 140). Audience studies have been concerned with issues of power from the beginning, as is evident in Hall's model (1980) and numerous empirical studies (among others, Lewis 1991; Morley, 1992; Kitzinger 1993; Philo 1990). Thus, the perception that to research audiences means to write power off the agenda is untrue. On the contrary, it is only through researching audiences that evidence about media power and its effects can be substantiated. As Lewis has observed:

The question we should put to textual analysis that purports to tell us how a cultural product 'works' in contemporary society is simple: where is the evidence? Without evidence, everything is merely speculation. … to put it another way, it is because I am interested in politics that I am interested in audiences (1994: 20).

However, there is some truth in the criticisms that audience studies have failed to address power thoroughly. Corner has pointed out a '… lack of consequentiality in the findings and an uncertainty of tone, perhaps even diffidence in the research conclusions' (Corner 1996: 298–99). If audience researchers were interested in power, they were perhaps looking for it in the wrong place. Despite their insights, audience and reception studies did not extend their focus beyond the point of contact between audiences and texts. They retained a highly mediacentric (or rather, text-centred) approach that did not look at wider social, economic and cultural processes of which the media and their reception are part. Audiences may interpret texts in idiosyncratic ways, but what does this tell us about changes at a wider social and cultural level? In short, while self-ascribing to the ritual model, underlying the work of some reception researchers was a transmission model of communication. Concepts such as the 'active' audience, which have been unhelpful and perhaps misleading on some occasions, are indicative of this approach (Livingstone 1998b). Silverstone has argued that '… instead of a simple term we need a theoretically motivated account of the dynamics of the place of television in everyday life' (1994: 157-8).

In order to answer questions relating to the reception process, we need to first find out more about how people use the media as objects in the first place. This leads to a consideration of questions of media as technologies and objects, as well as of issues of access and availability. The concept that takes the integration of media in everyday life into account is that of users and consumers, which some authors have proposed should replace that of audiences (Silverstone 1996). This approach, which examines media as technologies and objects, covered an area that was initially neglected by reception studies, but is now at the centre of audience studies.

MEDIA TECHNOLOGIES AND EVERYDAY LIFE

Technologies are shaped socially as much as they shape society (MacKenzie and Wacjman 1999). This binary function, present in all forms of mediated interaction, seems elusive as theorists tend to focus on either the social shaping of technology or the technological shaping of society. It is in this case, too, that the pendulum swings from models of powerful technologies (exemplified in medium theory and technological determinist arguments) to models of sophisticated consumers, who tailor and appropriate technologies to their own needs and cultures. Both are partially true, but it seems that authors always privilege one over the other in order to offer theories that can be operationalised and applied in a straightforward way.

The separation of the two approaches is problematic as technology and society are mutually constitutive (MacKenzie and Wacjman 1999: 23). MacKenzie and

Wacjman, however, are not too swift to dismiss technological determinism as it contains a partial truth:

> A 'hard', simple cause-and-effect technological determinism is not a good candidate as a theory of social change. … However, … to say that technology's social effects are complex and contingent is not to say that it has *no* social effects. (MacKenzie and Wacjman 1999: 3–4)

The challenge, then, becomes to ground the claims and assumptions of medium theory in empirical research. This study will combine both approaches by investigating the assumptions about the omnipotent role of the media in shaping identities and cultures in everyday life practices. There are now a number of studies that have examined the use of media as an integral part of everyday life, producing a wealth of data, although mainly in the context of Western Europe and North America (for an exception see chapters in volume by Ginsburg *et al* 2002). Studies of patterns of media use suggest a significant diversity in the way technologies (old and new) are used in the context of the household.

The emphasis here is on the *how* questions (Morley 1996). It is very often the answers to this how question that complicate the more deterministic approach that technologies shape identities. Media ethnographies, which have focused on the consumption of media in the context of the home, have emphasised a number of parameters that shape the viewing process. Consumption here is understood as the internalisation of culture in everyday life (Miller 1988: 212).

A key finding, on which many studies converge, is that media are hardly ever used in a pure and complete way with our full concentration (Bausinger 1984; Gauntlett and Hill 1999; Gunter and Svennevig 1987; Morley 1995), an observation that complicates the assumptions made about the effects of the media and the methodology used to investigate them. Perhaps more research is needed on the structural uses of the media,[1] which include the moments when television functions as an environmental source or background noise, as well as its role as a regulative source, which punctuates time and activity (Lull 1990: 35).

Another significant dimension that is often neglected in bottom-up work is the issue of availability and access. Although this is a concern traditionally associated with political economy, access and availability are central to the consumption process and can be relevant to identity articulations, especially when availability of non-national media is limited. An investigation of availability and access at the level of consumption is one of the instances when research with audiences can come close to a political economic perspective, a prospect encouraged by some authors both from within the political economy perspective (Golding and Murdock 1996; Mosco 1996) and media ethnographies (Miller and Slater 2000).

Studies on consumption point to the diversification of audience engagement. Gender is a category that has been found to cut across a number of other parameters that contribute to the viewing process (Morley 1996; Gray 1992), although more recent studies did not find significant gender differences in

---

1   The other social uses of television are 'relational', involving television's capacity to facilitate communication or conflict (Lull: 1990: 35).

viewing patterns and uses of technologies (Gauntlett and Hill 1999). Such findings indicate the importance of social change. Consumption patterns and social relationships change over time as media technologies (and media content) themselves change. Bovill and Livingstone have identified the rise of a 'bedroom culture' in media consumption (2001), which contrasts the notion of television as the hearth of the household (cf Barthes 1980 cited in Morley 1995). Change is also important in relation to age. There are significant generational differences in the ways people use and interact with media, with younger generations portrayed as more media literate (Gauntlett and Hill 1999).

TOWARDS A MEDIATIONAL APPROACH TO THE TELEVISION TEXT

The text, hitherto the focus of the bulk of media research, has recently received a somewhat bad press. This can be explained as the exclusive focus on texts had dominated the research agenda for a number of years and in some cases impeded other, primarily sociological, concerns about media from developing. Moreover, and more importantly, the problem with many text-based studies is that they make wider inferences about media and their effects on society. This textual determinism is what has led audience theorists to question the validity of the sole focus on texts in media research (Livingstone 1998b; Morley 1992).

There are also other problems related to the analysis of textual research. In an increasingly media saturated world it is not at all obvious which text should be the focus of analysis; why focus on some particular texts, rather than others? Even more importantly, why should an arbitrary selection and analysis of a particular media text tell us something meaningful about the complex societies in which we live? Moreover, the notion of a text in itself has been seriously contested. Intertextuality is highly significant and cannot be overlooked in the context of continuous flows of media texts. Is it possible to analyse a text without taking its (often endless) intertextual references into account? There are also problems regarding the role of the analyst who can 'magically extract the meaning of texts' (Couldry 2000a: 136). This last point echoes the persistent problem of the 'preferred reading' of the text. As Morley has put it, '. . . is the preferred reading a property of the text, the analyst or the audience?' (1992: 122)

Another related problem involves the linearity that textual analyses often imply. This is often the case even when the reception, as a form of textual realisation, is taken into account. This is a criticism addressed to Hall's encoding/decoding model (1980) and its empirical application in Morley's *Nationwide* (1980). As Morley himself put it in a critique of his own study:

[t]he encoding/decoding metaphor is unhappily close to earlier models of communication in the sense that it implies a conveyor belt system of meaning that is far from fulfilling the promise for a cultural, cyclical model of communication. (1992: 121; see also Hall 1994)

All these apparent limitations of textual analysis should not lead us to abandon the notion of the text altogether. What they imply is that the existing assumptions and research questions associated with textual analysis are inadequate. What we need, then, are new questions and a more sociological approach to texts, which would start with questioning the texts themselves. Which texts become meaningful and under what circumstances? Text has been traditionally conflated with content although it can be more than that. We could think of text as genre and form and even as technology (Silverstone 1988).

The challenge at this point is to incorporate the text into a mediational approach to communication. I argue that the text is an inextricable part of the communication process. It cannot be studied in isolation, for this would be incomplete, but to study the process whilst ignoring it would be equally flawed. Of course, it all depends on the questions being asked and the empirical case itself. The text need not be included in all media studies; but in this study, a number of reasons point to its indispensable inclusion.

The first reason that the text was taken into account is the assumption that nationalism and identity are reproduced through media content, a claim that calls for empirical investigation. Secondly, the importance of representation in the articulation of identity discourses pointed to the inclusion of the text in the analysis. As Hall reminds us, 'identity is always constituted within, not outside, representation' (1990: 222). Here the interest is not only in representation as a textual property, but also in the reactions it generates. How do people react to the ways they see themselves mirrored in the media? This is particularly relevant in relation to inclusion or exclusion from public life. Finally, another criterion for the inclusion of media content was the observation about the particular character of the Greek news, which will be discussed in the next section. First, we will examine the mediational approach to television news (Silverstone in press).

News

News is the most heavily researched genre. However, most traditional approaches to news '… rarely depart significantly from an – often unwitting – normative view that the news' primary function is to serve society by informing the general population in ways that arm them for vigilant citizenship' (Schudson 2000: 194). Schudson also notes that what is missing from the sociology of news is an account of its audiences and publics. This is not exactly correct, however, as there are a number of studies, some of which were path-breaking in their time, on the interpretation of news (*inter alia* see Gamson 1992; Lewis 1991; Liebes 1997; Philo 1990; for the interpretation of a news magazine programme, see Morley 1999 [1980]). According to Silverstone, what is missing is not research on news viewers, but rather a more ritual and mediational approach to news as a dynamic component of social and cultural life (in press: 17).

News as mediation

Silverstone suggests that a mediational perspective on the news should focus on news as a social phenomenon that has become an indispensable component of everyday life. He observes that:

[news'] particular, and remarkably globally homogenous, structures of story-telling, accounts of heroism and disaster, narrative closure, construction of the newsreader as the nightly reader of tales, and its fixed position in the radio and television schedules together define the genre as crucial in this subject (Silverstone in press: 19).

It seems that for Silverstone form is almost more significant than content (the most heavily researched aspect of the news). How something is said is as, if not more, important than what is said. Moreover, in this vein, the news is a ritual that punctuates time and everyday life thus providing an almost paradoxical reassurance to its audiences. Silverstone sees the news as the 'key institution in the mediation of threat, risk and danger' from the outside world (1994: 17). For Silverstone it is 'the dialectical articulation of anxiety and security' that results in the creation of trust (1994: 16).

> Our nightly news watching is a ritual, both in its mechanical repetitiveness, but much more importantly in its presentation, through its fragmentary logic, of the familiar and the strange, the reassuring and the threatening. In Britain, no major news bulletin will either begin without a transcendent title sequence ... nor end without a 'sweetener' – a 'human story' to bring viewers back to the everyday. (Silverstone 1988: 26)

This study draws from this mediational perspective on the news that also echoes the work of Scannell in relation to public service broadcasting and the BBC (1989). Such a perspective is significant as it adds a new dimension to media texts that extends beyond sheer content to incorporate form and phenomenology. However, it is also criticised for assuming the social effects of ritual news viewing among a homogenous audience (Morley 2000 – see Chapter 2 above). The only way to solve this is to match the analysis of the news with audience research. This is something that had been suggested by Fiske and Hartley (1989 [1978]) through the concept of 'bardic television', which they developed in order to encompass the integration of the analysis of messages, as much as the institutions that produce them, and the audience's response and the communicator's intention (1989: 85). Television is paralleled to a bard, who functions as a *mediator of language* (1989: 85).

Apart from the mediational perspective to the study of the news, this book is also informed by the work of Billig, in *Banal Nationalism*, and the discursive strategies through which nationalism is reproduced (1995). Chapter 7 will discuss the audiences' interpretation of the news and the discourses news generates at a local level.

Greece: Wall-to-wall news?

The context for this study is the Greek broadcasting landscape that partly shapes the consumption of news and its impact in public life. The commercialisation of the broadcasting system in 1989[2] brought sweeping changes in programming and also in the format of news broadcasts, which have been characterised for their

---

2   Greece was the last country in the EU to deregulate its broadcasting system. This was a political and contingent decision rather than the product of planning and public policy (Papathanassopoulos 1990: 387).

length (sometimes reaching up to three hours) and emphasis on 'live' reporting and studio discussions. News broadcasts are very popular in Greece and this is reflected in their proportion in the overall television programme, which reached 35.5% and 76.7% for the two public broadcasting channels (ET-1 and NET) and 43.5% and 40% for the two leading private channels (ANTENNA, MEGA) at the time of the fieldwork (1998–2000) (AGB Hellas Yearbook 1999: 37). Audience measurement studies have indicated that television is by far the dominant medium for information: 71% of the Greek population watch the news everyday compared to 17% who listen to the radio news and 16% who read the newspapers on a daily basis.[3] Given also that the internet connection rates continue to be the lowest in the EU,[4] it is not an exaggeration to talk about the dominance of television news and even the phenomenon of wall-to-wall news on Greek television. Although there have been efforts by the private channels themselves to self-regulate this phenomenon and to set standard times and duration for news broadcasts, the situation continues to be similar at the time of writing.

TOWARDS AN ANTHROPOLOGY OF THE MEDIA

This study follows the circulation of meaning in the context of discourses and practices about the nation and belonging. This involves understanding communication as a process of mediation. In so doing it will focus on the interrelated processes of media and consumption in the context of everyday life. The aim is to compare the discourses and practices generated in each moment of the mediation process in an attempt to locate the power of the media. This concluding section turns to the emerging field of media anthropology in order to identify a working approach for the study of the media as a process that might overcome limitations in the previous paradigms.

This section argues that the recent developments toward a field of media anthropology (Askew and Wilk 2002; Ginsburg *et al* 2002; Miller and Slater 2000) signal a return to a ritual model of communication. The introduction of ethnography in media studies was accompanied by a lengthy discussion relating to the proper application of the method and whether it actually deserved to be called ethnography in the traditional anthropological sense. Some have remarked that the term is often used to indicate qualitative methods in general (Lull 1988; Nightingale 1993), while only a few researchers have conducted participant observation, which requires a long immersion in, and investigation of, the culture studied. Moreover, media ethnographies, by focusing exclusively on the media, were criticised for ignoring or reifying other cultural determinants that shape everyday life (Radway 1988: 367). Given that ethnography has been successfully applied in the study of media production (Born 2004), consumption (Miller 1992;

---

3   The respective EU mean for television news is 68%, while for radio and newspapers it is 68 and 42% respectively. The figures reflect the period of the fieldwork but have remained unchanged (Eurobarometer 2000).

4   In 1999 the internet connection rate was 6% and although it has doubled in recent year (14% in 2003 according to the Eurobarometer survey) Greece continues to hold the lowest place in the EU together with Portugal (Eurobarometer reports 2000 and 2003).

Miller and Slater 2000; Abu Lughod 1995) and even texts (Altheide 1987; Pinney and Dwyer 2001), this chapter represents a step further in this debate. The concern here is with the move toward the field of media anthropology.

According to Marcus, media studies, and particularly the merging of the study of production and reception, have been one important arena in which multi-sited ethnography has emerged (1995: 103). Multi-sited ethnographic research – developed within the context of the postmodern turn in anthropology – moves from single sites and local situations of conventional ethnographic research 'to examine the circulation of cultural meanings, objects and identities in diffuse time-space' (Marcus 1995: 96). Note the emphasis on the 'circulation of meanings', which was also at the heart of the definition of mediation (Silverstone 1999: 13). Given that media power is diffuse, the ethnographic approach is well suited to identify the moments of media influence, but also of audience resistance. A multi-sited media ethnography can extend beyond the point of contact between text and reception and can examine the opaque presence of media in everyday life; for example, Couldry pointed out that media power is evident in people's personal contact with the media frame, rather than in the moment of reception (2000b). Such observations point out that media power might be located in spheres where it was not traditionally investigated and that we need a holistic approach in order to do so.

Ethnography requires a long term immersion in the cultures or sites studied and it is through this immersion that the strongest aspect of media ethnographies can emerge, that is, the unpredictability of findings, the possibility to be surprised by one's research conclusions (Ginsburg *et al* 2002). This is usually a good indication that the research has added something new to the existing body of knowledge. By adopting a bottom-up perspective, ethnography allows ideas and concepts to emerge from the field. Moreover, ethnography allows for an observation not only of people's discourses (what people say in an interview context), but also of their practices (what they actually do in their everyday lives) (Miller 1998). These are not always in agreement and such discrepancies are very revealing about the processes of consumption and media power in everyday life.

Through the immersion in the research field, ethnographers develop a long-term rapport with the informants. This in-depth perspective into people's lives allows for the development of a relationship of empathy and trust, which is vital for the understanding of the intimate and affective dimensions of everyday life of which the media are part. This is particularly relevant for this book, as the discourses about belonging and identification are largely emotional. It is quite surprising that the emotional aspects of communication have hitherto been somewhat ignored in media studies (for an exception, see Ang 1989 [1985]) given that emotions play such a central role in mediated communication.[5] This is

---

5   Uses and gratifications was the first theory that addressed the issue of emotions especially in
     terms of how the media can instigate an emotional release (see Blumler, Katz and Gurevitch
     1974). This approach, however, was individualistic and functionalist. A recent and
     innovative study on the emotional dimension of communication is by Lunt and Stenner on
     Jerry Springer as an emotional public sphere (2005).

perhaps because underlying studies of communication are normative ideas of how audiences should function as well-informed citizens. Ethnography can add an empathetic perspective on intimate processes and highlight nuances that might otherwise go unnoticed.

Moreover, the development of trust is crucial regarding issues of access, especially in the case of sensitive topics. In my fieldwork, given the sensitivity surrounding minority issues in Greece, it was only through an ethnographic perspective that I managed to gain people's trust and access to their homes. Given the resistance that I initially encountered in the field, especially among the Turkish minority, I was forced to revise what was a neat research design centred on in-depth and group interviews and decided to commit to a long-term immersion and participation in my informants' everyday lives.

It seems then that an ethnographic perspective can support the investigation of the media as a process of mediation. Ethnography allows for the integration of different levels of analysis in order to achieve empirical confirmation (Livingstone 1998a: 206). The integration of the levels of analysis is also linked to the micro/macro relationship. The ethnographic perspective on audience reception is valuable '… as it can inform our understanding of media power as it operates in the micro-contexts of consumption – without divorcing those issues from those of macro-structural processes' (Morley 1992: 40). As Morley notes, echoing Giddens' structuration theory (1979; 1984), 'the macro structures can only be reproduced through micro-processes' (1992: 19). Crucially, the comparison of the different levels, or moments, in the process of mediation might uncover the elusive – yet extant – power of the media. In this sense, this study is also a study of media power.

CHAPTER 5

MEDIATED EVERYDAY LIVES: MEDIA CONSUMPTION, BELONGING AND BOUNDARIES

In April 1998 I visited the city of Komotini in Thrace, in north-eastern Greece, as part of an exploratory trip before starting fieldwork. Komotini is the capital of the region, where the majority of the Turkish minority in Greece lives. From the top floor of the hotel where I was staying in the main square, I had a topographical overview of the whole town, which seemed to be split into two. There was no wall or barbed wire; there were no police patrols; it was rather a difference of landscape, a matter of aesthetics. In front of me was a neighbourhood of low-rise buildings, mainly houses connected through a maze of alleyways and dead ends. Houses had high facades and front doors, and often unorthodox extensions – an extra room behind the kitchen, in the internal yard, or on the roof; and on the roofs, an almost mandatory presence, satellite dishes. Throughout the sea of dishes in the low-built town were scattered numerous minarets, competing with each other for height. Behind me lay the rest of the town with reasonably organised roads, medium-rise concrete apartment buildings of four to five floors, Athens-style. Through these buildings rose church bell-towers, themselves competing for height with the minarets. In this part of the town there were no satellite dishes.

Back in Athens, satellite dishes helped me find my way to the neighbourhood of Gazi when I started fieldwork. Walking in the streets behind the old gas station during my first visit, I could tell where Turkish-speaking people lived from the presence – or not – of satellite dishes. Their presence was a reassurance that I was in the right place. The dishes served as a marker of recognition; in a sense, they objectified the community and its boundaries. It was only after entering people's homes that I realised that what was perceived as so different was, in fact, rather ordinary.

During that visit to Komotini in 1998, a Turkish journalist told me that satellite television is the 'umbilical cord' linking the minority to Turkey. This is a view that has become prevalent across Europe, among conservative thinkers, politicians, policy makers, minority leaders and the media themselves (Aksoy and Robins 2000: 351). The consequences of this approach are far-reaching and significant as they shape public policies, mould stereotypes and affect people's lives. Such a perspective echoes theories that favour powerful media; however, it is often challenged by the findings of empirical audience research.

This chapter, based on interviews with, and participant observation among, Turkish speakers, Greeks and Cypriots living in Athens, challenges the assumption that media determine identities thereby providing an 'umbilical cord' to identity. The uses of media and their integration in people's daily lives is a more complex process that involves a number of parameters, material, social and individual. However, although media do not determine identities, they do contribute in creating symbolic communicative spaces that either include or exclude, thereby affecting audiences' lives and discourses about their identities. This is the core argument of this chapter. In order to make this case, I will map people's media resources and examine how they are integrated in the informants' everyday lives. The emphasis here is on media as objects and the context of viewing. In this sense this chapter performs another function, complementing and contextualising Chapters 6 and 7, which address news content and news reception respectively. Of course, the distinction between media objects and media content is not clear-cut. Even though the primary focus of this chapter is on media as objects, media content will, inevitably, also be addressed.

The overall theoretical framework here is mediation. Media are understood as a process and emphasis is placed on their integration in everyday structures and the limitations posed by material conditions. Although media in general will be discussed, the emphasis of the chapter is on news media. The chapter takes into account the issue of access and availability. This chapter will also explore the informants' personal experiences with the media and journalists, which often shape people's overall interpretative framework.

The chapter is divided into three main sections, one for each group. This division does not imply that there are essential differences among the Greek, Cypriot and Turkish-speaking informants. On the contrary, one of the aims of the chapter is to identify themes common to informants of different backgrounds. Effort has been made to give voice to as many informants as possible, although selection was inevitable. This chapter should be read together with the description of the informants in Appendix II.

MEDIATED EVERYDAY LIVES: GREEK AUDIENCES

Any discussion of the uses and appropriations of the media needs to start with the issue of availability and access. As indicated in the introduction, the Greek media system is characterised by an excess of supply over demand (Papathanassopoulos 1999: 381). It should be noted that the broadcasting landscape is volatile as it is subject to constant changes. An interesting feature of the Greek broadcasting system is that a number of satellite channels (including CNN, MTV, Eurosport and the Greek-Cypriot public-service channel) are re-broadcast terrestrially for free. The other prominent feature is the system's national orientation – apart from the channels re-broadcast terrestrially, satellite penetration is low.[1] There is no cable television and digital television only began transmitting in December 1999, so it was not available during the two case studies. There is one subscription channel with a decoder that reaches 9.5% of households (AGB 2000: 30). This subscription channel shows only films, sport and children's programmes.

---

1   Satellite viewing amounted to less than 2% at the time of the fieldwork; see AGB Hellas Reports 1999 and 2000.

Of the mainstream available media, television is the most popular and heavily used. Radio came second and newspapers third. Internet penetration among the informants reflected the national figures at the time of the fieldwork (6%). Of the thirty-one Greek informants, only six had access to the internet. These were the only informants in the whole sample who had access to the internet. Of these informants, however, only three used it for reading news, albeit not regularly (Michalis, Sophia and Sergios).

A popular news culture

In Chapter 4, Greek television was described as producing a 24-hour news culture. This section will focus on whether the availability of news programmes is matched with an equally impressive viewership. As one would expect, none of the informants followed the constant flow of news programmes throughout the day on television and in the other media. Some informants, however, were heavier news viewers than others.

Ilias' and Eugenia's daily schedule seems to follow television programming as they watch the news and other programmes throughout the day. This is combined with the consumption of other media, such as newspapers and radio. Both are pensioners and have more free time than the rest of the informants. They start their days with a cup of coffee whilst watching the early morning news programmes. Later in the morning, Ilias visits his friends at the coffee house where he also reads the newspapers. Eugenia skims through one or two papers when she visits her sister who lives nearby. At 19:30 Ilias watches the news, most often together with Eugenia. Only during the summer months, they sometimes skip the evening news to have dinner in their garden.[2]

Haris, a high school teacher in his forties, describes his daily schedule as revolving around different media, as if the news punctuates his daily life.

> The moment I get in the car I will switch on the radio to listen to the news. Later, I'll read a newspaper, I might borrow it from someone at school, or I'll buy one to pass the time, or because I want to read about something in particular. Now, in the evening, as far as the news is concerned, I flick through channels.

Even if people do not watch the news continually, they usually watch it at some point during the day. The most common time is between 19:30 and 22:00 when the evening news bulletins are scheduled. In Haris' house, the television is on during most afternoons and evenings, even if nobody is watching at a particular time. Haris always watches the news, most often together with his wife and children. Many of the informants often watch the news whilst having their dinner. Lena mentioned that this perhaps generates a sense of security, that being 'I am well, thank God, I have my family, my job, I am healthy, secure and removed from the world's madness'. Spyros cannot sleep without the television on. His night-time viewing most of the time includes the last news bulletin, broadcast at around midnight. He often falls asleep with the television on.

---

2   Television viewing drops significantly in the summer months according to the AGB Hellas survey (AGB Hellas 2000: 16–17).

People do not just watch the news in a purposeful way, in order to be informed. Watching the news is also a habit, a routine, the same way that watching television in general is. News is associated with cosiness and relaxation (even if this was described as a hideous habit). As mentioned above, because of its scheduling, news coincides with the time people have dinner. In this context, the phrase 'watching the news' is perhaps misleading, as not everyone in front of the screen is watching. People often talk to family members about other issues; other informants talk on the phone, while others watch with the sound off and put it back on when an image attracts their attention. Older people (Ilias), or those living on their own (Michalis), turn the television on to keep them company.

'Addicted to news'

Many interviewees described themselves as 'addicted to the news'. By this, they meant that if they were at home and the news was on they 'have to switch the television on'. This 'addiction' was disrupted when people went on holidays, which they described as a 'period of detoxification'. As one informant put it, 'without the news it feels strange, that you have cut yourself off'. People attributed this 'addiction' to their need to 'keep up with reality', thus identifying news with reality. Even those critical of the news (and particularly of the sensationalist approach of the private channels) mentioned that they watch the programmes because they reflect Greek society.

> Nicos: One needs to watch SKAI. This is what our country produces, even if we don't like it. … If you want to be in touch with what is happening in your country you need to watch a bit of everything, including SKAI.

However, given the ubiquitous presence of the news in everyday life and the extent to which it is embedded in daily structures and practices, another interpretation is that the need to watch the news is a need to regulate one's life. Such observations point to an intimate dimension of news consumption that punctuates daily life thus providing its audiences with an almost paradoxical reassurance (Silverstone 1994). News can be the morning alarm clock, the voice that keeps company with those who feel lonely, the means through which to avoid having a conversation during a family dinner, a mindless ritual, or the organisation of everyday life itself, echoing Lull's 'structural uses' of the media (1990: 35).

Of course, news is not just on television. Many informants listen to the news on the radio in their cars, often stuck in the Athens traffic. Thodoris, a taxi driver, mainly listens to the radio during his eight-hour shift in the car. For some, radio is the preferred news medium at home. For Giota, a housewife, radio provides the background for her daily routines. As she is always busy preparing dinner or washing the dishes during the time of the evening television news, she mainly listens to the news on the radio, or listens to the news on television, thus using television in an aural way.

Tasos, a 'radio news maniac', wakes up at 5:30 in the morning and listens to the news programmes on various stations until 8:15 when he leaves for the office.

Tasos: I wake up early in the morning and because I know that some stations will have more information, some emphasise different aspects, there are also stations that are faster than others in breaking the news. I wake up early. I listen to ANTENNA at 5:30. At 6:00 I will listen to ERA1. At 7:00 SKAI. At 8:00 PLANET.[3] ... This way I have a complete picture of what is happening.

People use the different media to varying degrees. Fotini watches the late night bulletin before going to bed. She watches the 8 o'clock news if she is at home, but she is often out at that time. Even if she stays at home, she never watches the whole programme: 'in order to do that, you have to have three spare hours. Who can do that? I do not have the time'. Although she buys the paper everyday, she will only skim through it. She told me that she had recently been so busy that she only found out that there was a cabinet reshuffle when a friend told her. Michalis found out about the reshuffle from the coffee house waiter.

The different media combined provide a constant background in people's everyday lives. This highly mediated environment blends with the existing social networks; even if a news story escapes someone, they will find out through their friends, colleagues or people in the street. In this sense, news extends beyond the television programme and the screen and becomes an integral part of everyday life, in constant circulation – from the studio to the living room, the car, the workplace, the streets, the coffee houses and often back to the studio.

Direct experiences with the news media

What adds to the cosiness and informality of the news is the possibility of seeing oneself, or an acquaintance, on the news. This is more possible in Greece than in other broadcasting systems, such as the British, first, because of the ratio of population and channels (many channels for a relatively small country), and, secondly, because of the prolonged duration of news programmes. Shortly before I met Georgia, her son had been on the news as a witness to a fire near his workplace. Tasos' neighbour was on television when I visited his house, giving an interview as the head of the anti-smoking campaign. Nicos saw the daughter of his teacher, who was being interviewed as a Greenpeace activist. This perhaps explains why most interviewees referred to the news as gossipy.

Overall, Greek informants recounted positive (or neutral) personal experiences with the media. Television is also seen by some people as the vehicle for voicing complaints or criticisms. Yannis told me how a family acquaintance appeared on television to complain about an inflated bill he received from the water supply company. Only after he appeared on television was his complaint taken seriously. Nicos told me that a relative of his called the authorities with whom he had a dispute, threatening to call 'the channels' to complain. This case is not a direct experience with the media, but rather an indication of how the media can be used in a non-media related context for non-media related purposes, often

---

3   All names in capitals refer to Athens radio stations. ANTENNA belongs to the same company that owns the identically named television station. ERA1 is one of the three public service stations (part of ERT).

with successful results. It appears that the news, apart from information, is an integral part of everyday life providing many people with a common point of reference. This is contrasted to the experience of Turks when they see themselves misrepresented on television, which is a frustrating, rather than a cosy, or positive, experience.

'News programmes are no longer watchable': Viewing paradoxes

There are, however, a number of ostensible paradoxes associated with television viewing. Many informants told me that 'news programmes are no longer watchable' (*oi eidiseis de vlepontai pleon*). At a first level this phrase is in stark contrast to the high viewing rates news programmes attract and the heavy news consumption. How can one be addicted to news and then declare that it is no longer 'watchable'? This contradiction becomes less puzzling by distinguishing between two levels; 'news is no longer watchable' refers to the quality of news as information and is related to the critical stance of viewers, whereas 'news is an addiction' refers to the habitual, routine viewing of news programmes, every evening at the same time. This paradox points to a particular collision between the critical faculties of the viewers and their actual practices.

This paradox is further complicated in relation to the public channels. Although many informants mentioned that ET-1 and NET were the most decent channels, very few actually watched them.[4] Indeed, in none of my visits to people's homes were they watching the NET news. Marilena told me that sometimes she even forgets that ERT exists. Sophia described ERT's style as primitive compared to that of private channels, which 'have turned news into a spectacle'. 'It's sad, but ERT does not sell', Sophia added.

On the other hand, older informants described ERT as a government mouthpiece. This is reflected in the use of the adjective 'governmental' (*kyvernitiko*), which was sometimes used instead of 'public' (*dimosio*), or 'state' (*kratiko*), to describe ERT. One informant in his forties mentioned that he does not expect impartiality from the ERT channels as their position will be inevitably biased. Vassilis was sceptical of the clientelist relationships between ERT's administration and the government and pointed to the number of ERT's employees. 'The state is corrupt and inept because it employs 10,000 people in ERT whom we pay as taxpayers. They do nothing, they just sit on chairs.' The age difference between those informants who expressed a positive attitude towards ERT and those who associated the channel with the government can be explained by the latter's experience of the pre-deregulation era when ERT was tightly linked to the governing party's politics.

---

4   This is confirmed by a survey about viewers' satisfaction with television channels. The public channels had the highest percentage (NET 72.1% and ET-1 69.5%), followed by MEGA (67.1%) and ANTENNA (65.1%). Recall that the public channels' ratings are in constant decline (Taylor Nelson Sofres Metrisis, published in the daily *Eleutherotypia*, 29.5.02).

Most of the other informants, however, discerned a significant difference in ERT's news programmes and overall output in comparison with previous decades. They attribute this change to the privatisation of the airwaves and the proliferation of channels that increased competition for audiences. The ending of ERT's monopoly brought about more polyphony, also within ERT's own programmes. Still others were unconvinced about the quality of this diversity and expressed strong suspicions about the covert interests (*symferonta*) that still determine broadcast news (Thodoris, Alexandros, Vassilis). 'All channels show the same things' some informants told me, a comment reminiscent of Horkheimer and Adorno's arguments about the culture industry (1979). Moreover, some of the informants, notably those with middle class backgrounds, expressed their dissatisfaction about the populist style of news presentation.

> Sophia: Overall I cannot watch SKAI because it makes me depressed. . . . I cannot stand it when they degrade (*xeftilizoun*) the issues. Especially in the case of national issues.

> Nicos: Sometimes I am disgusted [and] I cannot watch for more than a couple of minutes. OK, perhaps you can have a laugh because it is ridiculous, but it is perhaps a bit too much.

In a rather different vein, Vassilis said that the proliferation of channels provides people with choice: 'one can watch TILETORA, a channel well known for its far right positions, or the channel of the Communist Party.' Andreas contested the homogeneity of television news by arguing that the particular format of the news, with its long duration and succession of invited guests, allows for a number of voices to be heard, even if this is for the sake of sensationalism and attracting viewers.

> Do you know what I believe about the Greek channels? That the news is certainly biased, but there are talk shows and the moments when news programmes become like talk shows with all these 'windows', and there you can get indirect information about the background of the issues. This is where you can see some weirdos . . . who tell their own story. This is when you can think about the other side of the events.

Alternative-to-national media

People do not rely just on national television, radio and newspapers for their daily information and entertainment. Greek audiences have access to a number of satellite channels that are retransmitted terrestrially via ERT. Digital television, through which subscribers receive a number of global media, had not been introduced at the time of the fieldwork. The other available medium was the internet.

Changing attitudes to foreign media

Global media are not so new. People have been accessing non-Greek media from the mid-war period. Some of the older informants pointed out that at some point in their lives they relied solely on foreign (non-Greek) media for their information. Tasos told me how his family would gather around the radio during the German occupation in the Second World War (and later the Civil War), in order to listen to the BBC news. In those turbulent times, local Greek media were not reliable and people could only find out about their own country from abroad. Tasos remembers that during the Civil War, in the town where he lived as a teenager, the left-wing coalition that controlled the area would put the BBC on loudspeakers and people would gather in the square to listen to the 9 o'clock bulletin in Greek. He remembers nostalgically how people would gather at the square in the middle of the winter to listen and discuss the news.

Aggeliki and Marilena point to a similar experience during the junta, between 1967 and 1974. They remember listening to the Greek programme of Deutsche Welle in order to find out about what was happening in the world and in their own country. People would stealthily tune their sets to these stations, often when gathered together at friends' homes. Similar patterns were observed by Mankekar in her ethnography of television consumption in India. She notes that before the advent of transnational television and when Doordarshan (the Indian public television channel) was censored by the state, 'when something momentous happened people would turn to the BBC World Service on their transistors to get the "true story"' (Mankekar 1999: 354).

Such experiences, often narrated with nostalgia, are contrasted with the informants' recent experiences with non-Greek media. While once the BBC and Deutsche Welle were regarded as the symbols of impartial journalism and people would turn to them to find out about their own country, today Western media are highly contested. CNN stands out from the rest of European and North American media as it received most negative comments.[5] Such observations point to the importance of a historical perspective in audience studies, which can cast light on the changing attitudes to media technologies and content (Livingstone *et al* 2001).

Even when CNN reports from Greece and the region, many informants regard its approach inadequate. Foreign media, and CNN in particular, were accused of ignoring the context and not going into depth when reporting Greek-Turkish relations.

> Fotini: [Foreign media presented the Imia crisis] in a general and vague way, like tension in the Balkans and tension in Greek-Turkish relations. Now, who, for what reason, and why, they do not care. They just mention the two parties, Greece and Turkey …, they do not go into depth … to examine whose fault it is, and for what reason [this is happening]. … They do not care. The only ones who care are us. And we have to care about ourselves.

The use and appropriation of Western media is shaped by Greek viewers' attitudes towards their content and particularly their representations of Greece. It is in relation to Western media that discourses about identity and Greekness come to the surface. Although from the previous pages the news appears to create a common point of reference, identity did not appear as a distinct category. These examples illustrate that it is always in relation to the other – and the other's representation of oneself – that identity is articulated, confirming that identity is relational.

---

5   Recall that CNN is freely available in most households (whereas channels such as BBC World require subscription on digital television, which was not available before the end of 1999).

Switching off

Not all informants were addicted to the news. Thodoris, a taxi driver and former heavy television viewer, told me that he had recently decided to stop watching television on a regular basis. He mainly attributed his decision to his lack of trust of journalists and media. 'It's all fake', he told me; and he added, 'I often feel television takes me for a fool' (*vlaka*).

> Television treats me like a fool. It tells me, 'you are an idiot'. That's how I feel I'm treated. How can I put it; I felt this way in the recent elections when I looked at those billboards with all those candidates standing over a design, discussing the major roadworks. Of course, this did not happen for real. They don't even care about the roads. It's all fake. It is in this way that television also calls me a fool. Literally. In my face: 'you are a fool'.

Thodoris did not read newspapers for similar reasons. He preferred to listen to the hourly news updates on the radio, which he considered less biased. Interestingly, even if he denied watching the news, he was well informed about current affairs. Even if Thodoris does not proactively switch on the television he will find out the latest news through friends, family, or clients.

Other informants who did not follow the news regularly were the working-class high school students, who attributed their lack of interest in the news to their loaded schedule as most of them were preparing for their final exams. Another reason for their disinterest, however, is that they lacked the contextual information with which to interpret the news, particularly the news on national issues. This made them more detached and less keen to follow the news and current affairs programmes, a phenomenon related to age and also evident among younger Turkish viewers (see following section). The lack of contextual information is also related to their limited information resources, and is also a class issue. For example, the middle class informants, who were studying in London and had access to a plethora of media, were 'addicted' to the news, while being only four years older than the students in the working class Athens neighbourhood.

Gendered consumption: women switching off

When I met Giota and her friends and tried to arrange an interview, I was explicitly asked not to visit them during the early evenings, as this is normally the busiest period in the day for Giota and Georgia. 'Don't you watch the news at that time?', I asked. 'Oh no, my girl, we only steal a glance at it every now and then' (*sta klefta*). 'At that time we're preparing dinner. There's no time for news. Only in passing we might catch a glimpse of what is going on'. Giota made a comment later that echoed Thodoris' words: 'Perhaps it is because [the news] makes a fool of us that we don't watch'.

Giota, Georgia and Rena told me that it was different for their daughters, 'who are educated, have their careers and know more about the issues'. However, the same gendered pattern in media consumption is confirmed by younger professional women. Aggeliki, a high school teacher, told me that she does not have time to watch the news, although 'her men' (husband and sons), who do watch, tell her what has happened. Gender differences also concern the power over choice or, rather, the remote control. Katerina cannot watch her preferred channel as there is only one set in the house and she has to watch the news on her father's favourite channel. A similar story is told by Sevasti; in her case it is her husband, Thodoris, who has a say over the choice of channels (or, over deciding whether to watch, or not).

Such patterns seem to confirm the findings of British researchers on gendered media use (Morley 1986; Gray 1992). However, gender differences do not pertain to all informants. In middle and upper middle class families and generally among the more educated informants, gender differences are no longer salient. In general, what emerges as the difference that cuts across all others is that of class as it relates to all the above cases of 'switching off'. It has to be noted, however, that these differences apply to issues of access and choice and do not necessarily translate into differentiated interpretations of the news programmes, as will be discussed in Chapter 7.

MEDIATED EVERYDAY LIVES : GREEK CYPRIOT AUDIENCES

All the media available to Greek audiences are also available to Greek Cypriots, who also have access to the Cypriot Public Service Channel (RIK/CYP SAT), which is retransmitted terrestrially for free via ERT. There are also a number of newsletters circulated by the various Cypriot organisations in Greece.[6] Finally, there are also newspapers from Cyprus that are available in kiosks in central Athens that distribute the foreign press. It has to be noted here that Greek and Greek Cypriot media are closely connected; a number of Cypriot media are owned by Greek media conglomerates. Such an example is ANTENNA, which airs a proportion of its Greek programmes in Cyprus (although the news is produced locally). ERT also broadcasts in Cyprus a programme modified from that broadcast in Greece. None of the Cypriot informants was a regular internet user at the time of the fieldwork.

Despite the reasonable presence of Cypriot media in Greece, most informants relied on mainstream Greek media for their daily entertainment and information. They said that they use Cypriot media when they are in Cyprus, and Greek when in Greece (although this distinction is not always meaningful as indicated above). Many switch to RIK's news when something particular happens. People exchange frequent phone calls with relatives and friends in Cyprus and these networks are key sources of information on Cyprus.

Anna watches the news every evening on her favourite channel, MEGA. Sometimes she will watch NET. She reads Greek newspapers regularly and never misses the Sunday editions. She only reads Cypriot newspapers when in Cyprus.

---

6   Most of the Cypriot informants were not members of these organisations, which they found too politicised.

> Anna: I am not the typical case of the Cypriot who lives in Athens, because I know from other Cypriots, they hang out together, they gather in the [Cypriot] student parties, they read the [Cypriot] newspapers, they watch every evening. I'm not like that. You might think that I've renounced my Cypriot identity, but I won't accept that. I'm just very involved in life here in Athens. And I watch the news to get informed, I want to be informed, I like watching the news and I try to watch at least once a day, both the local news and from Europe.

Despite Anna's – somewhat guilty – assertion that she is not a typical case, her routines are similar to those of other informants. Chryssa prefers to watch the news on NET and to a lesser degree MEGA and ANTENNA. She thinks that the news on NET goes more into depth and she attributes this to the increasing independence and impartiality of public television. She also watches CNN and reads British newspapers (she studied in the UK, which is where her sons were studying at the time of the fieldwork). Generally, Greek Cypriots' patterns resembled those of the middle class Greek informants.

Lia and Yannos have both lived abroad for some years. Lia found great differences between the experience of being Greek Cypriot in England and in Greece.

> Lia: England is a foreign country (*xeni hora*) and there is a need for the members of the community to bond. We do not feel the same as the Greek Cypriots in England. At least this is how *we* feel about this. Here we have families and we are close to them. We have friends. It's not like when you are in England and you feel nostalgic about your country. We feel at home in Greece.

Yannos adds that:

> In England, because we lived in a completely foreign environment, we had to be part of the community, it was a defence mechanism. We feel Greece is our home (*tin Ellada ti niothoume patrida*). Same language, same religion, same mentality.

Despite the centrality of mainstream Greek media, some informants are more likely to watch the Cypriot channel than others. Such cases were Orestis, Eva and Elpida, who had been in Athens for a shorter period as students. An exception is Yannos, who used to watch RIK regularly even though he has lived in Greece most of his life. Orestis also bought Cypriot newspapers, something none of the other informants would do proactively.

Informants did not observe significant differences between the private and the public channels, particularly in relation to how Cyprus is covered. Marianna and Ioanna stressed that both private and public channels ignore the issue. They provide, however, different reasons for this. Journalists have told Marianna that the Cyprus issue 'does not sell' because people are tired of the issue. For ERT, however, the reasons are political; Marianna said that 'the governmental channels are keeping their lips sealed' (*ehoune valei tsiroto sto stoma*).

Switching off

When I contacted Lia to arrange a joint interview with her husband, the first thing she told me was that they had no television at home. When we met, she and Yannos, her husband, told me that they had not watched television for almost two months. When their television broke down they neither fixed it nor bought a new one. Lia and Yannos felt disenfranchised with the sensationalist, and often politically motivated, coverage on all Greek channels and they decided to switch off.

The couple used to watch RIK regularly before they decided to ban television. Yannos described how he did not trust ERT, as it would often interfere in the transmission of RIK, when sensitive issues were mentioned.

> Whenever sensitive issues were mentioned in RIK's broadcast, the programme would be interrupted. … This was not by accident, because it only happened when sensitive things that should not become public were said.

Yannos added that in Cyprus all these 'sensitive issues' are discussed. 'Everything, the truth is said in Cyprus. Even during the dictatorship in Greece, we got different information from the people on the mainland.'

What is different in the case of the Cypriot viewers is that the reasons for switching off are less gendered or class based, but rather grounded on the dissatisfaction with the reporting of the 'national issues', particularly when Cyprus is involved. Another reason – though not as strong – was their personal experiences with the media.

Personal experiences with the media

Marianna expressed some bitterness towards Greek media and journalists because they did not cover adequately the Cyprus issue and related initiatives. Her experience was first hand, as she was involved in an organisation that aimed to increase awareness about the Cyprus problem.

> Marianna: Whenever we asked the media to cover our events, they hardly ever did. They don't even cover the political aspect of the issue. They just don't cover it. They prefer to have a report on two missing cows than something on Cyprus.

Her friend Ioanna adds:

> We will send 50 invitations and press releases to television channels, radio stations, newspapers and magazines and only two journalists will come, and they will not be from high circulation papers.

> Marianna: They simply do not care. That's it. There is a conspiratorial silence.

Marianna attributes this 'apathy' to the lack of education and awareness on the part of the journalists' who, she claims, are not well educated or trained. She adds, however, that responsibility also lies with the editorial policies of the media. Both Marianna and Ioanna say that this comes 'from above': 'There is a line that someone dictates (*mia grammi pou pernaei*). … Otherwise how come all newspapers and channels do not give priority to the Cyprus issue?'

MEDIATED EVERYDAY LIVES: TURKISH-SPEAKING AUDIENCES

Gaziots have access to all mainstream Greek media. There are no local Turkish language media in Athens.[7] None of the informants had access to, or used, the internet. The Turkish press is available in central Athens kiosks, together with the international press, but nobody in Gazi was reading it. There is also a video club in Gazi from where one can rent Turkish videos, although during the fieldwork its business had declined mainly due to the rise in popularity of Turkish satellite television channels.[8] In the last decade, the installation of satellite dishes, in order to get television channels from Turkey, has become very popular. In the mid 1990s, a dish cost around 60,000 Greek drachmas[9], an affordable price even for low income households.

I started by assuming that all people had access to Turkish channels, but I was quickly proven wrong as the picture was more complex than I had initially thought. Not all households had Turkish channels – and not all households had Greek. Younger couples do not always install satellite dishes, although they often watch Turkish channels at their parents' houses.

> Murat: My parents have satellite television, I don't. When I go there I sometimes watch [the Turkish channels]. But usually I watch the Greek [channels]. Most times, to be honest, I do not understand the Turkish. They speak [the language] differently, more clearly. When we speak and you tell me something that I don't understand, I will look it up in the dictionary and I'll find it. But in Turkish it's very difficult to find the word when there is no book or dictionary.

A reason younger people do not always have, or do not watch, Turkish satellite television is because of the language. Educated in Greek,[10] the younger generations in Gazi are more confident in Greek than in Turkish. Moreover, they often told me that the Turkish they speak is not like the Turkish spoken on television.[11] Murat's comment also points to the lack of resources in Gazi. It is not, of course, that there are no Turkish-language books and dictionaries in Athens, but rather that these are not accessible to the informants. Lacking a working knowledge of written Turkish, Murat and his peers do not feel these dictionaries would be of much use. Moreover, as there is no bookshop in the area, they would have to go to the central bookstores to get the dictionaries, which is not something they would do for Greek books either.

While the younger people feel more comfortable with Greek, older informants prefer Turkish. Nuriye, a woman in her 50s whose mother tongue is Turkish

---

7   In Thrace there are numerous local Turkish-language newspapers and radio stations.

8   Turkish satellite television channels started broadcasting in 1990. They were initially based outside Turkey, but targeted the home market, which was then monopolised by the Turkish public service broadcasting channel (TRT). As Aksoy and Robins have noted, the introduction of private channels opened up the opportunity for a shift from official Kemalist culture to a culture that reflected the diversity within Turkish society (1997).

9   This is equivalent to 173 euros, or £110. The price today is higher, but still affordable.

10   In 1996 the multicultural school, catering for all minorities in the area, started its classes in Gazi. This encouraging development only affects children who started school after 1996.

11   This is also related to the differences (in expressions and accent) between the Turkish spoken in Thrace and modern Turkish.

although she also speaks Greek, told me that she feels better watching Turkish programmes. 'It's my language. I understand better.' In the early 1990s, Nuriye and her husband bought a satellite dish to get Turkish channels. They have no aerial and therefore do not receive any mainstream Greek channels. Their son, who lives next door with his own family, has access only to Greek channels. Nuriye visits her son's house whenever she wants to watch the news in Greek.

Language is an important factor here; it is the reason Nuriye prefers to watch Turkish channels and Murat prefers to watch Greek. It is also the reason why the majority of people of all generations do not watch English-language channels – they are not competent in English. Nonetheless, linguistic boundaries are not rigid. Everybody in Gazi spoke fluent Greek (admittedly some more fluently than others). People shift between languages in everyday conversation and in relation to the media they use. Sometimes this is also related to the shifts between public and private spaces. People speak Turkish at home and a mixture of Greek and Turkish when they are in public, especially when Greeks are present.

I noticed that men watched significantly more television during the winter months. From April to mid-October, men were hardly ever at home in the early evenings. They would go for walks, to the cafeterias, or to the square. This is a pattern among Greek audiences as well, although among them it was not gendered. In general, gender differences were more salient in Gazi than among Greek audiences. Women spent more time at home and were less educated and less fluent in Greek than Gaziot men.[12] Generally, there was a discernible gender segregation reflected in the uses of space and the media; men play cards at the clubs, or drink coffee or beer in the square, while women go to the playground with the younger children, or stay at home. Younger men go out to cafeterias in different parts of Athens, while younger women have to be chaperoned by male relatives to go out in the early evenings.

While men spend their time in the square or around the city, women often exchange visits, or gather in their backyards to chat. Houses in Gazi are relatively small. It is common for different generations of a family to live under the same roof. Even if they live in separate flats or houses, these are close to each other and are sometimes connected through a common backyard. People exchange visits regularly and television is often a reason, or a pretext, for such visits, which take place mainly during daytime. In the evenings the family gathers together around the television set. Younger people, who are less likely to have satellite television, sometimes go to their parents' place to watch Turkish channels. Nuriye, in turn, goes to her son's flat, to watch the Greek channels. Her house is connected to his through a common backyard. Nazlı (Nuriye's daughter-in-law) and Bahar (her mother) visit Nuriye regularly and watch soaps or video clips in Turkish. During most of the visits, the television is on in the background as the women talk and gossip in Turkish, drinking coffee or ayran (a yogurt drink). On these occasions

---

12 This was particularly common among older women, some of whom had never been to school, like Nuriye. Younger women, such as Sevgi, have been to school for some years, although not all have completed the nine years of compulsory education.

television is used mainly aurally, often showing video clips of Turkish pop songs.[13]

'It's Just Television'

The most popular programmes in Gazi households are soap operas, television shows, films and sports programmes. Yılmaz, who described himself as a 'television addict' (*tileorasakias*) and owns a dish, mainly watches films on Turkish channels, usually Hollywood films dubbed into Turkish. He also watches sports programmes – football games in particular – but he hardly ever watches the news. Sports programmes (as well as sports newspapers) are highly popular among the young and older males, confirming a trend among Greek audiences. Generally, television viewing is mainly associated with relaxation for most informants.

A revealing comment comes from Sevgi, a woman in her 20s, who watches both Greek and Turkish channels. 'Turkish television is the same [as Greek]. Same game-shows, same music.' 'It's [just] television', she added. Such comments echo Öncü's remark that Turkish television, after deregulation, is 'banal', referring to 'the common denominator of global consumer television everywhere' (Öncü 2000: 296). Indeed, Turkish and Greek commercial channels share (together with many countries across the world) a number of programmes, such as *Wheel of Fortune*, and *Who Wants to be a Millionaire*, the difference being the actual production and language. Moreover, Greek and Turkish private channels have a number of common features, such as the form of some programmes (for example, extended news broadcasts and talk shows) and a general aesthetic.

The difference that news makes

It is in relation to news programmes (especially news on Greek-Turkish affairs) that informants identified differences between Turkish and Greek channels. This is explained by the fact that most informants had access to both broadcasting systems and could compare the news. Many informants watched the news on both channels although most preferred watching the Greek.

> Umut: Because I live here, and I want to learn about the country in which I live. Perhaps I will watch [the Turkish channels] when something weird happens. But I don't normally watch the whole bulletin.

When I probed Umut to tell me where he gets informed from, Umut replied, somewhat offended: 'We live *in this* society as well, you know.' The informants' preference for Greek news is partly explained by the fact that they – unlike most Turkish immigrants across Europe – have never left Turkey. They were born in Greece, in the space where their families have always lived as a beached diaspora. Therefore, news programmes are not a means to keep in contact with what is

---

13 Television's aural use is quite prevalent in Gazi households, especially among women. This is partly explained by the lack of Turkish radio. In order to listen to Turkish language or music, people have to switch the television on. This is also a common pattern among Greek working-class women – although not because of the lack of Greek radio. A suggestion is that the aural use of television has more of a gender and class pattern than an ethnic one.

happening 'back' in Turkey. The preference for Greek news can also be interpreted as a desire to be part of the Athenian or Greek public life, in the sense of being aware of current events and affairs that concern the overall population of the country. Umut's reply can be interpreted as an indirect reminder that he and his friends are citizens of Greece.

Overall, however, news programmes were not as popular in Gazi as they were among the general population. However, a talk-show called *Jungle* (*zougla*) is very popular among Gaziots. This programme tackles social issues in a sensationalist manner and perhaps resonates with the general dissatisfaction in Gazi relating to issues of unemployment, poverty and lack of resources. The show voices the criticisms and concerns that Gaziots are unable to raise themselves. Men often referred to Triandafyllopoulos, the journalist-presenter, in everyday conversation: 'as Triandafyllopoulos said…', or, 'he is the only one who tells the truth'. It is perhaps that *Jungle* functions as an oppositional public sphere for Gaziots, which explains its popularity in the neighbourhood (Livingstone and Lunt 1994).

Gaziots use both Greek and Turkish media and this consumption is not defined ethnically, but is common to audiences regardless of their ethnicity. Moreover, there are significant generational and gender differences, pointing to the importance of social change and the fact that the minority is not homogenous. Furthermore, the dimension of citizenship is significant; informants want to be in touch with what is happening in Greece (the country in which they live) and this desire shapes viewing patterns as much as language.

The next section disrupts this ordinariness of consumption patterns by examining the issue of boundaries; do media play any role in creating boundaries for inclusion or exclusion? I will discuss two examples in which the informants reverted to a binary scheme of 'us and them' as a reaction to either media content, or other media-related experiences. The examples discussed are those of direct experiences with the media and journalists, and the objectification of satellite dishes.

Personal experiences with the media and journalists

In one of our meetings Umut recounted an incident: he was once attacked by someone and fought back; both were arrested and taken to the police station for questioning. They later let him go. He stressed that the police arrived at the scene together with a journalist who asked him a few questions. The next morning he read an article in the newspaper and realised that to his surprise everything in the article was 'the opposite to what had actually happened'. He was presented as the attacker who intended to rob. Umut was particularly offended that they had described him as a homosexual. 'They have destroyed my life', he told me.

People from Gazi felt that there was distortion and falsification whenever the neighbourhood, or its inhabitants were represented in the media. Watching oneself or one's acquaintances on television did not invoke familiarity as it did for the Greeks, but rather exclusion. Reports on Gazi generated tension, frustration and even anger. 'We've been in magazines so many times, and there hasn't been a positive article even once', Yilmaz told me. 'They write whatever they feel like', said Süleyman.

> Süleyman: Journalists will hardly ever tell the truth. Once there was a show about the minority here and they interviewed me, they even showed me on television. What I said that they did not like, however, they did not show. For me, this is proof that all journalists are liars. All of them. They just don't show the truth.

Interestingly, there were a number of articles in magazines and reports in the media relating to the satellite dishes. Many informants referring to a recent article in a weekly magazine claimed that the dishes are provided by the Turkish Consulate or Embassy for free. Orhan remembers when the journalists came to Gazi and were taking pictures of the houses and satellite dishes. 'They did not bother to talk to anyone, they just took the pictures', he said. Another controversy involved *Ciao* magazine, where there was a piece on the Muslim weddings in Gazi. 'They were saying that we have guns and that we fire into the air, which does not happen', said Yilmaz.

While Greek informants only had positive direct experiences with the media to refer to, Turkish informants recounted only negative ones. This is a fundamental difference between the different groups, which shapes trust in the media and the overall interpretative framework, as will be discussed in Chapter 7. The ordinariness with which Turkish informants use the media, both Turkish and Greek, is in stark contrast to the ways in which they see themselves represented in the media. The next section further explores this symbolic exclusion of the Turkish viewers.

Objectifying satellite dishes

The articles and reports about satellite dishes are in stark contrast to the actual use of these technologies at home. Watching Turkish satellite television may be an ordinary viewing experience for the majority of the informants, but it is a highly contested practice in the eyes of fellow Athenians. Satellite dishes are seen as markers of difference, reminders of the other within the 'mythically homogenous' nation state, and hence are perceived as polluting and dangerous (Douglas 1966). Hargreaves and Mahjoub (1997) have described how satellite dishes among the immigrant communities in France were objectified by the authorities and the public and became '... the symbol of ... immigrants as an alien cultural presence, threatening the integrity of French national identity'.

A perspective that objectifies Turkish channels as an umbilical cord that links the minority to Turkey is deeply flawed as it ignores the fluidity and movement between languages and media settings. A comment made by Nuriye is revealing in this context: 'I love Turkey the same way a boy loves a girl.' She continued: 'I thought that all people there live like they do on television. But when my son visited he told me that it is not like this.' Nuriye has never been to Turkey. For her it is a mental space to which she escapes through television. It is important to understand where she escapes from: an everyday life (grim and unglamorous in many cases), but also, in her case, a difficult everyday life characterised by unemployment and exclusion. In this context, Nuriye does not only escape from her Greek identity to her Turkish, but rather from a real space, with all the difficulties it entails, to an imaginary, fantasised space which allows for all sorts of possibilities and solutions to her problems.

It is not so much the technology itself that shapes identities, but it is the fact that it is taken so much for granted (by lay people and also by academics) that makes it powerful. Much of the theory, policy and public opinion about the impact of technologies on identity are driven either by speculation – or speculative theory – or by moral panics. Satellite television from Turkey does not make people 'more Turkish'; nonetheless outside the Turkish neighbourhood, satellite dishes are perceived as a marker of difference. I started with this assumption myself as is evident in the introduction to this chapter. Satellite dishes objectify consumption, making what is usually a private practice, public. This observation resembles the moral panics associated with the introduction of satellite television in the UK (Brunsdon 1996).

The case of satellite dishes is significant because it locates media power beyond the area of media content or political economy, where it is usually researched. The objectification of satellite dishes can be seen as an example of the mediation process whereby a media technology (the satellite dish) is invested with a certain negative meaning by the print media and is subsequently reified as something threatening. This suggests a processual and diffused model of media power. The following example further illustrates this point.

When I asked if people in Gazi had thought of setting up a Turkish-language radio station in Athens, Orhan said: 'We haven't thought about it. And even if we plan it, I don't think we will be able to. *They* will probably shut us down.' This phrase exemplifies a number of points that pertain to the minority. First, the remark that they had never considered setting up their own local media is indicative of the lack of confidence and assertiveness within the neighborhood. This lack of confidence is manifested in the projection of a negative result. Such a projection, however, is justified if one takes into account the accumulated negative experiences with journalists and the media and the authorities in Greece in general. This is an example of the mediation process, where different media-related experiences interconnect, affecting people's lives. Media power (in this case the power to exclude) is not only located in one moment of the mediation process, but is seen at different, although interrelated, levels. Thus, the negative experiences with the journalists affect the informants' trust in media, which in turn shapes the decoding of the news. Moreover, as seen in the case above, the negative media experiences and the lack of trust affect people's confidence in establishing local media that can make their voices heard. This finding connects with the work of Couldry (2000b) on lay people's interactions with the media institutions. Couldry approaches media power not as a property that media institutions simply possess, but as a broad social process that operates at many levels (2000b: 39). The similarity with the work presented here is that he identifies media power in people's direct interactions with the media.

BELONGING AND CITIZENSHIP

It emerged earlier in this chapter that the media create some form of common communicative space (Schlesinger 2000a), which was termed as the creation of a common point of reference in which the majority of the Greek informants participate. In this context informants did not feel the need to express their identity. It was in relation to the Western media, and particularly in relation to the non-Greek media's representation of Greece, that some Greek informants became more vocal about their identity.

Cypriot informants fell into two categories. Those more integrated into Greek society were those who mainly used Greek media. The other category included those who had been in Greece for a shorter period of time and those who for personal reasons were more involved with what was going on in Cyprus and who used the Cypriot media more frequently. Such was the case of Yannos, who is deeply interested in Cypriot politics. His attitude is marked by his experience as a refugee in 1974. Overall, however, there were no differences between Greeks and Greek Cypriots, especially in relation to entertainment programmes. This is also reflected at a macro level as there is synergy and cross ownership between Greek and Cypriot channels. In this context many informants expressed an affinity with Greece, as Lia's comment indicates: 'We feel Greece is our country'. Recall that Greek Cypriots are not Greek citizens.

This phrase by Lia is in stark contrast to what the Turkish informants, Umut and Nihat told me: 'Greece *is* our country – but we do not feel it'. Turks are Greek citizens, but they 'do not feel it' in the context of social marginalisation and media exclusion. This exclusion was also expressed in relation to Turkey. When Süleyman and Mumın went to Turkey they were called 'bastards' or 'Greeks' (*Yunanlı*). Turks continually negotiate their identity both toward the Turkish and toward the Greek media and they often feel excluded from both. These negotiations are exemplified in Süleyman's phrase: 'We are in the middle.'

In the context of such negative experiences many Turkish informants repeated the phrase: 'When this happens, I become a Turk.' This phrase is revealing, as it is a wordplay with the word Turk; in Greek 'to become a Turk' also means to become angry. I interpret this phrase, not as a claim to ethnicity, but principally as a claim to citizenship, equal treatment and access to resources. Turkish informants emerged not only excluded from the common communicative space that the news created, but were sometimes even mistreated. In this sense their reaction is interpreted as a struggle for membership and participation in the community (Held 1991: 20). In the following paragraphs I include a couple of examples in which Gaziots negotiate their position in Greek society, continually shifting positions.

Many Turkish-speaking men also have a Greek name, which they use interchangeably. Gaziot women sometimes have a Greek name as well, but this is less common. This is explained by the fact that Greek names are primarily used in public and in relation to the Greeks, so it is mainly women who work outside the household who adopt a Greek name. The only two female informants who had Greek names were Ayşe and Sevgi, who I first met in their workplace. Many of the informants initially introduced themselves to me with their Greek names. Double names provide Gaziots with some flexibility. This practice, however, is not something to be celebrated; it is a result of a dominant view that privileges Greeks with Christian names in the job market. Double names are a pragmatic decision, rather than a freewheeling choice and expression of hybridity. On the other hand, once forced into this system, people cope rather well and sometimes in unpredictable ways. Thus, when I met Süleyman he introduced himself with his real (Turkish) name, only to hear his Turkish friends call him later with his Greek name. In some circumstances and for some people, double names, initially a hegemonic practice, became a casual practice that is not necessarily taken that seriously – although this should not be interpreted as some form of empowerment. People learn to move across spaces and identities and this is often determined by needs and is for practical purposes. It can also become playful, proving again that identities are relational.

People's loyalty to football clubs is also revealing of the multiple layers of identity. Many men in Gazi support Greek teams, especially teams from Thrace, which is where they are form. Xanthi's team, from the second largest city in Thrace, is doing well in the Greek premiership and has many fans among Gaziots. At a European level however, Gaziots often support the Istanbul club Galatasaray, which has performed better than Greek teams in recent years.

CONCLUSIONS

The perspective 'from below', which this chapter is based on, suggests that media and identity are not linked by a causal relationship. The use of media and their integration in people's daily lives is a more complex process that involves a number of parameters, material, social and individual. Although media do not determine identities, they do contribute in the creation of symbolic communicative spaces (Schlesinger 2000a) that either include or exclude, thereby affecting audiences' lives and discourses about their identities. Television is a common point of reference, but, as inevitably happens in all public spheres, it is more common for some than for others.

One such communicative space is that of the news, which not only is a constant background to Greek viewers' lives, it is also a part of their lives. People often see themselves in the news and use such programmes in order to make their voice heard. Greek viewers are 'addicted to news' and conflate news viewing with 'being in touch with reality'.[14] Moreover, news seems to be in constant circulation. The life of some news stories does not begin and end in the living room, or wherever viewing takes place; news stories often become subjects for discussion and retelling in an everyday context. In this sense, news can be seen as a common point of reference.

---

14 The audiences' need to 'keep up' with reality is confirmed by Gans (1979) and Jensen (1998: 58).

However, this is not a process which all people living in Greece experience the same way. Whereas news invokes comfort and cosiness to some, confirming arguments by Silverstone (1994), it excludes those who 'feel like fools' when watching the news (Rena, Giota, Georgia, Thodoris). The cases where people switch off are the most revealing. They involve people who do not connect with the media, in general, and the news, in particular. Although the reasons that have led people to withdraw from the dominant news culture are diverse, this withdrawal is not determined ethnically; rather what these informants share in common is their feeling of disenfranchisement. Thus their decision to disengage with mediated information is a reaction to a discourse that does not reflect their reality. Such examples are Giota, Georgia and Rena (the Greek housewives); Thodoris (taxi driver); Lia and Yannos (Cypriot middle class), and Nihat, Süleyman, Mehmet, Murat and Yilmaz (Turkish working class).

Although it is difficult to sustain a causal relationship between technologies and identity, technologies are enabling. They offer choice and enable people to switch to different languages and broadcasting systems. Satellite television brings 'a bit of the world' to Turkish-speaking homes. In this sense, technologies are enabling rather than determining. For the Turkish speakers, television facilitates moving across spaces, between Greece and Turkey. Turkey is for many of the Gaziots an imaginary place, a place where they do not come *from*, but a place that they symbolically escape to, in avoidance of their everyday reality. This is not necessarily an 'ethnic' practice, but rather an escaping from the difficulties of everyday life and social exclusion.

Most Turkish-speaking informants watch the news about the country in which they live. Shifts in viewing patterns do not necessarily relate to strategies about belonging, but are often contingent and pragmatic decisions. There are also material limitations to the use of technologies relating to one's education and literacy. Language is of paramount importance here. Television provides comfort to some of the elder Gaziots who feel more comfortable speaking in Turkish. The extended use of television as an aural medium partly explains this. Conversely, younger Gaziots feel more comfortable in Greek and aspire for more integration in Athenian society. Choosing Greek media is an indication of their wish to participate in Greek society.

In this chapter exclusion is evident in the context of the direct experiences with the journalists and the media. It is in this context that the ordinariness of television viewing observed in the Turkish speaking households and coffee houses is transformed into frustration and sometimes anger. In this sense the media manage to raise the boundaries for exclusion as interviewees revert to an 'us and them' binary scheme of thought. This function of the media echoes Barth's theory (1969b) on the construction boundaries in the formation of ethnic identities. Of course, the exclusion that the media bring about is not only their responsibility. Media operate at a symbolic level that reminds informants of their exclusion at a material level and at other symbolic levels as well. This is part of the mediation process where different moments interconnect; people's direct experiences with the media shape people's trust, which in turn influences their interpretation of the news content, which is what the next chapters will explore.

CHAPTER 6

NEWS AND THE PROJECTION OF A COMMON IDENTITY

This chapter focuses on identity discourses in the news, analysing news programmes as one of the key moments in the mediation process. A number of studies have examined the role of the media in the symbolic construction of a common identity. Morley and Brunsdon have shown how the nation is evoked, through the analysis of a current affairs programme (1999). Billig has argued that the nation is constantly flagged through the national press (1995). Scannell has stressed the role of public service broadcasting in shaping national identity (1989) and Dayan and Katz have demonstrated how media events bring the nation together (1992). Silverstone has argued for a mediational perspective that examines news as a central cultural component of social life, which punctuates everyday schedules and offers ontological security (1988; 1999 and in press).

This chapter investigates the construction of a common 'we', both through the textual features of television news in Greece and an analysis of news form. Most of the studies on media and identity have focused on media texts as the locus of identity construction. Although there are studies that have examined the relationship between media and identity by focusing on form, broadcasting context or technology, there are few studies that have combined both the emphasis on texts and on form. Form is understood here as the generic characteristics of the news broadcasts, including the mode of presentation, the duration of broadcasts (which are sometimes lengthy), and whether the broadcast is recorded or live. Attention to form is crucial as the news in Greece borrows elements from other types of programming, notably talk shows. Form is also related to the particular broadcasting culture in which the news is produced. This is why the flexibility in programming and even the domination of news broadcasts in the programme mix will be discussed, as broadcasting context affects news form.

This chapter is about one of the moments in the mediation process and should be read in relation to the chapters that discuss the reception of the news (Chapter 7) and the integration of media in the daily lives of the viewers (Chapter 5). Instead of extracting with certainty the meaning of the news in order to make assumptions about its effects on the audiences, this chapter describes some features of the news, which will be then examined in relation to the viewers' responses. This is an important distinction as the point here is not to argue that television is projecting a common identity, which is then unquestioningly adopted by the audiences. The aim, rather, is to stress the dialectic nature of communication as mediation.

The chapter is divided into three sections. The first deals with the textual properties of the news. The second analyses news as genre and form. The third brings the two previous sections together in the analysis of a media event. The analysis draws on news reports that have been analysed by a combination of quantitative and qualitative methods. In the paragraphs that follow I discuss the selection of the events and the reports on which the analysis is based.

The reports sampled represent news from two periods. One period was in October 1998 during the 'violation of national airspace by Turkish planes' and the other was in March–April 1999, during the first month of the NATO intervention in Kosovo and Yugoslavia. For reasons of convenience these reports will be referred to as the *airspace incident* and the *Kosovo conflict* case studies.

The two case studies are intended to complement each other in the analysis. At a first level the *airspace incident* represents a relatively routine event and the *Kosovo conflict* a crisis. This is evident from the media attention that they received. While the Kosovo conflict literally took over news programmes during the seventy-nine days for which it lasted (news often featured items only on this issue), the airspace incident was reported for a maximum of four days (on ANTENNA) and a minimum of two (on ET-1). Moreover, the events in Kosovo had wider repercussions in Greek society (especially the reactions towards the NATO air campaign), while the airspace incident caused no obvious controversies.

It should be mentioned that the routine/crisis distinction is not definite as there is an element of crisis in the *airspace incident* and a routine element in the *Kosovo conflict*. The *airspace incident* should be seen in the context of the relations between Greece and Turkey, which despite the recent rapprochement saw a number of crises in the 1990s. Disputes have included the Cyprus issue and control over areas of the Aegean Sea (Rozakis 1988). Airspace incidents like the one described in this chapter are common, especially during military exercises. Thus it could be argued that this incident was routine, to the extent that incidents like it take place regularly. By the standards of other Western European countries, however, it would be considered a crisis as such incidents involve a significant proportion of the countries' armed forces and sometimes result in casualties. Maybe a better way of describing these events is that they are routinely not routine.

Conversely, the Kosovo conflict did not involve Greece directly or pose any immediate threats to Greek sovereignty. However, it was widely perceived as a crisis. The difference between the Kosovo coverage in Greece and the coverage in other Western media, was that a large number of the reports did not just focus on Kosovo as a regional and international conflict, but rather on related, but not urgent issues, such as the Greek minority in Albania, or the popular expressions of anti-Americanism in Greece and elsewhere. The conflict triggered a number of reactions and reports that could be characterised as routine or banal, in the sense that there was nothing critical about them.

To summarise, through the airspace incident it is possible to observe the reporting of the nation in a routinely not routine internal issue. Through the reporting of the Kosovo conflict the nation is evoked in the context of an international crisis in which Greece was only involved indirectly (as a neighbouring country and a NATO ally).

First, the interpretive analysis of the airspace incident will be presented followed by the content analysis of the Kosovo conflict. The quantified data will be illustrated with examples from the interpretive analysis of the same reports.

NEWS AS TEXT

Banal nationalism: the reporting of the airspace incident

The incident took place in the third week of October 1998 and involved 'the violation of Greek airspace and Athens FIR in the area of the Aegean Sea by Turkish military planes, during a joint military exercise of Greece with Cyprus'. This is the definition provided by the channels in the actual reports. ANTENNA covered this incident most extensively with four reports in four consecutive days (22–25 October 1999). MEGA reported on this incident in three days' broadcasts (22–24 October 1999), while ET-1 had two reports (22 and 23 October 1999).

The dominant theme in these reports was an 'us and them' frame confirming the finding of a number of studies on news in general, and news about conflict in particular (Gamson 1992; Liebes 1997; Neuman *et al* 1992). As there were three main actors involved in the incident (Greece, Cyprus and Turkey), I shall apply discourse analysis to see how the 'us and them' binary scheme is constructed. In particular, I shall examine the uses of pronouns through a deictic analysis (Billig 1995).

The term 'deixis' (which comes from the Greek word for 'pointing' or 'indicating') is used in linguistics to refer to the function of personal or demonstrative pronouns, of tense and of a variety of other grammatical or lexical features that relate utterances to the spatiotemporal co-ordinates of the act of utterance (Lyons 1977: 636–37). Although the use of pronouns in the context of face-to-face conversation is usually straightforward, as it is clear who is talking and who is being addressed, in the case of political or journalistic discourse, deixis is more complex (Billig 1995). 'We' does not just include the speaker and the hearers, but becomes abstract. 'We' may be extended to include the party, the community, the nation or the people. Deixis in media or political discourse may become the vehicle to imagining the nation. Billig, in his study of the national press in the UK, shows how the newspapers employ a routine 'deixis', which continually points to the national homeland as the home of the readers (1995: 11). Of course, if nationalist discourse reminds us who 'we' are, it also tells us who we are not. As much as it is inclusive, this discourse is also exclusive, as Morley and Robins have noted (1995: 25). In the following paragraphs I will discuss how a common identity is projected through an 'us and them' frame sustained by deictic expressions.

Deictic words were commonly used in the reports to demarcate 'us' (in this context the Greeks and Greek Cypriots in the joint military exercise) and 'them', the Turks, who were reported to be obstructing the exercises. The following examples illustrate this: *'Our* aircraft managed to break through the Turkish air barrier after intense and dangerous air-fights.' (ANTENNA, 24/10/1999)

> Dozens of Turkish aircraft attempted today to obstruct the flight of the aircraft of *our* airforce to Cyprus. The third wave of Greek planes passed the Turkish 'wall'. The Turks responded swiftly. The provocations of the Turks did not prevent the Greek and Cypriot forces from continuing with the exercises. Ground forces and units of *our* navy managed to complete the exercises with live ammunition.' (MEGA 24/10/1999)

This quotation, typical of the discourse of these reports, points to 'us', the Greek nation, and 'our' aircraft that are battling with the Turkish. This possessive pronoun, used in the reports of both private channels, but not on ET-1, makes the contrast between us and them even more salient. The 'us' implied in these reports embraces Cyprus as well. Greece and Cyprus are seen as a united force against the common enemy. The following quotation is indicative of this climate. It contains the statement of the then minister of defence, Akis Tsohatzopoulos on ANTENNA, on 25 October 1999: 'Turkey has to understand that Greece will not tolerate its threats. Neither will Cyprus.'

Another word in the reports that connotes the special relationship between Greece and Cyprus is *Meghalonisos* (literary meaning 'Large Island'), used to refer to Cyprus. This word was mentioned in both ANTENNA and MEGA programmes, but not by ET-1. Its use, instead of the proper name Cyprus, implies a relationship of intimacy. This is enhanced by the fact that in some reports Cyprus is not referred to as a separate state. The following quote is indicative: 'The Turkish aircraft attempted unsuccessfully to cut off *Meghalonisos* from the mainland.' (MEGA, 25/10/99 and ANTENNA, 24/10/99) *'Meghalonisos'* appears as an integral part of Greece that can be cut off only with the intervention of Turkish planes. The following quotation is in the same vein:

> Turkey is orchestrating a war scene in the triangle between Cyprus, Rhodes and Crete. Ankara, through the Turkish Air Force, is actively contesting the common defence dogma between Greece and Cyprus. The intention of the Turkish pilots was to intercept each Greek airplane that was heading to Cyprus. (ANTENNA 23/10/99)

The sense of tension is heightened with other phrases, such as 'Turkey orchestrated a war scene over the Aegean again today … with 200 super-modern and armed aircraft' (ANTENNA, 24/10/1999), and 'Ankara's audacity has no limits' (ANTENNA 24/10/1999). The 'us and them' frame is made more salient through the visual material that accompanies the footage. Most of it contains images from air force exercises and air combat (this is archival material although it is not explicitly mentioned), creating a feeling of tension and threat. There are some shots where we see the pilot in the cockpit and in the background can hear him saying 'I have locked them' (*tous egglovisa*), which refers to him targeting the Turkish planes in a dogfight. This is not clearly heard, but even the sound of the anxious voice creates tension.

Most importantly, none of the reports mention the background to the dispute between Greece and Turkey over the Aegean. The reports do not even mention the background to the related issue of the Cyprus problem and the 'common defence dogma' with Greece in the context of which the military exercises take place. The lack of contextual or background information is common practice in news in general and does not apply to the Greek case solely (Philo 1990).

The airspace incident reports are an example of banal nationalism where small words and pronouns establish and naturalise the nation and its others (Billig 1995). Moreover, because these reports were about conflict that involved the armed forces, visually they extended beyond the 'banal nationalism' thesis as they showed images that evoked conflict. The images used in the reports mainly consisted of archival footage from past military exercises and, in the case of ANTENNA images, from a flight simulator programme and a video game. In short, the images that accompanied the banal reports were nothing but banal in the sense that they emphasised a clear separation between 'us and them' that evoked conflict and war.

It needs to be noted, however, that there were significant differences among the channels with ANTENNA being more vocal about the dangers of the incident and Turkey's threat, and MEGA and ET-1 being more restrained.

Global conficts – local worlds: the reporting of the Kosovo conflict

This section will present the findings of the thematic and interpretative analysis of the news reports on the Kosovo conflict. A description of the qualitative and quantitative methods applied can be found in Appendix 1. The analysis identified a number of themes in the reports, which are presented as follows:

- *Bombs and Casualties* (BOMBCASU).[1] This includes items with a reference to the NATO strikes and the casualties of those strikes.
- *Serbs* (SERBS). This includes any reference to the Serb people.
- *Military issues* (MILITARY). This includes references to the military aspect of the conflict and details about the operations.
- *Refugees* (REFUGEES). This includes all references to the refugees.
- *Reasons refugees are leaving* (REFUGREA). The categories are:
  (1) NATO strikes;
  (2) ethnic cleansing;
  (3) mixed reasons; and
  (4) reasons not mentioned.
- *NATO*. This category refers to the way the reports present the coalition. The items were coded as *negative, neutral, positive, combined* (negative and neutral) or *absent*. The combined category was needed as some reports contained a mixed portrayal. Negative refers to any objections or ironic comments towards the coalition and its actions. Neutral refers to a descriptive item that does not make evaluating remarks about NATO when presenting its actions. Two further categories were derived from this, NATONEG (the negative depiction of NATO) and NATONEU (the neutral items), both coded as present or absent.

---

1   The names in the parentheses are the codes needed to decipher the graph presented in Figure 7.1

- *Diplomacy* (DIPLOM). This includes items which refer to the diplomatic efforts.
- *Regional Destabilisation.* (DESTREG) This refers to fears for regional destabilisation, change of borders and movements of population.
- *Effects in Greece* (GREFFECT). The effects of the conflict in Greece and effects on the environment, the economy and tourism are included.
- *Initiatives* (GRINITIA). The initiatives of the Greek government and Greek non-governmental organisations (NGOs) at a diplomatic and humanitarian aid level.
- *Reactions against the bombings* (GREACT). The reactions against the strikes in Greece, both at a political and general population level.
- *Cyprus.* This includes items with references to Cyprus as a reverse parallel to Kosovo.
- *North Epirus* (NORTEPIR). This comprises of items that made references to the Greek minority in Albania and how it might be affected by the events in Kosovo.
- *Church.* This includes items referring to the common religion of the Serbs and Greeks (Orthodox Christians), as well as initiatives and/or reactions of the Church of Greece.
- *Flags.* Items with images of flags were coded in this variable. Categories include:
  (1) Greek flags;
  (2) Serb flags;
  (3) US flags; and
  (4) no flags.
- *Russia.* This includes items with a reference to the role of Russia in the diplomatic efforts and Russia's reactions to the NATO strikes.
- *Ethnic cleansing.* This includes items with references to ethnic cleansing or genocide.

Identifying discursive patterns

From the content analysis, it emerged that the most prevalent themes were those of *bombs and casualties* (32.1%) and *NATO negative* (25.2%). Interestingly, *NATO positive* was not mentioned even once. *NATO neutral*, on the other hand, was more popular with 21.6%. *Diplomacy* was also a prevalent theme, especially in the case of the public channel where it was the most common variable, as it reached 34.8% while the overall percentage of the theme was 21.8%. The least prevalent theme was that of *ethnic cleansing* (2.8%).

What is important, however, is to identify discursive patterns in the news, that is groups of themes that often co-occur in the same report. For this purpose a cluster analysis was performed that revealed two clusters, or groups of themes, as can be observed in the dendrogram in Figure 7.1.[2]

The themes that form the first cluster are: *bombs and casualties, Nato/negative, Serbs, reactions, flags and live*. *Live* was included in the cluster analysis, despite the

---

2   For a discussion of the method used, refer to Appendix I.

fact that it is not a theme, so as to see which themes received extended live coverage. The second cluster consists of the following variables: *diplomacy, Nato/neutral, Greek initiatives, refugees, destabilisation, effects (of the conflict in Greece), Russia and military.*

The themes which co-occur in Cluster 1 are as follows: references to the bombs and casualties of the NATO strikes usually co-occur with a negative portrayal of NATO, along with references to the Serb people and with the reactions to and demonstrations against the air strikes. Images of flags also occur in the context of the above themes (mainly with *reactions*). Conversely, in Cluster 2 references to the diplomatic activity surrounding the conflict co-occur with neutral references toward NATO and references to the initiatives of the Greek government and NGOs (at a diplomatic and humanitarian aid level). These also cluster with references to refugees, destabilisation, the effects of the crisis in Greece, the role of Russia in the conflict and military issues.

In most cases, themes from the two clusters do not co-occur in the same item. For example, *refugees* are commonly referred to either in the context of diplomatic activity or in the context of regional destabilisation (that is, concerns about the settlement of refugees and how that might affect the populations of other Balkan countries and, in particular, the Greek minority of Albania). On the other hand, *Serbs* are presented as either the victims of the NATO strikes or as the people who are courageously attending concerts in the squares of Belgrade despite, and against, the bombings. Similarly, NATO is presented in a negative way in the context of what is happening to the Serb people and in a neutral way in the context of diplomatic activity and collaboration with the Greek government.

These thematic patterns are further confirmed in the cross-tabulations of theme couples. In Table 7.2, the relation between *destabilisation* and *refugees* mentioned above appears as statistically significant (p<0.0001, see Table 7.2). The same goes for the relationship between *NATO-negative* and *Serbs* (p<0.0001, see Table 7.3) and *Serbs* and *Church* (p<0.0001, see Table 7.4). These relationships between themes suggest the existence of a particular frame of identification, an 'us and them' frame. The Greeks are presented as close to the Serbs through religion (*church*), resistance to foreign interference (*reaction* and *NATO negative*) and *flags*. The Kosovan refugees are presented in a more detached way (*diplomacy*), or even as a threat (*destabilisation*). Greece is negative towards NATO in relation to the bombings and the casualties of the Serb side (*bombs-casualties and Serbs*), but neutral in relation to diplomacy and governmental co-operation (*Greek initiatives*) (see Table 7.5).

(ANTENNA, MEGA, ET-1)
Squared Euclidean Distance used
Dendrogram using Ward Method

Cluster 1 appears in bold; Cluster 2 is in normal type face

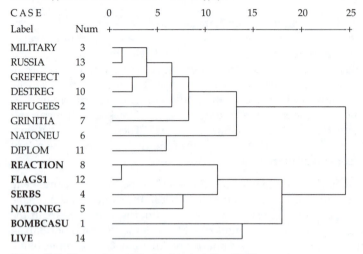

Figure 7.1 Hierarchical Cluster Analysis For All Channels

Table 7.2 Cross-tabulation of thematic variables
Refugees and Regional Destabilisation (DESTREG)
for all channels and chi-squared test
($x^2 = 27.554$, df=1 p<0.0001)

		REFUGEES		
		PRESENT	ABSENT	TOTAL
DESTABILISATION	PRESENT	27 (40.3%)	40 (59.7%)	67 (100%)
	ABSENT	55 (13.9%)	342 (86.1%)	397 (100%)
TOTAL		82 (17.7%)	382 (82.3%)	464 (100%)

Table 7.3 Cross-tabulation of thematic variables Nato-negative and Serbs
for all channels and chi-squared test
($x^2 = 22.051$, df =1, p< 0.0001)

		NATO-NEGATIVE		
		PRESENT	ABSENT	TOTAL
SERBS	PRESENT	42 (43.8%)	54 (56.3%)	96 (100%)
	ABSENT	75 (20.4%)	293 (79.6%)	368 (100%)
TOTAL		117 (25.2%)	347 (74.8%)	464 (100%)

Table 7.4 Cross-tabulation of thematic variables Serbs and church
for all channels and chi-squared test
($x^2 = 33.907$, df=1 p< 0.0001)

		SERBS		
		PRESENT	ABSENT	TOTAL
CHURCH	PRESENT	14 (73.7%)	5 (26.3%)	19 (100%)
	ABSENT	82 (18.4%)	363 (81.6%)	445 (100%)
TOTAL		96 (20.7%)	368 (79.3%)	464 (100%)

Table 7.5 Cross-tabulation of the themes Diplomacy and Nato neutral for all channels and chi-squared test ($x^2 = 30,843$, df=1, p<0.0001)

| | | NATO NEUTRAL | | |
		PRESENT	ABSENT	TOTAL
DIPLOMACY	PRESENT	42 (41.6%)	59 (58.4%)	101 (100%)
	ABSENT	58 (16%)	305 (84%)	363 (100%)
TOTAL		100 (21.6%)	364 (78.4%)	464 (100%)

Differences among channels

An important finding from the content analysis concerns the differences between private and public channels. Differences included both the distribution of theme frequencies and the overall presentation style, although this section discusses only the former. Recall that the audience ratings for the public channels have dropped dramatically since deregulation and their audience share is only a small fraction of that of the private channels. In terms of the theme frequencies, ET-1 had significantly fewer references to the themes *Serbs* and *NATO negative* (see Tables 7.6 and 7.7 respectively, p<0.001 in both cases). Conversely, the themes *diplomacy* and *Greek initiatives* were more prevalent on ET-1 (the differences are statistically significant, p<0.0001 in both cases, see Tables 7.8 and 7.9). These findings indicate that the public channel chose to emphasise the diplomatic activity surrounding the conflict and the related initiatives of the Greek government, while the private channels stressed the effects of the air campaign on the Serb people and projected a stronger anti-American stance.

The 'us and them' frame takes a different shape in the context of ET-1. The public channel stresses the Greek side, but in relation to the diplomatic initiatives of the government toward the resolution of the conflict. The identification with the Serbs is not as strong as on the private channels, nor is there evident unfriendliness towards the refugees or NATO. Instead, ET-1 adopts a reassuring stance towards the conflict, which was to a large extent the same as that of the government at the time. ET-1 emphasises the work of the government at the diplomatic level and the role of Greece as a stabilising factor in the region (instead of emphasising effects and destabilisation).

Table 7.6 Cross-tabulation of variables Serbs and Channel and chi-squared test
($x^2 = 13.893$, df $= 2$, p < 0.001)

		SERBS		
		PRESENT	ABSENT	TOTAL
CHANNEL	MEGA	39 (23.1%)	130 (76.9%)	169 (100%)
	ANTENNA	47 (26.1%)	133 (73.9%)	180 (100%)
	ET-1	10 (8.7%)	105 (91.3%)	115 (100%)
TOTAL		96 (20.7%)	368 (79.3%)	464 (100%)

Table 7.7 Cross-tabulation of variables Nato-negative and Channel
and chi-squared test
($x^2 = 12.804$, df $= 2$, p < 0.002)

		NATO NEGATIVE		
		PRESENT	ABSENT	TOTAL
CHANNEL	MEGA	53 (31.4%)	116 (68.6%)	169 (100%)
	ANTENNA	49 (27.2%)	131 (72.8%)	180 (100%)
	ET-1	15 (13%)	100 (87%)	115 (100%)
TOTAL		117 (25.2%)	347 (74.8%)	464 (100%)

Table 7.8 Cross-tabulation of variables diplomacy and Channel
and chi-squared test
(x^2=18.022, df =2, p < 0.0001)

		DIPLOMACY		
		PRESENT	ABSENT	TOTAL
CHANNEL	MEGA	36 (21.3%)	133 (78.7%)	169 (100%)
	ANTENNA	25 (13.9%)	155 (86.1%)	180 (100%)
	ET-1	40 (34.8%)	75 (65.2%)	115 (100%)
TOTAL		101 (21.8%)	363 (78.2%)	464 (100%)

Table 7.9 Cross-tabulation of variables Greek initiatives and Channel
and chi-squared test
(x^2 =23.012, df =2, p<0.0001)

		GREEK INITIATIVES		
		PRESENT	ABSENT	TOTAL
CHANNEL	MEGA	20 (11.8%)	149 (88.2%)	169 (100%)
	ANTENNA	20 (11.1%)	160 (88.9%)	180 (100%)
	ET-1	35 (30.4%)	80 (69.6%)	115 (100%)
TOTAL		75 (16.2%)	389 (83.8%)	464 (100%)

'Us and them'

The main function of the 'us and them' frame in reporting is the simplification of a significantly more complex situation. This frame is common in the news (Neuman *et al* 1992), and even more so in the reporting of conflicts and wars (see *inter alia*, Liebes 1997; Katz 1992). The 'us/them' frame was dominant in the Western media as well, where it was coupled with references to the SecondWorld War. Katz (1992: 5) has remarked that the Second World War took over as a dominant frame since the end of the Cold War and the collapse of the ideological frames between the Western and Eastern blocs. Thus, Milocevic was commonly referred to as 'Hitler,' and the fleeing of the refugees was paralleled to the Holocaust (Nohrstedt *et al* 2000: 394–95). The Greek media, especially the private television channels, also made references to the Second World War. In this case, however, the roles were reversed; in the Greek media Clinton was Hitler, the plight of the Serbs was paralleled to the Holocaust and the American flag was sometimes depicted with a swastika.

A common framing mechanism associated with the 'us and them' frame is that of 'personalising', which Liebes defines as the 'asymmetrical portrayal of the humanity of the two sides' (1997: 73–74). The human suffering of 'our' side is emphasised (the victims have names, age, families), while the 'others' are depersonalised. In the sampled reports there was a strong emphasis on the plight of the Serbs as the victims of the NATO strikes, while the refugees were seen in the background of the crisis. Moreover, the images of the Serb and Greek flags that often appeared tied together were a metonymy for the friendship of the two nations (Billig 1995: 41). The identification with the Serb people was also invoked by the references to the church and the common religion, and by the reports on the visits of Greek people in Belgrade to participate in the daily concerts against the air strikes.

This 'personalisation' is evident from the analysis of the titles[3] that introduce the reports on Serbs: 'The Mum of a Hero'; 'Both Serb and Refugee'; 'The Damned of the Balkans'; 'They are still singing'; and 'The Calvary of the Serbs'. In the report entitled 'The Mum of a Hero'(ANTENNA, 15 April 1999), the focus is on the family, and particularly the mother, of a Serb soldier who died whilst on duty. The journalist comments off the screen that the family is '... in deep mourning as is appropriate in the Serb tradition'. He adds: 'The name Tepanovac [the family's name] will not be continued' (the 'mother of the hero' had no other sons). This emphasis on mourning and the continuation of the family's name, Greek traditions as well, underline the identification with the Serbs.

The common religion between Serbs and Greeks was invoked in a number of reports. One example is a video clip broadcast on 25 March 1999, which opened the news broadcast of ANTENNA. That was the second day of the bombings, which coincided with a Greek national holiday (commemorating the anniversary

---

3   It is common practice on the private channels to start each report with a title/caption accompanied by music. These captions condense the dominant frame of the news into a few words. In Barthes' terms, it is the caption that anchors the meaning (1977).

of the revolution against the Ottoman rule). The events in Yugoslavia and the national character of the day merged in the symbols juxtaposed in the video clip, which started with the caption 'Freedom or Death', which was one of the slogans of the Greek revolution. The caption appears in Serbian (Cyrillic) fonts against a background of Byzantine Christian icons (connoting the common religion) and then in Greek fonts (against a visual background of military planes). Then a Greek flag is double printed on an image of the Acropolis, before we see the Head of the Greek Church making a statement about the NATO offensive.

There were even a number of explicit pro-Serb reports. In one, while we are watching images of the mock funeral of NATO, with a swastika on the coffin, enacted by Serbs, the reporter says: 'Serbia must stay strong; Kosovo must remain Serbian; it is the cradle of their civilisation.' (ANTENNA, 24 April 1999) In the same vein, in another report from Prizren, the journalist says: 'Kosovo belongs to the Serbs.' (MEGA, 24 April 1999) The private channels sometimes even screened propagandistic video clips from the Serbian television.

Conversely, report titles referring to the Kosovan refugees were descriptive, rather than emotionally charged: 'New wave of refugees'; '[Diplomatic] Mobilisation for the refugees'; 'Kosovars in Italy'; and 'The caravan of the refugees'. In these reports the refugees are only seen in the background while other people (politicians or NGO representatives) speak on their behalf. There are very few reports where the refugees talk directly to the camera to narrate their stories. Moreover, there were even cases where refugees were presented as a possible threat, as the dendrogram (Figure 7.1) and Table 7.2 have suggested. Such an example is the caption: 'Northern Epirus:[4] the settlement of refugees poses new threats [to the Greek minority]'. Indeed, all the reports from Southern Albania, where there is a Greek minority, describe the arrival of the refugees as a threat to the ethnic homogeneity of the region. Although there are not many such reports (twelve in total, corresponding to 2.6% of the sample), it is interesting to examine them as they project a particular discourse about the conflict, invoking an essentialist understanding of difference and belonging. The representation of refugees as a threat and danger has also been observed by other researchers (Malkki 1995). Refugees are seen as the stateless people who challenge the naturalisation of the nation state and its borders and are thus considered as a threat to national security and harmony.

In one of these reports from Southern Albania, ANTENNA's reporter mentions that 'there are plans to change *the* population' (that is, the Greek population of the region) (ANTENNA, 31 March 1999). This concern is also raised in a report on the otherwise rather moderate ET-1. This item voices the concern to 'protect the rights of *the* minority … in order to avoid demographic changes' [emphasis added]. It should be noted that ET-1 does not use the term Northern Epirus, but uses Albania instead (ET-1, 31 March 1999). These items link with another theme, the 'conspiracy theory'. In this context, the arrival of refugees is not accidental; rather it is the result of a planned strategy to change the population mix of the region.

---

4   'Northern Epirus' is what Southern Albania, where the Greek minority lives predominantly, is popularly called in Greece.

There is no specific reference to who is behind this strategy; but what emerges from this item is a way of thought that combines the projection of insecurities and fears about the stability of the region, that are grounded in the history of previous Balkan conflict, and competing nationalistic projects.

Refugees were mentioned in 17.7% of the items. What is important, however, is the way they were represented. In the majority of these items (64.4%), there was not a single reference to the reasons refugees were leaving Kosovo. When reasons were mentioned, in the minority of the items, these were ethnic cleansing (14.9% of the category and 2.8% of the sample), the NATO bombings (9.7% and 1.9% respectively), the combination of the two previous categories (8.7% and 1.7%) and, finally, other reasons (2.1% and 0.4%). It should be noted here though that ethnic cleansing was usually mentioned in passing or within the discursive pattern, for example 'as the refugees themselves claim…', or, 'as NATO allegedly claims…', thus weakening the credibility of the explanation. The following is such an example:

> [The refugees are fleeing] terrified from the NATO strikes, but also from the Serbs, as they themselves are claiming …. Their stories, recorded by foreign journalists as the refugees cross the borders, make the round of the world in order to justify to public opinion NATO's attacks against Yugoslavia, through the emotions that human suffering creates. (ET-1, 31 March 1999)

The following is an item about Pristina and refugees, which appeared on 31 March 1999, one of the days when the number of refugees fleeing Kosovo was increasing dramatically. In one of the long and concluding scenes (the item's duration was just under seven minutes) we see a man waving farewell to his wife and child who are about to leave on a bus. Afterwards, the man, dressed in a Serbian army uniform, talks to the journalist in Serbian. Although this is seemingly a report on refugees (one would readily assume that this meant Kosovan Albanians) it is, in fact, about Serbs. It is easy for the viewer to conclude that the refugees are Serbs. If this is a report on refugees, and everyone in it is Serb, then the refugees must be Serb. The report was captioned 'The Damned of the Balkans', followed by a second title, 'The moment of farewell'. In the same report the journalist meets a Serb soldier, who says in front of the camera, 'I want to send my greetings to the Greek people and the Orthodox Church for all they've done for the Serb people'. Then the journalist follows the soldier and meets more Serb people hiding in the shelters. The 'damned of the Balkans' are the Serbs. The refugees are mentioned, but it is easy to think that the refugees are the Serbs, who are leaving Pristina because of the bombings and the tensions (MEGA, 31 March 1999).

The 'us and them' theme runs through the above reports. The identification with the Serbs on many occasions (mainly in reports that refer to the people, not their leadership) emerges as the unified 'us', sharing the same traditions, religion and spirit. The 'other' in this context is NATO. These reports project onto the crisis in Yugoslavia and the NATO intervention, the relatively recent experience of the Greek Civil War (1945–49). Foreign interference (mainly American) in Greek politics continued in the following decades leading to the military dictatorship and the events in Cyprus.

Nationalisation and conspiracy theories

The way in which the refugee issue was represented was one of the most important differences between the Greek and Western media. Regardless of one's position towards the NATO bombings, and despite the refugees being used for both NATO and Serb propaganda (Thussu 2000), the fact that there was a mass fleeing of refugees is undeniable. The lack of an account by the Greek media as to *why* the refugees were fleeing gave rise to a number of conspiracy theories, in order to explain why NATO was bombing Yugoslavia, thus increasing the levels of anxiety. Because no reason for the bombings was provided in more than half of the reports on the bombings, NATO's intervention appeared irrational and incomprehensible. This explanatory gap allowed for conspiracy theories to emerge. A report claimed that NATO was dropping bombs in order to dispose of the missiles that would be made redundant by the millennium bug (ANTENNA 23 April 1999). Most commonly, there were references to the 'secret interests' that were the real cause of the military intervention. In this context of irrationality, comments that 'Greece would be the next victim', and that 'borders would be redrawn' were heard (ANTENNA, 26 March and 26 April 1999). The fear of the effects of the crisis on Greece internalised the conflict, thus making it a national issue as well. What is important is not the quantity, but the emotional intensity of these reports. Interestingly, even channels with conservative political orientation adopted these frames, confirming an earlier study that found that anti-Americanism was strong in the conservative press (that had traditionally supported the US in previous decades) during the controversy surrounding the name Macedonia in the mid 1990s (Demertzis and Armenakis 1998: 130).

Recently, Marcus and others have argued for the understanding of the concept of conspiracy theory not as an irrational and paranoid mode of thinking, 'but *within reason*, as a reasonable component of rational and commonsensical thought and experience in certain contexts' (Marcus, 1999: 2). Many of the above reports, along with those that are negative towards NATO, echo popular perceptions and feelings about foreign intervention in Greek politics, especially in relation to Cyprus and the military dictatorship (1967–74). In other words, there was an emotional realism in the ostensibly unrealistic conspiracy theories.

Global sources, local meanings

The content analysis revealed that a significant proportion of the visual material used in the news came from international news agencies and television networks, most notably CNN (30.4%). This percentage does not include the images re-transmitted from Serbian television, which formed a category of their own (18.5%). The figure of 30.4% reflects the globalisation of news and news images and suggests that Greek viewers, even indirectly, watch non-Greek, 'global' images from the international networks and agencies. What is interesting here is to examine the ways in which these images were appropriated by the Greek channels.

The two most prominent themes in the visual material originating from 'global sources' were those of *Diplomacy* and *NATO neutral*, with percentages of 51.5%

and 50% respectively. Considering that the majority of Western media did not object to the NATO air campaign, the prevalence of the above themes indicates some consistency with the intentions of the original producers of the material. However, the theme *NATO negative* appears in 33.3% of this material. This suggests that there was a parallel oppositional usage of the 'global' images and a local appropriation of their content. Conversely, such oppositional usage is not observed in the images from Serbian television.

An alternative discourse

The coverage of the events in Kosovo was not homogenous or monolithic. There were many neutral items on NATO (21.6%), particularly in the context of *diplomacy* and the *initiatives* of the Greek government and NGOs (see Table 7.8). In these items the European identity of Greece as a member of the EU and NATO was stressed. Greece was also portrayed as a significant and stabilising force in the region. The presence of these themes suggests that there was an alternative discourse about the crisis, which complicates the above 'us and them' frame. These reports maintained a reserved attitude towards the air campaign without ever endorsing it. Instead of Greece (*us*) opposing NATO (*them*), as was evident in the anti-Americanism of the previous examples, Greece is presented as an active member of NATO and the EU. However, this alternative discourse, which was more prominent on the public rather than private channels, did not carry the emotional weight of the previous frame and involved fewer, shorter and recorded (rather than *live*) reports.

How the others see 'us'

A number of reports (4.5%) were concerned with the way foreign media (Western European and North American) reported the conflict. These reports were often critical or even sarcastic (3.4%) and also commented on how Greece and its regional role were portrayed. This is particularly interesting as such reports are indicative of the local-global dialectic and the media's response to Greece's perceived position in the world. The negative references to Western media are often reactions to the ways they had portrayed Greece and the Balkans in the context of this conflict. Greek journalists often implied that Western media, and the West in general, are ignorant of the particularities in the region and were making erroneous judgments while ignoring local history and politics.

Three reports on the same topic (present on all three channels) are indicative of the reactions to negative representation of Greece in the foreign media. The reports were all in the news on 26 March 1999 and were about an account that had been broadcast on CNN regarding a possible spillover of the Kosovo conflict into the Balkans, which could draw in Greece and Turkey. All channels showed the visual part of the report from CNN with an added voice over that commented on the original report. In MEGA's report, which was entitled 'Arsonist propaganda', the journalist stressed that many questions were raised with CNN's 'maps of fire' trying to involve Greece in a possible spillover. He dismissed these claims, which he interpreted as 'Western propaganda in order to justify the war'. ANTENNA's report is captioned 'The maps of fire' and makes similar points. Both channels gave priority to this item as it was fifth in the order of programming on MEGA and third in order on ANTENNA. ET-1's reporting was more reassuring, emphasising that there was no real danger.

Cultural intimacy and the moral prohibition of dissent (abroad)

The image of the country abroad is the topic of other reports, including those that focus on Greek diplomatic initiatives. There was one particular item, a live studio discussion, which revealed the sensitivities regarding the image of Greece abroad, which also related to the concept of cultural intimacy (Herzfeld 1996). The discussion was between MEGA channel's then most prominent newscaster and Andreas Andrianopoulos, a former minister with the conservative government in the early 1990s, about an article that Andrianopoulos wrote in the *New York Times*, which criticised the stance of the Greek media during the crisis. Hatzinicolaou, the newscaster, asked Andrianopoulos:

> Why did Mr Andrianopoulos criticise the Greek media during such a critical period ... when Greece is on a tightrope ... and when the national interest is under threat ... and all this in a newspaper abroad that is not renowned for its pro-Greek sentiments. (MEGA, 28 March 1999)

With this phrase the journalist emphasises the dominant view, and the importance of national homogeneity. The Kosovo crisis is presented as a national issue and dissenting views are not acceptable, especially outside the confines of the nation state. This example is indicative of the concept of cultural intimacy that Herzfeld has developed (1996) to explain the paradox of how a country, where dissent and rebelliousness towards the state are considered the norm, will not allow the same practice by foreigners. Discussing internal affairs of the state abroad is like exposing the 'dirty linen' of the domestic sphere in public. Cultural intimacy means that dissent is allowed only within the confines of the nation state.

Observing the 'us and them' frames prevalent in the news reports, and particularly the identification with the Serbs through religion and customs, one is reminded of theories such as Huntington's *Clash of Civilisations* (1996). Is it that perhaps there is something truthful in this much-discredited theory? The last two reports discussed might shed some light on this issue. First of all, it helps to be reminded that historically Greece has not always had peaceful relationships with its Christian Orthodox neighbours (recall the Balkan Wars in 1912–13). As mentioned in Chapter 3, the Pomak minority issue was more sensitive in past decades due to hitherto hostile relationships with Bulgaria. More recently the dispute over the Macedonian issue was another example of the 'us and them' binary shifting to exclude Orthodox Christians who then became the enemy.

Greece is also not monolithically anti-Muslim as suggests the support towards the Kurds and the Palestinians. It is perhaps more useful to think of the identification with the Serbs as an expression of the deep anti-Americanism in

Greece, which is rooted in US interference in Greek politics in the recent past.[5] Interestingly however, many Greeks, including the Greek media, attributed this differentiated reaction towards the conflict to a cultural affinity with the Serb nation. This is perhaps because such explanations have become particularly prominent as the dominant discourse about culture has become central in popular discourses (Baumann 1996). Moreover, the extract from the Andrianopoulos interview, and the reports of the journalists' reactions to Western reifications of Greece and the Balkans, are indicative that identification with the Serbs cannot explain the prevalence of the 'us and them' binary. Apart from the historically-grounded anti-Americanism it seems that the essentialist approach to culture and the media in the Greek media is a reaction to the equally essentialist Western media. The global–local dialectic becomes an exchange of essentialisms and counter-essentialisms. In this context the 'us and them' frame is not determined by culture, but rather by politics. What is important, however, is that it masks itself as a cultural issue because explanations grounded in culture and ethnicity have gained credibility and can thus attribute legitimacy to their causes.

NEWS AS FORM

The focus in this section is on the particular form of the news in Greece. Three issues will be highlighted in this context: the use of 'live' links and reporting in news broadcasts; the length of the broadcasts themselves in the context of a loosely regulated system that allows flexibility and interruptions of programming; and the mode of presentation, which borrows elements from other genres, such as talk shows or current affairs programmes. The overall argument is that, through its particular form, news naturalises its own practice. By seemingly following the events in real time, interrupting the broadcasting schedule to transmit the latest news and by addressing the audience in a chatty and informal way, news programmes create a sense of immediacy and perhaps a common point of reference. In the previous sections the focus was on how the television text points to a common identity through the 'us and them' frame and deixis. In this section the argument is that the form and the technology of the news and television are implicitly invoking a common 'we'.

Form in this context refers to the generic characteristics of the news broadcasts, including the mode of presentation, the 'live' and lengthy character of the broadcasts, and the interruptions in the programme schedule. It also includes the broadcasting of public rituals in the context of a news bulletin. These features are common to commercial television channels in general; the difference in the Greek ones is a matter of degree. This discussion applies *only* to the private channels and *not* to ET-1, whose news broadcasts adopt a more conventional format (fixed duration, moderate use of live links, etc).

---

5   A similar argument has been made by Sutton, who argued that the attitudes of Kalymnians (inhabitants of the Greek islands of Kalymnos) towards the war in Bosnia were shaped by existing attitudes towards the 'Great Powers' and particularly the USA (1998: 167).

Live news

It has been noted that, during conflicts, television channels in their quest to broadcast 'live' neglect the more critical and analytic dimensions of journalism (Katz 1992: 13). There is also another dimension associated with the 'liveness' of the news. 'Live' plays with the connotation of 'real', as if the immediate transmission removes the constructedness of the programme (Feuer 1983), attributing an aura of objectivity and naturalness to the broadcast. Television producers are aware of this dimension and emphasise it when they stress that they are 'bringing the news as it really happens'. Considering that the items that were reported live were those of cluster 1 (Figure 7.1), it is possible to assume that this was an indirect way of adding emphasis. Live is also linked to urgency. On the first day of the NATO intervention in Yugoslavia the broadcast was full of interruptions. One live link would follow the other, creating a sense of obligatory viewing. Moreover, 'live' reports were those most easily dramatised (human impact stories, bombings and casualty updates, and protest marches and rallies) and the live coverage enhanced their emotional framing, evoking the distinction between 'us and them'. This is further stressed by the observation that the live reports were also the longest ones in the sample. Approximately one-third of the reports of the private channels were 'live' (32%).

Debunking the concept of live television is quite important in this discussion. Corner has observed that:

> most 'unscheduled' events, have happened by the time the journalists arrive on the scene, so in these cases news typically recounts *what happened* against images which show spaces and places *after* the event. (Corner 1995: 59)

Feuer is also critical of the claims about the 'live' character of television. She argues that:

> … to equate 'live' television with 'real life' is to ignore all those determinations standing between the event and our perception of it – technology and institutions to mention two. Television's self referential discourse plays upon the connotative richness of the term 'live', confounding its simple or technical denotations with a wealth of allusiveness. Even the simplest meaning of 'live' – that the time of the event corresponds to the transmission and viewing times – reverberates with suggestions of 'being there'… 'bringing all to you as it really is'. (Feuer 1983: 14)

These remarks echo the debates about realism and the classic realist text (cf MacCabe 1981). As MacCabe has argued, in realist cinema the story is told in such a way that the viewer is unaware that the narrative has a narrator. In the classic realist text, narrative conceals its status as a discourse and is presented as complete knowledge. The story speaks for itself (1981: 221).

Feuer remarks that network television never truly exploits its capacity for instantaneous and unmediated transmission. She recognises that: 'only the ideological connotations of live television are exploited in order to overcome the contradiction between flow and fragmentation in television practice.' (1983: 14) Although this is true to a great extent, news in Greece seems to be making an effort to exploit the actual capacity for instant transmission, which explains why items might last for up to forty minutes (for example, MEGA 26 March 1999). Still, this does not mean that what is actually presented as 'unmediated and unedited' material is necessarily eventful or particularly meaningful. In the report that lasted for forty minutes, the screen was showing scenes from some – not particularly violent – incidents during a demonstration in Athens against the NATO air strikes. The report consisted of images of protesters and policemen gathering outside the US Embassy. In fact, not much happened in these forty minutes. By reporting an event 'live' for forty minutes, television is attributing importance to a (rather uneventful) event. Perhaps what was most eventful about these incidents was their reporting. Interestingly, at some point during the forty minute coverage, the newscaster noted in disappointment that 'these events at the centre of Athens are taking valuable time away from the coverage of the significant events in Kosovo', thereby confusing the incidents themselves with the channel's decision to broadcast them live for forty minutes. In other words, there was nothing natural or self-evident in the channel's decision to focus on these incidents for such a long period of time.

Marathon news? Lengthy broadcasts and flexible programming

Long reports usually imply long broadcasts. The duration of the news programmes, which have at times reached three hours, bears many similarities to the phenomenon that Liebes calls 'disaster marathons' (Liebes 1998: 71–72), where the anxious society gathers around the television set to follow the news as it unfolds. Long broadcasts mean that the rest of the schedule will change, giving absolute priority to the news. Long broadcasts and live reports, especially when most commercial channels broadcast at the same time, create a sense of obligatory viewing as there is not much else on television anyway, invoking the concept of simultaneity and its relation to the construction of imagined communities (Anderson 1991 [1983]).

In Greek 'television disaster marathons' the programme is interrupted and often suspended to follow the events as they unfold. Such cases have been natural disasters, such as earthquakes and floods, the crisis with Turkey over the rock island Imia in 1996, the arrests of the members of the terrorist organisation November 17 in 2002 and even political speeches and resignations, to name but a few. There is no doubt that some of the events mentioned were very significant. However, the practice of suspending the original programming to broadcast live the 'breaking news' is quite common, even if the event concerned is of minor importance.

Moreover, the long broadcasts and the live studio discussions and links have contributed to the development of a particular mode of presentation, which is based on a chatty informality that is perhaps more typical of news magazines and talk shows (Morley and Brunsdon 1999 [1978]).

CELEBRATING THE NATION

This section will analyse a media event, a public concert for 'peace in the Balkans' that took place in the central square of Athens on 26 April 1999, in the context of the reactions against the NATO strikes in Yugoslavia and Kosovo. It was co-organised and broadcast live by one of the private channels (SKAI, now renamed ALPHA), although all other channels, private and public, repeatedly interrupted their news broadcasts and programmed schedules to transmit parts of the event. This is the event described at the beginning of the book. The reason this event is presented separately from the other data is because it brings together a number of issues discussed previously, namely the textual and formal characteristics of the news. At the same time this section introduces another feature of broadcasting, which is the ritualistic character of television. This event can be seen in the context of other public rituals that took place in Greece on different occasions (that is, the rallies against the recognition of the neighbouring state of Macedonia (FYROM) in 1992 (Tsagarousianou, 1997) and the funeral of the cinema star and politician, Melina Mercouri (Tsaliki 1995)).

This event can be seen as a 'media event' in the sense that it was broadcast 'live', interrupting the broadcasting routine and creating an atmosphere of ceremonial viewing (Dayan and Katz 1992: 5–8). The concert in Athens was undoubtedly a moment that projected and celebrated the nation, confirming the consensual character of the media event (Dayan and Katz 1992). This is evident from journalists' comments, such as 'this war has united us' (ANTENNA, 26 April 1999). It is also evident from the juxtaposed symbols, of diverse ideological origins, representing different sections of Greek society: the flags of the Byzantine Empire (associated with nationalist and religious groups) and those of the communist party. This consensus was symbolised in the leading figure, Theodorakis, who had served under both socialist and conservative administrations and was highly recognised for his music. The nation was celebrated as united and homogenous and it asserted its identity to itself and to the world. ANTENNA's main newscaster at the time, Terence Quick, remarked that this consensus reached people with both conservative and progressive political affiliations. Prompted by the journalist of ANTENNA, one of the members of the organising committee stated the message of the event as follows:

> The message is that a people (*o laos*) who have history and memory, like the Greek people, do not forget what they have gone through in various prosecutions. Of course, we are wholeheartedly standing by our friends, the Serbs, for the injustice that has been inflicted on them by Europe and the Americans.

Another journalist from ANTENNA, the private channel with a centre-right wing orientation, stressed:

> What must be mentioned, as you can see on your screens, is that there are people [here] of all ages, of all political and party affiliations. Because, as the organisers of the concerts said in the beginning: This war has united *us*.

ET-1's reporter says emphatically, 'Greek history is encapsulated in these moments …', while we are listening to 'the songs with which the post-war generations were brought up'. He continues: 'Three generations of Greeks meet here today'. Television framed the conflict by anchoring the events in Greek history and collective memory.

Another way of evoking the nation was the presence of flags at the concert.

There were mainly Greek flags, but also some Serb. Towards the end of the concert the two flags were tied together, with the camera close up. This was a clear metonymy for the nation, as Billig has remarked (1995: 41, 86). In this case the nation was aligned with the Serbian nation, confirming once more one of the dominant themes in the reporting of the conflict discussed above. 'We' the Greeks and 'our brothers, the Serbs' are unified against 'them', the Americans and NATO.

CONCLUSIONS

This chapter has discussed the construction of a 'common we' through the analysis of the textual features and form of the news. It is, however, interesting to examine who belongs to this common 'we', as its confines appear to be porous. The first obvious category is the Greeks, although this begs for some clarification. In the airspace incident, 'us' included Greece and Cyprus. Cyprus appeared as a natural extension of Hellenism, in the same way that the Greeks of Southern Albania appeared in the reports in the Kosovo case study. In the Kosovo reports, religion emerged as a determining parameter; 'us' in many reports included Serbs as Orthodox Christians. The alignment with Serbs was also justified more generally through the sharing of common traditions and experiences. Interestingly, however, there was no reference to Greek citizens, irrespective of religious affiliation. Moreover, in some of the Kosovo reports, 'us' included Europe and the West (in the context of Greece's membership of the EU and NATO). These reports, however, did not have the emotional intensity of those that emphasised the 'national/cultural' attributes.

This chapter has suggested that the emphasis on a cultural definition of belonging (that is, a definition that is grounded on cultural traits that are considered as givens) should not be interpreted as a confirmation of Huntington's theory of the *Clash of Civilisations* (1996). This theory cannot explain a number of instances when Greece has been involved in disputes with other predominantly Christian Orthodox nations (the more recent example being the Macedonian issue), and moments when Greece has aligned itself with Muslim populations, such as the Kurds or the Palestinians. The discourses emphasising cultural homogeneity should be seen in the political context of the anti-Americanism that is present in Greece for historical reasons. Moreover, the reporting of the conflict in Greece can be interpreted as a popular reaction to a reified discourse about the Balkans and Greece itself in the Western media.

What is surprising is the homogeneity of the private channels. While it has been argued that the media have become more polyphonic after deregulation in 1989 (Tsaliki 1997), it seems that when it comes to national issues there is an overwhelming consensus across the channels. Although it is true that the media have made public aspects of Greek culture that were downplayed in the pre-deregulation era, this does not seem to be paralleled with a wider polyphony on national issues. It seems that the diversity that deregulation brought about was limited. The Greek media are still highly concentrated in Athens. It is indicative that, today, it is almost impossible to hear any other accents in the broadcast media apart from the Athenian. It is perhaps surprising that the only alternative voice in the reporting of the two case studies, and particularly in the Kosovo case study, was that of the public service broadcaster, ET-1 which had traditionally been associated with the official state policy.

This chapter has not attempted to locate the preferred reading of the news. Rather it has looked at the various narrative patterns and the transformations of the 'us and them' scheme in different instances (airspace and Kosovo) and on different channels (public and private). Although I embrace the scepticism about extracting the meaning of texts with certainty, a number of features point to the emergence of a particular discourse in the news. This is determined by the prevalence of some thematic patterns (for instance, the claim that refugees are most often associated with destabilisation or threat). In a similar fashion, absences from the news reports also point to a degree of closure. Absences here include the lack of any reference to the background of the Cyprus issue in the airspace reports, or to the background to the Kosovo conflict. All this should also be seen in the context of the particular form of the news which naturalises its own practice.

Examining the circulation of discourses about the nation, it is possible to discern a certain discourse in the news about who belongs to the nation and who does not. It is also possible to identify who is implied as the natural audience for the news. However, what becomes imperative now is to examine how these public discourses are interpreted by the people, the actual audiences. The next chapter will examine the types of discourses that the news generates at a local level, as part of the exploration of the mediation of discourses about the nation.

CHAPTER 7

NEGOTIATING THE NATION: CRITICAL VIEWERS, CULTURAL INTIMACY AND IDENTITY EXPERIENCES

This chapter brings together the theoretical framework on identity discussed in Chapter 2 and the research on audiences (Chapter 4), in order to examine whether the news influences the ways people talk about the nation and their position within it. What happens to the relatively open identity discourses identified in Chapter 5, when they come into contact with the dominant discourse about the nation analysed in Chapter 6? Do critical viewers contest the 'banal nationalism' (Billig 1995) and the essentialist projection of the nation in the news? In which circumstances do people become more essentialist about their own identities and those of others?

Chapter 2 argued that the theories which support the reproduction of nationalism adopt a top-down approach. In this chapter I examine the perspective from below in order to test this assumption with empirical evidence. Does the nationalism in the news affect viewers' discourses, and if so when? In order to answer this question I draw on the developments in audience studies and particularly on the concept of the critical viewer (Livingstone and Lunt 1994), which is helpful as it captures the increasing sophistication and media literacy[1] with which audiences approach media texts. 'Critical designates a distanced, informed or analytic approach to programmes, rather than simply a negative or rejecting one' (Livingstone and Lunt 1994: 71).

Liebes has noted that theories of communication are full of dichotomies 'that seem to be inspired ... by some notion of open and closed' (1996: 178). She reviews the major dichotomies, starting from Eco's distinction of naïve and smart readers, which focuses on the reader's work at the aesthetic, rather than the ideological, level of the text (Eco 1985). While the 'naïve' reader takes reality as given, the 'smart' reader discerns the constructedness of the text.

Another dichotomy, between the interpretive and the analytic viewer, is proposed by Neuman. The interpretive viewer relates the programme to their life or to broader issues of society and culture, while the analytic focuses on the syntactic elements of the text and the quality of scriptwriting and acting (Neuman 1982: 471–87). The oppositional category takes an aesthetic dimension in Neuman's model; it is concerned with the viewer's cognitive ability rather than

---

1   According Livingstone media literacy 'and indeed literacy more generally is the ability to access, analyse, evaluate and communicate messages in a variety of forms (2003: 6).

anything political or ideological (Liebes 1996: 179). On the other hand, there is Hall's encoding/decoding model (1980) and Morley's empirical confirmation in the *Nationwide* study (1980). Hall's concern is with the political and ideological elements in communication. Drawing on Gramsci's theory of hegemony and Parkin's model of meaning systems, Hall identified the oppositional, negotiated and dominant decoding positions.

The above dichotomies seem to be divided in relation to aesthetic and ideological concerns. Liebes and Katz (1993), in the *Export of Meaning*, proposed a fourfold typology as an attempt to integrate elements from all the previous dichotomies and, in particular, to integrate the aesthetic/ideological divide. They distinguished between the real, ludic, ideological and constructional positions. Liebes has applied this typology to the reception of the news (Liebes 1997; Liebes and Ribak 1991). Real decodings are hegemonic, as they take for granted the depiction of reality in the news. Ideological readings attempt to uncover the ideological manipulative message hidden in the text. Ludic decodings view characters and events in the news as entertainment, while constructional decodings point to the journalistic and generic conventions that 'determine the relationships between reality and its construction on the screen' (Liebes and Ribak 1991: 206).

There are, however, some difficulties with the application of this typology to the news. The ludic category seems to be more easily applied to fiction and drama reception than to the news (although some viewers may develop playful or imaginary relationships with newscasters). Moreover, the term 'real' is not necessarily opposed to both 'ideological' and 'constructional'. Finally, this typology does not include a category that addresses exclusively viewers' reactions to media content. All categories are related to media content, but also include an aesthetic dimension. A category that addresses reactions toward media content is significant for this study as it is in relation to media content that discourses about identity are articulated.

In this chapter the dichotomy will be between critical (or not) readings in relation to news as a genre and journalistic practices, and critical readings (or not) in relation to news content. Viewers who are critical about the news, recognising its constructedness (through journalistic and generic conventions), operate primarily at an aesthetic level, although this is not always the case. For instance, when viewers make comments about the economics of television and media's symbiosis with the political system, and how they affect news presentation, the decoding is both 'ideological' and 'aesthetic'.

The category of critical readings towards news content is subdivided into further categories. In this study, the focus is on identity discourses, thus viewers who accept the dominant, official discourse about the nation and its 'culture' presented in Chapter 6, are making 'dominant' decodings. Conversely, interviewees who challenge this dominant discourse make 'demotic' decodings. Viewers who have a contextual knowledge of the events presented in the news make contextual readings. Viewers who juxtapose their historical knowledge of the events presented in the news make historical decodings. Finally, analytic viewers are those who attempt to read through the events and provide the reasons for their presentation – or not – in the news (this category is similar to what Liebes and Ribak name ideological (1991)). Of course all these distinctions are for analytic purposes as the aim is to examine their interrelation.

The analysis presented here also takes into account the viewers' discursive shifts between the news and their own experiences, echoing the concept of 'commuting' as developed by Liebes and Katz (1993). These shifts, from text to context, are significant as people relate to the news through their personal experiences and it is during these moments that identity discourses and experiences are articulated. These shifts manifest the types of discourses (dominant or demotic) that the news generates at a local level. As Livingstone remarks, the focus on text and context 'cannot be an either/or choice but remains a tension at the heart of the field which should be productive not destructive of understanding the connections among audiences, media and contexts' (1998c: 251).

The chapter is divided into two parts, one for the airspace incident and one for the Kosovo decodings. Each section is further divided according to the three different groups. The aim is not to stress differences. The concluding section draws links among the different groups. Effort has been made to represent all informants and the chapter should be read together with the description of the informants (Appendix II).

AIRSPACE INCIDENT DECODINGS: CONTESTING BANAL NATIONALISM

Greek viewers: contesting banal nationalism

The first observation in the *airspace interviews* is that most interviewees described the incident as routine. This contrasts with the tone of the news reports where words such as 'provocative', 'dangerous', 'worrying' and 'intense' were used (see Chapter 6).

> Christos: It was simply a report on some plane interceptions. Ordinary sensationalist reporting.

> Irini: OK, people are used to this . . . every week they watch the same reports.

Although most interviewees agreed that these incidents were routine, some voiced a concern about the dangers involved.

> Fotini: This was very intense, there were one hundred aircraft involved, and they were sending another eighty, and I am thinking that perhaps someday something will happen. It is almost inevitable.

> Sergios: We just saw instances from a war. Someone who did not understand Greek, or had been cut off from Greece for the last two or three years, would think that we are at war.

Note that Sergios said that someone 'would think that there was a war, if they had been cut off'. The point is, however, that viewers are not 'cut off from Greece' or, rather, its televised communicative space; on the contrary, as Chapter 5 showed, people are often addicted to television news. Even when they are not, they are informed through the interpersonal networks of which they are part. It is because people are familiar with Greek reality, both mediated and unmediated, that they express indifference towards such reports.

There is a degree of gender differentiation in the reactions to these reports. Women, like Fotini above, are more concerned than men about the dangers involved in such incidents. Men draw on their experience in the army, which they contrast with what they watch on television, thus challenging the reports.

> Christos: As a specialist, I did my service in the air force; I can say this, this situation is just a game … The same way they violate our airspace, we violate theirs. It is part of the game, a rehearsal. … I've heard from some [Greek pilots] that they know the Turkish pilots by name. They talk on the radio. They're playing a game.

> Thodoris: When I was doing my service, I was in the navy, and we were patrolling off the shores of Turkey, between Samos, Chios[2] and Turkey, and the Turkish ships would approach us, we would approach them, they would then threaten to ram us. It was like a game, without any substance.

The interpretation of the news is firmly grounded in personal experiences. Contextual knowledge affects comprehension and interpretation and explains the gender differentiation mentioned above. This finding connects with Philo's empirical study (1990) on the reception of the reporting of the English miners' strike in 1984–85. Philo found that people with first-hand knowledge of the strike remembered the picketing as peaceful, while those who depended on television had perceived it as violent (1990).

Viewers critical toward journalists and generic conventions

All Greek interviewees expressed criticisms about the journalists and the media and were largely aware of the generic conventions of the news. Most interviewees described the news reports as sensationalist and recognised that the reports used footage from past exercises, as well as images from a flight simulator programme, to reconstruct the air fight. Only the oldest informant, Tasos, did not recognise the use of animation, which suggested that media literacy might be related to age.

Haris recalled a documentary on the fabrication of news stories broadcast by NET that other interviewees had watched as well. 'In an hour they showed all the tricks that they can do with images', Haris said, suggesting that media literacy is linked to media use. It is through watching television that he became critical of the news' conventions and journalistic practices.

> Haris: [The programme] showed how the news is manufactured. In the end it showed that even Greek journalists are not innocent. They showed what happened in Albania … after the collapse of the pyramids scheme. The Greek journalists reporting the unrest were asking local Albanians to gather around the camera at 8:30, when they were on air, and start shooting with their rifles. The shootings reported live from Albania those days were not for real. It was all staged.

---

2   Greek islands in the Aegean Sea.

Other interviewees said that the report used images, and perhaps even text, that were taken from the Ministry of Defence, pointing to a close relationship between media and the government.

> Christos: This video was taken from the Ministry [of Defence]. Obviously they also got the text from the Ministry.
>
> Sergios: Not necessarily the text. At least not the whole text.
>
> Stelios: But the video [they got] for sure.
>
> Christos: Because how else would the journalists know?

Some of the interviewees expressed a social constructionist perspective on the news and the reporting of such incidents. Some argued that the issues themselves would not exist if television did not emphasise them.

> Thodoris: If there was no television there would be fewer air fights like these. Because of television more of them happen and are made more salient; ... if there was no television no one would know about them.

Moreover, people were aware of the economy of media institutions and how it affects the content and the agenda of news programmes. The following excerpt from a discussion expresses a political economy perspective.

> Haris: They show incidents like these to fill up the duration of the programme. When they have one and a half hours of news, they have to find some issues to fill it up.
>
> Lena: They have to make up something. That's what it comes to. But we should not fool ourselves, we should not think that those working in the media are socially altruistic.
>
> Spyros: They are companies.
>
> Lena: Exactly. And companies have to have profits. Otherwise what's the point. They'll shut down. This is what we need to remember. In order to make profits they will do anything, even illegal things.

Analytic viewers

One of the dominant patterns in the interviews with the Greek viewers was the identification of the reasons why the reports were seen to be presented in a sensationalist manner. Another dominant theme was the identification of the deeper causes of the air fights themselves, something that the news reports did not address, pointing to the fact that viewers were more analytical than the news reports.

In accounting for the reasons behind the airspace incident informants said that it was related to the politics between Greece and Turkey and their governments' attempt to divert attention from social and economic issues. Giota said: '[t]his is some form of terrorism so that we do not speak up.' Other informants argued that such incidents were the result of Turkey's opportunistic foreign policy. Interestingly, most interviewees implied a synergy between the Greek government and the media. This was often expressed through the use of the pronoun 'they', which includes journalists, media owners and politicians. '*They* show these incidents because *they* want to distract our attention from other matters', Dafne said. '*They* want us to be in constant tension with Turkey', Fotis added. '*They* are misleading us' (Giota). All the informants mentioned that there are covert interests, often implying a symbiosis between politicians and the media. 'We cannot even imagine the hidden interests', Irini said.

A frequent explanation for the prevalence of such reports in the news and what the interviewees interpreted as its sensationalist style, was the commercialisation of the media and the concomitant competition for audiences and advertising revenue. 'They do it for the ratings', was an oft-repeated phrase. 'These are everyday incidents which the media exaggerate in order to attract viewership', many viewers argued.

Viewers are analytical in attempting to add the missing pieces to the incomplete puzzle that is the news. They seek and provide explanations for the events and try to identify the causes, something the news does not do. Of course, as most of the interviewees admitted, this kind of thinking is often speculative and only those involved know what the 'hidden interests are'.

Contextual knowledge

The analysis of the 'airspace incident' news reports (Chapter 6) revealed that there was no reference to the historical context of Cyprus and Greek-Turkish relations. Many viewers juxtaposed their historically informed perspective with the ahistorical news, and based their critical interpretations on their knowledge of the issue. Tasos, one of the older informants, gave an alternative perspective on the Cyprus problem that challenges its naturalisation in the news. 'When I was young, there was no Cyprus issue. There was only the 'Northern Epirus' issue back then.' Informants were aware of the context that shaped the events, although not everyone was as well informed, as the following excerpt shows:

> Sergios: The pretext for the invasion was a Greek coup in Cyprus orchestrated by the colonels' junta in Athens. And, this is my personal view, Turkey had the right to intervene, she was covered by the Treaty. She was one of the guarantor powers.
>
> Interviewer: Do people know about this?
>
> Christos: I think that most people of our age know about this.
>
> Sergios: Not of our age. Older people do.
>
> Stelios: I did not know.
>
> Sergios: It is not well known. It has been carefully hushed up.

The younger interviewees did not know what had happened in Cyprus in previous decades and what caused the events of 1974. This is not something taught at school and, as Sergios mentioned above, it is not something that is often discussed publicly. It is even common for people in Stelios' generation (mid-twenties) not to know the background of the events. Stelios heard some of the facts surrounding the Cyprus conflict for the first time in the context of the interview.

Lack of contextual knowledge is not only related to age; it is also a generational issue, affecting people who were born after 1974. This means that those with no experience of the conflict have limited resources to learn what happened. Since the media do not present the historical context, younger informants rely on either education or personal networks. However, Tatiana, a high school student, remarked: 'The history we are taught at school does not cover the Cyprus issue.' Dafne added: 'Textbooks ... only mention the achievements and the triumphs of the Greeks.' Even older interviewees such as Rena, who was an adult when the events in Cyprus took place, expressed frustration with her lack of knowledge. She feels that there is nowhere to turn to when she wants to be informed. She admits that she does not even try to ask, but at the same time she said: 'Of course, I would like to know more. It's like when you ask a blind person, do you want to see?'

Contextual knowledge affects the comprehension and the interpretation of the reports (Livingstone 1998b; Morley 1999). Those with poorer information resources could not explain why the interceptions took place and why the planes were there in the first place.

Demotic discourses

Greek viewers contested the discourses about Cyprus in the news. In the airspace news reports there was a constant deixis, a rhetorical pointing to the nation, which included Cyprus and Greece. Cyprus was referred to as 'Meghalonisos', the 'Big Island', as part of the national imagery. Conversely, interviewees contested the official discourse that advocates continuity between Greece and Cyprus. When I asked Thodoris if he thought Cypriots are Greeks, he replied: 'I believe they are. I am not sure if they do.'

> Thodoris: When [the invasion] happened, [Cyprus] was a national issue. Today, I don't think it is. Because Cypriots themselves don't want us to have them as a national issue, and the Greeks are also tired of this Cyprus issue. It will never be resolved. What is the Cyprus issue? That half of Cyprus is Turkish. It will always be. Or, will Denktash ever leave Cyprus? It is more probable that he will take the whole of Cyprus. ... There is no Cyprus issue for me. I think that they have accepted this; this is how things are. Either things will stay the same, or they will worsen. ... What I've been listening to since I was a child is the 'resolution of the Cyprus issue'. Before Cyprus they put the word resolution. But I don't think this will ever happen. The resolution of the Cyprus issue will never take place.

'So why is there a fuss every time Cyprus' application to the EU is challenged?', I asked Thodoris. 'There isn't a fuss. If you do a survey I believe that not everyone will react. Especially young people. Even Cypriots do not care if Greece reacts or not.' This view was shared by other informants, who also thought that Greece cannot do much about Cyprus.

> Dafne: We have so many problems in Greece now I'm not saying that we should not be involved with Cyprus, I'm not saying it's not worth it, but perhaps we should resolve some other issues first and then look at Cyprus.

Stelios: We shouldn't be too preoccupied about the Cyprus issue because the Cypriots are not particularly preoccupied with us. Why should we be the parents of the Greek Cypriots? ... The educational level in Cyprus is very high, they don't need us.

Interestingly, Michalis wonders why such a prevalent attitude is never heard on television, revealing the power he attributes to the media. His question can also be interpreted as how can something so prevalent not be part of media reality.

Michalis: I do not know how, because I've never watched such a thing on television, but in the last twenty years a negative attitude towards Cypriots has developed, which I cannot understand ... So all these years, wherever I go, people of my age don't like Cypriots ... Everybody scorns the Cypriots.

Fotini: I have heard this as well. At university. A Cypriot would ask a question in the amphitheatre and it would cause gales of laughter.

Michalis: [Greek people] make fun of their accent. Similarly, Cypriots do not like us at all and have their reasons for this. Because of the '74 invasion. They don't care which government was in power then and who inspired it, who let this happen. They don't care if it was the Greeks, the government, the junta ...

The following excerpts are interesting as they point to a demotic discourse about the nation, while in parallel they reveal an 'us and them' dichotomy that renders the Cypriot as the 'other'. In this sense the following quotes are 'demotic' and, at the same time, essentialist as they objectify Cypriot people.

Michalis: Meanwhile, Cypriots do not like us, and at a practical level they have nothing to gain from us, they are much better off on their own. If they were a part of Greece they would be just like Crete, an affluent region of Greece with a high standard of quality of life. Even though they have bad taste and they are *nouveau rich* ... they are having a good time. They have no reason to want Greece. [. . .] They feel Greek when it's in their interest.

Fotini: This is what I suspect as well, and I am not sure if it is true, but I sense it, not because I've been to Cyprus, but once I gave private lessons to a Cypriot family, and their relatives, aunts and uncles would come by. Cypriots have strong solidarity among them. And they would all refer to Greece in the third person. They never said 'us Greeks'. Never.

Cyprus is not the only issue about which demotic discourses concerning the nation are expressed. Sergios referred to the army as a 'dump', while Christos called it 'a brothel'. Andreas, who works for the army, said that '[t]here's nothing exceptional in working in the army; it's an ordinary job'. Everyday personal experiences contest a nationalist perspective in which the armed forces are considered the bastion of the nation.

Moreover, some informants challenged the assumption that it is only Turkey that violates Greece's airspace. Many interviewees mentioned that they know – from personal contacts and experiences – that when Turkish planes violate Greek airspace, Greek planes violate Turkish space. All the interviewees acknowledged that they did not expect to hear this on the news, suggesting that people are aware that the news presents a more formal account of events, a dominant discourse.

Dominant discourses

Not all Greek informants challenged the dominant discourse of the news. Tatiana, a high school student, regarded Cyprus as a national issue. Note that she considers Cyprus a part of Greece that could be 'lost' if Greece is not interested.

> Tatiana: Greece has to be interested in the continuation and preservation of the Hellenism of Cyprus. We need to make sure that we will not lose other lands.

Georgia also expressed a dominant perspective taking the 'us and them' dichotomy in the news for granted.

> Georgia: We've seen incidents like this before, Turks chasing our planes, because we are enemies, Turks and Greeks and we seek to harm each other. We don't really want to, but the Turks chase us so …
>
> Rena: I am Greek and I will defend Greece's rights – not Turkey's.

Marilena argued that the news cannot show everything because national security has to be taken into account. According to her, a form of censorship would be acceptable in order for the national interest not to be compromised. Her case is similar to that of the 'deniers' that Liebes describes (1997). Deniers are the viewers who believe that the news is credible, but nonetheless support censorship (Liebes and Ribak 1991: 209). By putting the national interest above everything else, Marilena does not challenge the dominant categories of the news and thus makes a dominant interpretation.

Greek viewers generally were critical of media practices and journalistic conventions. This critical stance was coupled with a critical perspective concerning news content. The majority of the Greek informants contested the banal nationalism of the news reports by juxtaposing their own personal experiences and contextual knowledge. Overall, their accounts were more historically informed than those of the news reports. Viewers expected the news to present a dominant perspective. Contextual knowledge affects comprehension and interpretation; the least resourceful viewers found it more difficult to challenge the news and were ambivalent, often oscillating between discursive positions within the context of the interview.

Greek Cypriot viewers

The ordinariness attributed to the airspace incident reports by the Greek viewers is in stark contrast to the reaction of most Cypriot viewers' reaction. Cypriot viewers were critical of the news, albeit in a different way from the Greeks. While Greek viewers contrasted their reality to what they described as an exaggerated report, Cypriots interpreted the report as one that did not reflect the seriousness of the issue and their own experiences in Cyprus. They compared the report to the information they got from Cyprus (through satellite television and personal networks). There were, however, differences between those who had lived in Athens for longer and those who had left Cyprus more recently.

> Orestis: It was not stressed. In Cyprus it would have been first on the agenda.

Eva: This is not an issue that concerns only Cyprus, it concerns the whole of Greece. It is the infringement of Greece's right to have an alliance with Cyprus. It is the common defence dogma.

Elpida: They are not as interested here. They consider it less important.

Orestis: Generally when you watch Greek news, you notice that the priorities are very different. They start with the robberies . . .

Orestis: SKAI might not show it at all.

Yiorgos: The channels here start with robberies, or prostitution, or the police. Yesterday they were looking for someone who had escaped.

Elpida: Today they had this woman who was threatening to jump from her window to commit suicide. Forty minutes of live reporting.

Eva, Elpida and Orestis were students living in Athens for three years at the time of the interview. Their recent experiences in Cyprus were key in their interpretation of the news reports. A similar comment was made by Anna, who had lived in Athens for a decade at the time of the interview.

Anna: They show what is happening, they do not distort it. But it is detached. As if this happened miles away. In Cyprus they would present it as the event of the day. There would be interruptions in the programming. ... When I am in Cyprus, whether I want it or not, because this is a major issue, I get informed everyday. Everyday you wake up and you know that Cyprus is as it is and you say, let's see what the news is today, if there are any developments.

Other interviewees, however, were more detached. Dina, having lived in Greece for almost thirty years, found the report exaggerated. Thalia thought that the report was neither exaggerated, nor understated.

Viewers critical towards journalists and generic conventions

At the same time, all the Cypriot interviewees demonstrated a critical ability to recognise the generic conventions of the news. They pointed out that the images used in one of the reports were from archive footage. Orestis recognised exactly where this footage had come from. The critical views that the Cypriot interviewees expressed toward the media were also the result of their low trust in the Greek media in relation to how Cyprus had been reported. Greek Cypriot informants combined media literacy with their existing attitudes towards the media. Elpida noted that the report was problematic; instead of focusing on the political aspect of the crisis, they showed 'all these fancy images'.

Contextual knowledge

Interviewees were not just critical at an aesthetic level. Orestis objected to the report as it was only a description of the incident and it did not show the reactions it caused in Cyprus, or in the diplomatic field. The respondents gave me all the background about the reactions of the politicians in Cyprus and the procedure that is followed at the diplomatic level every time such an incident takes place. Some criticised the report for being too short. For example, Orestis said:

> The reporting was flawed. They spoke of interceptions. Do people know what interceptions are, what a dogfight is (*emploki*)? We can think of up to four different meanings for this word. I know from an air force pilot, that a dogfight is when you follow a plane and you 'trap it' on your screen.

The students were particularly knowledgeable about the political and military aspects of the process and found that the report lacked all this information. All Greek Cypriot informants had a historical knowledge of the background of the Cyprus issue, which determined their interpretive framework. In the following excerpt, the students argue that, because the coverage of the Cyprus issue is flawed, Greeks do not understand what the problem is.

> Orestis: The Cyprus issue is played down on Greek television. ... Greek people need to understand that the Cyprus problem exists, and it *is* an everyday problem. It is being experienced by Greeks, who live at the other end of the Mediterranean, but it is a Greek issue.
>
> Eva: There are Greeks who know nothing about the Cyprus issue.
>
> Elpida: On Greek television only occasionally, like now with the exercise, or when there were some events. And the reporting is always problematic. Some things are presented wrongly. I've never met anyone who knows what 'federation' means, or which are the possible solutions from which we have to chose. The political aspect of the problem is unknown. They only know the problem.
>
> Yiorgos: That the Turks came and harmed the Greeks.
>
> Elpida: Some people think that we still want union (*enosis*) with Greece. Things that are completely untrue ...

From this excerpt it also emerges that the Cypriot interviewees, albeit emotional about the incident itself, were not 'in line' with the report, but were challenging it both at a content and an aesthetic level. The interviewees challenged the way the Cyprus problem was reported, by stressing that the media never discussed the political aspect of the issue. In this sense their interpretations are similar to those of the historically informed Greek informants. In the case of the Greek Cypriots, however, age and generational differences were not as important as with the Greek viewers. The Cypriot university students who were twenty-one or twenty-two were all familiar with background information about the conflict, because it had affected and still affects their lives. Recall that most of the younger Greek informants had a scanty knowledge about Cyprus. This is an indication of media power, as the Greek viewers relied mainly on the media for learning about Cyprus.

Analytic viewers

Some interviewees attempted to identify the reasons why the Cyprus issue is downplayed in the Greek media. The most common reason emerged from the previous excerpt; most Greeks ignore the situation in Cyprus and the media are partly responsible for this. Some informants mentioned the role of the educational system as well. Thalia said that: 'Cyprus is too costly. Nobody cares.'

The reality of experience

In their interpretations, all the Greek Cypriot interviewees continually shifted to their experiences in Cyprus. Men referred to their army experiences, which often involved violence and conflict.

Yiorgos: I served in the Green Line,[3] this is an experience (*vioma*).

Orestis: It is an experience. I saw Turks, I spoke to the Turks across the line.

Yiorgos: You see the Turkish flag when you wake up in the morning.

Orestis: Four months before I was moved to a new army base, a soldier had been killed. They tricked him and he entered the Green Line to exchange cigarettes for spirits; someone there was waiting to kill him. This is how it is. When I went there his best friend was in that checkpoint.

Overall, gender differences are not prevalent among the informants. People referred to a common 'reality' of tension that transcends gender differences.

Anna: I live opposite a military base in Cyprus. Our boys, when they finish high school, they go directly to the army. Sometimes I hear them at four o'clock at night when they are doing exercises. You cannot escape in Cyprus. When I go there I say, here I am. Today we are well, tomorrow there might be war.

Yannos underlined the importance of his experience by stressing the use of deictic pronouns, clearly differentiating between Greeks and Cypriots. Yannos mainly refers to past events that the news reports evoked.

I see analyses that they write about *my* country, Cyprus. And I realise that *we* see things very differently from *them*. The way they present them is completely different from the way *we* experienced them.

Dominant readings

The 'us and them' dichotomy was present in all the interviews, even among those who were more detached. For most interviewees these dichotomies were grounded in personal experiences. People said that they had lost relatives and friends in the conflict, some even recently. 'Every family has lost someone in the conflict, some families more than one' (Thalia). Anna's family became refugees in 1974 (she was two years old) and lost their home and assets. Her uncle is one of the 'missing people'. Orestis noted that he knew one of the people who got killed in 1996 in the Green Line during an incident.

Most of the Greek Cypriot viewers were emotionally involved in the decoding of the report. They contrasted their own experiences with the news and found the news unsatisfactory. The emotional interpretation of the news content does not mean that Greek Cypriots are not critical viewers. On the contrary, they were very critical, both at an aesthetic and content level. This indicates that viewing can be both critical and emotional. Moreover, the affective dimension of the Cypriot informants' interpretation should not be conflated with an acceptance of the banal

---

3   The Green Line is the UN buffer zone that separates the Greek and the Turkish side of Cyprus.

nationalism of the news. Informants challenged the content of the news by juxtaposing their own experiences and dominant discourses.

Turkish-speaking informants

Most Turkish-speaking viewers watch the news, albeit to varying degrees as Chapter 5 showed, on both Greek and Turkish channels; this is how they knew that Greek planes violate Turkish space as well. Ayşe told me that in the Turkish media such reports would normally be presented as a violation of Turkish airspace by Greek planes.

> Orhan: You never hear on the Greek news that Turkish airspace has been violated by Greek planes. They never say, look, we violated their airspace. But I see it on Turkish news.

> Hasan: They have reports like this on the Turkish channels. Here it said that the [Turkish] planes were intercepted. In the Turkish news they will say that they did not know that there was an exercise in Cyprus. That Greece is accusing us wrongly. It's all propaganda.

Watching the news on two 'national media systems' makes viewers more sceptical, but does not provide any certainty. As Ayşe remarked, 'Who knows the truth?'

> Hasan: Sometimes I watch both. … Here they hide [information], and we compare when we watch the Turkish. Where is the truth? We have to think, what is their interest, what is our interest … There is nothing else we can do, to untangle the tangled knot. We just have our opinion, we watch, but we are not always convinced. God said that you need to see it with your own eyes to be convinced. Not just to listen.

Analytic viewers

The Turkish-speaking viewers attempted to provide explanations both for the reasons these incidents take place and are shown on the news. Orhan, in the same vein as some of the Greek informants, identified a symbiotic relationship between the media and the political establishment. The difference is that Orhan's comment is based on his experience with two different broadcasting systems.

> Orhan: These incidents are presented whenever we have internal problems. It's the same in Turkey. We are privileged to have the [satellite] dishes. Whenever we have an internal problem in our country we stress these incidents to distract the public's attention. Simitis[4] has a problem, the Turkish government has a problem, they show these, and then people do not think about the government and the problems. They worry about the air fights.

The Turkish speaking interviewees noted that there are 'interests' involved in Greek-Turkish relations and it is in this context that Hasan's comment, 'it's all propaganda', should be understood. For the Turkish speaking informants, both the Greek and Turkish channels present whatever is in the interests of the media and the respective governments, which echoes the comments by the Greek viewers who implied a symbiotic relationship between the media and the government.

---

4   Kostas Simitis was the Greek Prime Minister from 1996–2004.

Viewers critical toward journalists and generic conventions

The Turkish-speaking viewers were aware of journalistic conventions. Their critical stance stemmed largely from their negative experiences with journalists (see Chapter 5). Interviewees constantly referred to such experiences whenever the issue of trust and objectivity was raised. All men had a story to tell. Women also expressed their dissatisfaction with journalistic reporting, although they mainly repeated the stories where men were the protagonists.

Contextual knowledge

Most of the Gaziot male informants were familiar with the historical context surrounding the Cyprus issue and drew on this when discussing the airspace reports. Hasan had fought in Cyprus in 1974 and had first-hand experience of the events.

> Mumin: Who went to kill Makarios? The Turks? The Greeks bombed the palaces where Makarios was staying. ... Greece started it all. Not Turkey. The landing[5] in Cyprus happened afterwards. And I've heard that many Turks got killed. I heard in the news about a five year old child, who got forty bullets. A little girl. All this in the Turkish news, of course. Here, they do not mention this.

Female informants were not as vocal in their interpretations. Like some of the Greek high school students and housewives, they seemed to lack the historical and political knowledge with which to interpret the events. In the interview, Ayşe, Bahar and Nuriye repeated constantly: 'Who knows? We do not know these things.' This suggests a lack of confidence to express their views; for this reason they preferred to shift the discussion to other topics with which they felt more comfortable.

Discursive oscillations: dominant and demotic

In his account of his experience in Cyprus in 1974, Hasan told me that 'the army had changed his name.[6] 'I was not Hasan. I was Haris Vlachos', he said. Hasan told me that he did not know with whom he was fighting. 'With the Greeks? With the English? With the Americans? With the Turks, or with the Turkish guerrillas?' Through his personal experience, Hasan underlines the complexity of Greek-Turkish relations, the Cyprus problem and his own position in this situation (a Greek Turk, fighting under a Greek name, against the Turks in Cyprus). Through his personal experience he expresses dissatisfaction with the dominant divisions, which do not reflect his complex reality.

Often, however, interviewees oscillated from a demotic to a dominant discourse, as some Greek interviewees did in the previous section. In the following extract Hasan challenges the dominant definition of who is Greek and

---

5   Mumin uses the word 'landing' to describe the Turkish incursion, whereas all the Greeks used the word invasion.

6   See section on double names in Chapter 6. This is a different case as the decision about Hasan's Greek name was not his, but rather taken by the Armed Forces

proposes a new definition based on the concept of citizenship. Mumin, however, reverts to an 'us and them' scheme, objectifying and reifying the Cypriots.

> Hasan: In relation to what we just watched, Greece and Cyprus, are they relatives? Are we cousins? What are we? . . . For me they are just Cypriots, not Greek Cypriot. There are no Greeks *and* Cypriots. They are [just] Cypriots. Haven't they got their own flag? Haven't they got their own currency? How, then, can Cypriots be Greeks?
>
> Mumın: Some even call themselves English.
>
> Interviewer: Some call themselves Greek.
>
> Hasan: And we say that we, who were born here, are Greek.

These comments echo some of those made by the Greek interviewees. Similarly, the comments here reflect both a dominant and a demotic discourse. On the one hand, informants are challenging the dominant discourse about the nation, but, on the other, they are reifying the Cypriots.

Experience

Turkish-speaking men drew upon their army experience when interpreting the news. The difference from the Greek interviewees is that they referred to the army to express the negative experiences that the reports invoked. Turkish-speaking informants shifted to their everyday life in Greece – in the same way that the Greek Cypriots talked about their Cypriot reality. The comment by Hasan in the previous section ('we say that we, who were born here, are Greeks') is illuminating. Turks in Gazi are Greek citizens, while Greek Cypriots are not. It is as Greek citizens that the Turkish interviewees react to a discourse that does not reflect their reality. In short, what the Gaziots are saying is that the news is more concerned about the non-citizen Cypriots than about the citizen Turks. It is in this context that Ayşe's comment has to be interpreted: 'Why should we feed the Cypriot children, if we cannot feed ours?'

Ayşe found the airspace incident report irrelevant to her reality. Umut (below) made similar comments. What these interviewees are saying is that the reports are banal compared to their 'grave' problems of everyday life, which never make it to the news.

> Umut: God has forgotten about us here, as Muslim Greeks. We want jobs. ... This is evident in the news. It is as if we do not exist. They don't even mention us. ... Sometimes I feel I have no desire to live anymore. I'd rather die than have a life like this. Nobody can give us a job. We have served [the army] here, we grew up here. We will die here. They have slammed many doors in my face because my name and my religion are different. But I do not cease to be and to feel Greek, maybe even more than you, maybe more than anybody. ... They call us Greeks, but in practice they are kicking us around. That's what I know.

The Turkish-speaking interviewees, in their 'commutings', make claims to citizenship and equal rights. They also claim that their reality should be represented in the news. Their interpretations and overall critical stance is more anchored to their own personal experiences and not so much in the decoding of the text, although some people stressed that the constructedness of the news. Most of their criticisms derive either from their symbolic annihilation from media discourse ('as if we do not exist' (Umut)), or their unfair depiction by television and the press in some cases.

THE RETELLINGS OF THE KOSOVO CRISIS

Greek informants

Emotional and critical viewers

The ordinariness of the news and its reception in the first case study is contrasted to a more emotional reaction in the Kosovo retellings by some Greek interviewees. The emotional reaction toward the content affected some interviewees' attitudes toward journalists and the media.

> Ilias: They have to show you the news. The buildings. The corpses. How can these be lies, all these things that they show on television. The camera cannot lie. It shows the building destroyed.

In Ilias' eyes, the fact that journalists get emotional is further confirmation of the reality that television conveys. He noted, 'How can they not be emotional when they see people digging in the rubble to find their loved ones? Is this a lie? All these monstrosities that I see on television I believe them all. They are not exaggerated.' (Ilias) 'Of course, we believe them', added Eugenia.

Other interviewees, however, expressed more critical views toward the media and journalists. People were aware of media conventions and journalistic practices, as was the case in the airspace interviews. Informants mentioned that there is no objectivity in the news. 'It is biased and hypocritical', said Vassilis. Sophia said that the media are 'the last thing that one will trust in their life'. Andreas noted that Greek television is well known for 'trading in horror' and this practice is attributed to the commercialisation of television. 'The more horror, the higher the ratings', Andreas said. He also remarked, rather cynically, that he believed that there was a tariff for each sigh and sob in the news. 'A sob, 300,000 drachmas[7], two sighs ... Journalists will do whatever to sell their goods', he added.

As in the airspace incident discussions, it was through media use that people criticised the news. The more people watch, the more critical they become towards media practices. Andreas said that during the first Gulf War the channels that supported the Alliance, as well as the Greek channels, showed a picture of a heron covered in tar and crude oil. In the end, this picture was proven to be from a different incident, but was used to exemplify the ecological disaster in the Gulf. This is something that Andreas read in a magazine, which made him very sceptical of journalistic practices. 'Journalists uncovered other journalists', he said.

---

7   Around £550.

Viewers were also aware of the economics of media production and their effects on media products and use, articulating a political economy perspective.

> Alexandros: The media in Greece are controlled by a small group of people, MEGA is owned by Vardinogiannis, ANTENNA by Kyriakou, Channel 5 by that guy who publishes Avriani, Kouris, and so on. They are the ruling classes, they have lots of money and interests. Through their media, they promote a certain idea about Greece.

Interestingly, even the informants who were critical of the media in the reporting of the conflict often agreed with the content of the news. There is a paradox here – while people were critical of media and journalistic practices, they watched the news and were convinced by its emotional reality. The reason that people identified with the media (even those who expressed doubts about the objectivity of the news) is that the media echoed emotions, popular perceptions and fears prevalent in Greek society. In other words, the exaggerated reports had an emotional realism for the viewers. The quote by Andreas is illuminating: 'Of course the coverage is biased. Of course I know this. But I am pro-Serb.'

Dominant and demotic negotiations

Not all the viewers were convinced by the news content. In the following excerpts different views are heard as the informants are debating the coverage.

> Alexandros: I cannot stand this populist stuff, we have the impression, and the media reinforce it, that we are Orthodox, and Serbs are Orthodox and Russians are Orthodox, so we are all a happy family.
>
> Sophia: But isn't this the culture of our people?
>
> Alexandros: This is the culture of our people that the media convey and reinforce. The media reproduce this idea because their owners have interests and this is what they want. They cannot accept any other idea.
>
> Katerina: Maybe we are only looking at one side of the story, because we think that [the Serbs] are being wronged in this case.
>
> Andreas: Look, the Greeks were always the people who were driven by emotions. On the other hand there is the historical relationship that binds us with the Serbs.
>
> Zoe: The same religion ...
>
> Andreas: The emotions prevail.
>
> Katerina: If it is only emotional then why aren't we emotional in relation to the others [the Albanians]? ... Aren't they people as well? They leave their homes and their belongings and they are even bombed while they are on the road.
>
> Andreas: Let's not forget that the Greeks were always on the Indians' side and not that of the cowboys. Always.

In these excerpts it is possible to observe the competing discourses about the nation and its culture and how they relate to perceptions about the role of the media. While in the airspace case study there was relative homogeneity within the groups and most interviewees challenged the news and the incident itself, here the voices were more mixed. Some viewers were more sceptical and critical of the coverage, while others drew on a dominant view of Greek culture to justify their stance and that of the media. In the second extract, it is possible to discern one of the reasons why the Greek viewers were more sympathetic towards the Serbs in the Kosovo conflict. Andreas' comment about 'cowboys and Indians' suggests that it is anti-Americanism, rather than 'culture', that determined the support for the Serbs. Andreas is projecting his experience and knowledge about US involvement in Greek politics in past decades, in his interpretation of the conflict, a comment made by many of the informants.

Some, however, were clearly oppositional to the coverage and the pro-Serb feelings expressed in the Kosovo reports. For example, Vassilis said:

> Channels distinguish according to religion. I can't understand this. This is the most ridiculous thing ever. ... We should not distinguish between Christians, Buddhists or Muslims. Why should we become racist? ... This is tragic and disastrous.

Resourceful viewers

During the Kosovo conflict I noted an increased use of foreign (news) media. The issue of access is important here, as not all the informants could follow foreign language media. However, even those who did not really watch channels such as CNN expressed opinions about their coverage based on how this was reported in the Greek media.

> Alexandros: I do not identify [with any channel]. I do not believe in anything they say. I do not believe it when Blair announces that there are 250,000 refugees, I do not believe that. When Greek television announces that 1,000 Serbs died because of a bomb, I do not believe that, either. Everything is misinformation.

Having access to both Greek and non-Greek media provided Alexandros with a measure of comparison. On the one hand, he identified problems in the Greek coverage, but on the other, he also identified problems with the British media, which he criticised for ignoring, 'perhaps with NATO's orders', the diplomatic initiatives undertaken by the Greek government.

By identifying the reasons why the British media ignore Greek initiatives Alexandros' comment is analytic. It emerges that analytic interpretations are made when viewers are dissatisfied with the content of the news. Although Greek viewers were critical about media practices during the Kosovo conflict, they did not elaborate the reasons why this was happening and what role the media play, at least not to the degree that they did in the airspace interviews. This confirms the dissonance between the critical level of interpretation toward media practices and the sympathetic interpretation of media content.

Contextual knowledge and alternative resources

Many of the informants attempted to identify the causes of the conflict, thereby appearing more historically informed than the news, even if there were occasionally inaccuracies in their accounts. All the informants noted that the conflict had its roots in past decades. The difference was between those who had alternative resources for finding out about the conflict and those who were more dependent on the media. Vassilis' account was an open one, avoiding the 'us and them' dichotomies prevalent in the news.

> Vassilis: Years ago, Serbs and Kosovars had no problems living together. It was a few years ago that some people, for their own interests, created nationalist sentiments on purpose and the confrontations began. The Civil War started as a result. Two peoples lived together in the same land for 1,000 years without a problem and now there is a problem. … People do not have inherent problems with each other.

Vassilis knew that there was ethnic cleansing of the Kosovans by the Serbian army and this was the reason they were leaving. He had heard this from some Albanians in Greece, whom he employed in his business. Reflecting upon his own history (his mother's family had arrived from Asia Minor in 1922), he told me: 'These things have always been happening. Here in Greece we are all refugees and foreigners.' This comment, in stark contrast to the news reports that depicted refugees as a destabilising threat, evokes the successive population displacements in recent Greek history.

Alexandros knew about the conflict and its background through a branch of his family who live in the Republic of Macedonia (FYROM) and whom he sees every summer when they visit his home town in Northern Greece. Alexandros knew that there was ethnic cleansing against the Kosovans; his family in the Republic of Macedonia had also been harassed because they were part of the Vlach minority – a linguistic minority that lives in Greece as well. Alexandros' experience exposes the arbitrariness of the national and ethnic boundaries. His family is divided into two parts, one living in Macedonia and one in Greece, after finding themselves on different sides of the border, when the border was drawn.

Some interviewees mentioned that the refugees were leaving because of ethnic cleansing and prosecution by the Serbian army (Nicos, Andreas, Katerina). The rest said that the refugees were leaving because of the NATO strikes (Zoe, Ilias, Eugenia, Sophia). The following section examines how they related the conflict to their experiences and knowledge.

Dominant discourses

Some of the informants drew a parallel between the intervention of NATO in Kosovo and its lack of intervention in Cyprus in 1974, or thereafter. Interestingly, while Greece's relationship to Cyprus was contested in the 'airspace incident' interviews, it was reinstated in the Kosovo case study. Note how Sophia used the personal pronoun to include both Cyprus and Greece in her discourse: 'What did the Americans do for Cyprus? They left *us* alone then.'

All the interviewees (apart from Vassilis) made a parallel with Western Thrace, expressing a fear that there might be problems with the Turkish minority there. The parallel was made to justify the Serb reaction to the development of KLA. Most of these discourses are 'dominant', identifying and reifying communities. The use of pronouns is indicative of the 'us and them' dichotomy that evokes segregation.

Ilias: The same way *we* have the Turks in Thrace. If the Turks ever revolt and demand *their* own state, will we say, of course, go ahead? We will not. That was the problem.

Andreas: I know that something will happen. I am not afraid that *we* will have war with Turkey over this issue. Because *we* are a member of the EU. . . . In the worst case scenario, *they* already have *their* mufti in Komotini and in Xanthi, in the worst case scenario *we* will give *them* new representation in Parliament. And nothing else.

Sophia: The same way *we* have Greek Muslims. *They* are not Turks. *They* are Greek, only Muslim in their faith.

These quotes reveal an underlying tension and also an obvious essentialist discourse on ethnicity and belonging. The minority is objectified and is considered a threat because it threatens ethnic homogeneity and thus contests the very essence of the nation that is thought of as natural and taken for granted. To use the terms that Douglas has developed (1966), minorities are thought of as impurities polluting the pure state; they are a symbolic danger threatening the discourse on which the nation is based. The power of naming (Muslims *not* Turks) and the use of pronouns are very significant. By insisting on calling them Greek and Muslim, people symbolically reduce the threat. These examples are reminiscent of the reports about Northern Epirus discussed in Chapter 6, although Northern Epirus was not mentioned in the interviews.

Overall, the discursive patterns identified in the news analysis (Chapter 6) were not repeated identically in the viewers' interpretations. However, there were similarities especially among those informants who had no other alternative resources for finding out about the conflict. Thus, some interviewees reacted to the refugee issue as if it were a threat. The difference is that, while the news reports focused on Northern Epirus, the interviewees focused on Western Thrace and drew a parallel with the events in Kosovo.

Cultural intimacy

In the context of discussions about media objectivity and the possibility of expressing different opinions about the conflict, some interviewees recalled the controversy with the former conservative Minister Andrianopoulos and the article he wrote in *The New York Times* (analysed in Chapter 6). Ilias said that 'Andrianopoulos is an agent of the Americans', with Eugenia agreeing and saying, 'He has sold himself to the Americans' (*poulimeno tomari*). Interestingly, informants, who were critical of the Greek media coverage, were against an open criticism of the Greek media abroad.

Sophia: ... did he have to say this in America? Couldn't he just say it in Greece?

Nicos: This ... is how a negative image is created about Greece.

Greek-Cypriot viewers' interpretations

Many informants reacted to the reporting of Kosovo in an emotional way, which was reflected in their assessment of the coverage.

> Marianna: ... Not only were [the journalists] objective, but they also added their own emotional reaction, without which, the reporting would be flawed. You cannot see corpses mutilated and burnt for no reason and not react as a human being. If you do not, then you are as subhuman as Shea and Clinton and all the rest.

In the same vein, the correspondent who reported the bombing of the Chinese Embassy was praised for crying. Marianna and Ioanna said that this way 'he proved that he is a human being'. They added that they themselves were also crying when watching the report. However, not all the interviewees made emotional interpretations. Chryssa was critical about some aspects of the Kosovo coverage, although overall she thought that the Greek media were more objective than the Western.

All informants drew parallels between the events in Kosovo and the invasion of Cyprus, thus appropriating the conflict through their own personal experiences.

> Marianna: There are similarities. Turkey invaded Cyprus and now NATO unlawfully invades Yugoslavia.
>
> Ioanna: In a sovereign state, a foreign, third party comes and invades just because they want to (*me to etsi thelo*).
>
> Marianna: The ethnic cleansing committed by the Turks is not condemned by NATO. And then we say that Milocevic did ethnic cleansing.
>
> Ioanna: NATO did not even react then. When 200,000 left Northern Cyprus.
>
> Marianna: [They were] refugees. I have many doubts about the ethnic cleansing they accuse Milocevic of. Because this is what the English and Americans told us. We don't have enough information.

Apart from anchoring the Kosovo conflict to the events in Cyprus, the two women expressed their distrust towards 'the English and the Americans', a comment that includes both politicians and the media. Distrust is grounded again on experience and the lack of support and attention that the Cyprus issue received. Yannos, who is a refugee himself from the Northern part of Cyprus, makes a similar comment. 'We feel there is hypocrisy. When they speak about human rights and I cannot go to my home, then what human rights?'

> Yannos: The problem is that the Great Powers apply double standards. They say that Kosovan Albanian refugees are different from Cypriot refugees. In Kosovo they run to protect the rights [of the minority], but they don't care that in Cyprus there are refugees who cannot return to their homes. There is a UN resolution which says that the refugees can return, but it is never applied. This is how it is for us. You can't help making the comparison. Even Greece has double standards. We are hurt because we see that we are the weak ones, at the end of all this. Cyprus is divided *de facto*, but there will probably also be a *de jure* as things go. When they take away your last hope, that we are not going to go back to the house where we were born, what can I say, humanitarian rights are great, but reality, unfortunately, is not compatible with them. ... When did the Great Powers come to support Greece? Never. Greek people support Serbia out of a gut feeling.

Apart from making references to Cyprus, informants also connected the refugee issue to the minority in Thrace, echoing the comments by the Greek informants.

Again the same discursive strategy is applied through naming (Albanian-speakers *not* Albanians, Muslims *not* Turks) and the use of pronouns in order to neutralise the perceived threat. These are examples of a dominant, closed discourse:

> Marianna: [the refugees are leaving] because they [NATO] are bombing. Of course, this is widely known. 20% left before the air campaign started and now 80% is leaving. It's obvious.
>
> Ioanna: And why did the 20% leave before?
>
> Marianna: Because there was some fighting between the Serbs and Kosovars.
>
> Ioanna: The separatist groups of KLA were formed there. They operated for some time and they caused troubles; they were a source of anomaly. Let's make a parallel with things in Greece. If there was a separatist group in Thrace, where we have many Muslims. Because Kosovars, we call them Albanians, but they are not Albanians, they are Albanian-speakers. They belong to the Yugoslav state. They are Yugoslavians.
>
> Marianna: They are Yugoslavians.
>
> Ioanna: The same way we have Greek Muslims. They are not Turks. They are Greek, only Muslim in their religion.
>
> Marianna: They are Muslim Greeks.
>
> Ioanna: Even if they learn their own language and Turkey intervenes to cultivate the feeling that they are a Turkish minority etc.

Demotic discourse

Only one of the interviewees reflected upon her personal history in Cyprus and articulated a more open and historical discourse. This suggests that it is not culture that determines the decoding, but rather experience and the ways that it can be transformed into something constructive. I should note here that this is not always possible, or rather, it is more possible for those with the necessary resources.

> Chryssa: If there was a degree of hatred between the Serbs and the Kosovars, now this has multiplied. This is no solution to such problems. More tension is created. The same happened with the Cyprus problem. ... In order to be able to live with someone, you have to familiarise yourself with them. This also applies to the Muslims of Thrace. They can very happily live with Orthodox Greeks, as long as we respect them. This attitude towards minorities, which the Greek governments upheld to a certain point, was mistaken, extremely mistaken, as well as a source of misery. Because there would still be some nationalists among them ... But if the majority of the minority were happy and living in dignity, there would be no reason [for tension]. Now everybody is talking about Thrace and the danger of Thrace. But why 'the danger of Thrace'? ... Not assimilate, I do not talk about assimilation, because assimilation means that I change you in order that you become like me. But I do not want you to become like me. To respect means that although different, we will be able to live together. You have to integrate the others as citizens, respecting their differences, their religion, their cultural processes, and everything else.

Turkish-speaking viewers

The emotions expressed by some Greek and Cypriot interviewees were not present among the informants. The retellings of the Turkish-speaking interviewees were often characterised by a degree of hesitation, which can be attributed to their lack of confidence and contextual knowledge and also to their difficulty in expressing views that might be considered controversial. The emphasis in the following extract is not on the bombings and the plight of the Serb people, themes that were prevalent among Greek and Cypriot interviewees – albeit at varying degrees as noted previously – but on the persecutions of the Kosovan minority by the Serb authorities.

Yilmaz: There is a minority.

Murat: There is a small minority in Kosovo. Yugoslavia did not allow them to be autonomous.

Faruk: And what did Clinton want? War?

Murat: He wanted to give freedom to the Albanians.

Yilmaz: That's it.

Murat: To have their own freedom.

Yilmaz: So that Kosovo belongs to the Albanians. Wasn't this how it all began?

Critical viewers

As in the airspace incident interviews, the Turkish-speaking viewers had a double perspective, having access to both Greek and Turkish media. This informed their judgements of the journalists' role ('they only show that NATO is bombing'). Many of the male interviewees argued that the news is sensationalist because of the increased commercialism and covert interests.

Mehmet: I believe that they write whatever suits them. Whatever is more sensational, whatever will attract higher ratings, that's what they show. Sometimes they choose not to show some things and they show only what NATO is doing. You know, television cannot show us everything. But OK, they show what is in their interest.

Yilmaz: Whatever is in our interests, you are right to say.

A lot of the criticism was grounded on the fact that most informants had access to the Turkish channels. Many informants noted that 'they did not see both sides' on the news although, again, such comments were not made by women.

Mehmet: I feel that some of the things they show are right. Others they shouldn't show because we become anti-NATO … Perhaps NATO is right and we are only presenting the other side. We only give justice to the others [the Serbs].

Murat: The issue is that we do not see both sides. We only see one side. You cannot get the truth like this.

Yilmaz: First we should find out what is happening and then we should be against NATO.

Yilmaz: We in Greece support Yugoslavia. We do not show some of the things that Yugoslavia has done, so we only show what NATO has done by invading Yugoslavia.

For Murat the Turkish channels are also driven by interests. Watching both Turkish and Greek channels makes people more sceptical, but still does not provide any certainty. Many of the interviewees, and women in particular, were hesitant to express opinions about the events because they found them confusing and they thought they did not possess the necessary knowledge to express an opinion. For some of the informants, and particularly the women, this is related to the limited resources and the lack of contextual knowledge.

Bahar: There are differences between the channels. … But we don't watch CNN. Not all houses get CNN in Gazi. I get it but cannot understand the words.

Gaziots shift to their everyday severe reality of marginalisation, unemployment and poverty. One evening in the spring of 1999, I was watching the news with a group of young men. During some reports on the Kosovo conflict my informants became silent. After a few sporadic remarks on the sensationalism of the reports, Ismail said: 'Let us show you something.' They showed me a videotaped documentary aired on one of the private channels a few months before the interview. It was after this that the discussion became heated, centring on the inaccuracies in the programme. All those present expressed their disappointment, and in some cases anger, about the distortion of reality. Characteristically, Nihat said: 'I watch this and I become a Turk. They make me a Turk.' Some of the informants were interviewed for the documentary and what they had said had been turned around. In the context of such negative experiences many informants repeated the phrase: 'When this happens, I become a Turk.' This phrase is revealing, as it is a wordplay with the word Turk; in Greek 'to become a Turk' also means to become angry. I interpret this phrase, not necessarily as a claim to ethnicity, but principally as a claim to citizenship, equal treatment and access to resources. Gaziot informants felt not only excluded from the symbolic communicative space that the news created, but even mistreated. In this sense their reaction to the news is interpreted as a struggle for membership and participation in the community (Held 1991: 20).

This example shows that the informants were ostracised and alienated from the dominant discourse, as they did not relate to the emotional intensity of the news reports. This symbolic exclusion evoked other instances of their material exclusion from Greek society and explains why they showed me the video. These informants were the same people who in our other interactions were reflexive and sometimes ambivalent about their identities. What the above example suggests is that news reporting raised the boundaries for exclusion in a similar way that the negative experiences with the journalists did. People reverted to an essentialist discourse about belonging and difference as a response to an equally essentialist representation of identity and difference. This did not apply only to the Turkish speakers; it was the same for most of the informants regardless of their nationality. The difference is that, while the Greek and Cypriot informants who reverted to essentialist categories as a reaction to the news coverage were included, Turkish speaking informants were excluded from the common communicative space that the news projected.

It is remarkable that, although the informants made claims to citizenship when they reacted to the news content and their experiences with journalists, they used ethnic categories in order to make this point. The finding that the dominant discourse is often challenged should not mask its pervasiveness at a local level. Baumann observed in his fieldwork in Southall (West London) that the dominant discourse 'represents the currency within which people must deal with the political and media establishments on both the national and the local level' (1996: 192). The dominant discourse then becomes a hegemonic discourse within which people from minorities must explain themselves and legitimate their claims.

The following quotation reveals how Turkish-speaking interviewees used a dominant discourse and an 'us and them' binary scheme in their references to Western Thrace as a parallel to the Kosovo conflict. Süleyman was an informant who had repeatedly told me that he felt 'in the middle, both Greek and Turkish'. Note the difference in content with the discourses of the Greeks and Cypriots to the issue of Western Thrace.

> Süleyman: One day *they* will have a problem here in Greece as well. With whom? With the Muslims.

The coverage of the crisis led another informant, Mehmet, to express what he already knew from personal experiences. The difference from the previous informants is that Mehmet challenged the coverage as it was based on dominant categories that did not reflect his complex experience. Like Süleyman above, Mehmet distanced himself from the Greeks, referring to them in the third person ('they'). So, even if Mehmet did not reproduce a dominant discourse himself, his comment reveals that the news coverage made him distance himself, and perhaps feel excluded, from the dominant discourse.

> Mehmet: Greek journalists distinguish according to religion. The Albanian speakers are Muslim. Greeks only help the Christians.

CONCLUSIONS

A number of issues were raised in this chapter and will be brought together in this last section. The emphasis will be on the themes of critical viewers, personal experiences and cultural intimacy. First, however, the differences and similarities between the two case studies and among the groups of informants will be discussed.

Differences between case studies: Greek viewers

The Greek informants were more detached and critical of the news content in the airspace incident case study, while they were more emotionally involved in relation to the Kosovo reports. While most interviewees challenged the banal nationalism and dominant identity discourse present in the airspace incident decodings, they reverted to a dominant discourse themselves in their interpretations of the Kosovo conflict. The emotional reaction and the dominant discourses that the Kosovo news coverage generated coexisted with critical comments about media practices and journalistic conventions, indicating that the affective and the critical need not be considered as contradictory. The difference between the airspace and the Kosovo case studies was explained partly through the theory of cultural intimacy (Herzfeld 1996). The airspace incident was an affair that concerned Greece and Turkey. Informants interpreted it as an internal affair that concerned the army and Greece's relationship with Cyprus – rather than to Turkey. In this context, they were highly critical of the news and its depiction of the army and Cyprus. To use a metaphor, people were discussing the dirty laundry of the nation within the confines of the 'home'. This internal consumption of the news allowed people to be critical of the nation and some of its symbols and thus challenge the banal nationalism in the news.

Conversely, Kosovo was not a national issue, but an international and regional affair that was heavily reported in Greece, often in an emotional way. As the news analysis suggested, the Kosovo news reports were highly nationalised and were based on the 'us and them' dichotomy. 'Us' included the Serbs and the Greeks, while 'they' were the Americans and, in some cases, the Kosovan refugees. In this context, Kosovo was an affair whereby Greek viewers defined themselves in relation to the world and, particularly, NATO and the United States. This explains why some viewers referred to experiences or historical instances that were related to US involvement in Greek politics and the effects this had on people's everyday lives. For other interviewees, Kosovo was a reminder that NATO 'applies double standards' in its interventions; an interviewee paralleled Kosovo to the events in Cyprus in 1974 when neither NATO, nor the UN, intervened to stop the humanitarian disaster. Finally, some interviewees sympathised with the Serbs, by projecting their fears of succession by the Turks of Thrace.

Thus, in the Kosovo retellings people adopted a more dominant discourse than in the airspace interviews. Many of the Greek informants interpreted the events in Kosovo as a threat to their identity and reacted by asserting their own identity and experiences to the rest of the world. They were reacting to an international conflict (instead of a local affair) and in this context there was not much room for challenging identity and national symbols.

How are these identity articulations related to the news? Would people relate the same way to the events in Kosovo, even if they were not mediated? This question begs an impossible answer. We cannot even think of 'unmediated' wars these days. Without the media, perhaps wars would be altogether different and here the discussion enters the hypothetical sphere. What is important is that the news offers viewers a continuous flow of discourses and representations to which they can relate, or not. It is as if the media instigate a continuous (potential) reflexivity. People are invited to articulate their identities and to juxtapose their own experiences to every report in the news. In the Kosovo case study, people related to news reports that were, in their majority, highly nationalised. Moreover, during the Kosovo conflict the media were the main source of information for most informants, notwithstanding a few exceptions (Alexandros, Vassilis and Nicos), who either had contrary personal experiences or access to alternative resources. In the light of this observation, the viewers' reactions to the conflict itself are reactions to its mediated coverage, insofar as people did not have any other means of finding out about the conflict. This is another difference between the two case studies, as in the 'airspace incident' most informants' decodings (and those of men in particular) were informed by personal experiences in the army. Interpretations depend on the range of available information resources, mediated and unmediated.

Differences were observed according to the resources that people had access to. Irini, a student from a working class neighbourhood, said she was 'in the dark' implying the lack of alternative resources with which to interpret the news. Although students were critical at an aesthetic level, they did not have the confidence to confront the news with their experiences or historical knowledge. Nicos, a middle class student in London, who also lacked historically grounded experiences, benefited from a rich media infrastructure, which informed his interpretations and shaped his confidence to challenge the news.

People were critical about television news and journalistic practices and at the same time they watched the news a lot – in some cases they depended on it as their sole source of information. On many occasions it is through media exposure that people have become critical of the media (media literacy). Younger people were media literate and thus critical of media output; older people were often more emotional in their encounters with the media (Ilias and Eugenia), or less media literate (Tasos). Younger people, on the other hand, were more dependent on the media to get information than older people whose experiences provided the interpretative framework within which the decoding took place. The variety of resources affected interpretation and comprehension.

Being critical towards news at an aesthetic level does not imply a more critical approach concerning its content. Many critical decodings were as essentialist as the media texts themselves, particularly in the Kosovo case study (Sophia, Andreas, Marianna and Ioanna). Andreas and Yannos, who were highly literate viewers, interpreted Kosovo reports in an emotional way, pointing to a dissonance between different levels of decoding.

Greek-Cypriot viewers

Most of the Greek-Cypriot interviewees were emotionally involved in the decoding of the airspace report. They contrasted their own reality to that portrayed in the news and found it unsatisfactory. However, Cypriots do not form a homogenous category. Those informants who had lived in Athens for longer were less emotionally involved. The emotional interpretation of the content of the news does not mean that Cypriots are not critical viewers. On the contrary, they were very critical, especially at an aesthetic level.

Greek-Cypriot informants were also emotional in their interpretations of the Kosovo coverage, drawing a parallel to their own experiences in Cyprus. In short, there were not as many differences, as there were among the Greeks, between the interpretations of the two case studies. The concept of cultural intimacy can be applied to explain this case as well; while for the Greek interviewees the airspace incident was a banal, internal issue, for the Greek-Cypriots it was an issue that they had to defend as it concerned their country and what they perceived as a misrepresentation of their reality. In other words, had the airspace incident been discussed in Cyprus, in relation to the Cypriot media, some of the informants might have been more detached and critical about its content. In the case of the Kosovo conflict, the Cypriots' interpretations were very similar to those of the Greeks, as discussed above. It is interesting, then, to note how Cypriots are excluded from the national narrative in one case (airspace incident) and included in the other (Kosovo). Finally, it should be observed that experience emerges as a key notion. It is not simply a common (in this case, Cypriot) identity that determines the above interpretations, but the different ways in which people have experienced their common history and political circumstances. This is why Chryssa expressed a balanced, anti-essentialist and learned opinion on the Kosovo conflict and the Cyprus problem, indicating that identity is not the prison from which there is no escaping.

Turkish-speaking viewers

The emotional, dramatised and nationalised presentation of the Kosovo conflict echoed the emotions and popular perceptions of the Greek and Cypriot viewers. However, there was little emotional identification among the Turkish speakers. The reports were for many a confirmation of their exclusion from society at other levels. It was also a reminder of their negative first hand experiences with the media. Of course I cannot talk about the whole range of media and media texts available. It is possible that television drama might be experienced in a more inclusive way; but given that the news is such a dominant feature of public discourse in Greece this observation becomes significant. The drawing of the boundaries is relevant not only to the Turkish minority of Greece, but perhaps also to the large number of immigrants who have been living in Greece in recent years.

Criticisms at an aesthetic and content level were also related to trust and personal experiences with the media, which, in the case of the Gaziots, were always negative. In this context, an argument about mediation, the attempt to see the media as a process, is emerging; the interpretation of the media text is but one of the moments in this process, which is determined itself by other moments and processes (such as the experience with journalists). Moreover, mediation has an impact on unmediated processes, such as the discourses and practices about identity. Given that identities are relational (Barth 1969a), this chapter argues that the media, together with other institutions and structures, can play a role in creating boundaries.

The reality of experience

The readings of the news content are influenced by existing interpretative frameworks which, in turn, are shaped by people's experiences and life histories. All the viewers drew upon their own experiences to make sense of the news. This suggests that reception and context cannot be separated, but are part of the same process.

The concept of experience emerges as particularly useful here. Experience allows for both fluctuations in identity positionings and diversity within ethnic categories. It also foregrounds the personal dimension and the possibility that the same events can be experienced differently by people of the same ethnic group. Interpretative frameworks were not determined by ethnicity, but by people's experiences and the ways in which they had integrated them into their lives. Yannos and Anna, who were refugees from Northern Cyprus, used the dominant 'us and them' frame in their interpretations. Chryssa, on the other hand, who had similar experiences, transformed them through her work (as a counsellor) into a different perspective that accepted difference and avoided the 'us and them' dichotomies. Similarly Nuriye, Ayşe and Umut had a different perspective from Orhan and Mehmet, which depended on their degree of integration in Greek society. The frustration that some Turkish speaking men and women articulated towards the news was similar to that expressed by some Greek interviewees (working-class housewives and students). In short, there was not a homogenous Greek, Cypriot or Turkish-speaking interpretative framework. On the contrary, there were overlaps and differences that were determined by a number of factors: gender, age, class, experience.

Overall, however, it can be argued that viewers' decodings were more open than the encoding. Viewers' interpretations were more analytic and historical than the news itself. This happened more regularly in the airspace incident interviews, at least for the majority of the Greeks and Cypriots. The Turkish-speaking informants were equally critical in both case studies, although it has to be noted that the women were not particularly vocal in either case.

Given this diversity, it is not possible to identify a causal relationship between the media text and the reproduction of nationalism at a local level. People often, and sometimes forcefully, challenge the banal nationalism of the news. This does not mean that interpretations are random and arbitrary, but rather that they do not depend solely on the abstract categories of nationality and ethnicity.

Text did not determine interpretation. A number of extra-textual factors, such as historical and contextual knowledge, alternative resources and personal experiences, contribute to interpretation. There is, however, another, broader way that media content is related to interpretations and people's discourses. The media make available a number of discourses and representations about the nation, its place in the world and its relationship to its 'others'. Identities, being relational, are constantly negotiated in relation to media texts. There are, however, limits to this reflexivity. The concept of cultural intimacy casts some light on these discursive oscillations.

Cultural intimacy

The concept of cultural intimacy (Herzfeld 1996) explains some of these discursive shifts from openness to closure. During the airspace incident (an internal incident that also involved Cyprus) people were critical of the role of the Greek army, the relationship between Greece and Cyprus and the politics between Greece and Turkey. Such discourses are very different from the more formal discourse about Cyprus in the news. Recall that in the news reports Cyprus was referred to as *Meghalonisos*, the 'Big Island' – Cyprus was part of 'us'. In people's discourses, however, Cyprus and Cypriots became 'them'/'the others'.

Conversely, in the Kosovo study, whenever the interviewees mentioned Cyprus spontaneously, it was in the context of 'us'. Cyprus was incorporated into the symbolic national corpus in many of the respondents' discourses. When discussing identity and difference 'within the home', people were keen to contest the dominant discourse about the nation and its symbols. Conversely, a different discourse emerges when identity is challenged from the outside. During Kosovo, many Greeks felt they had to assert their identity to what they thought was an external threat to their culture.

More importantly, the dominant discourse has an effect that is often ignored in the literature on media and identity: exclusion. Chapter 5 argued that television provides a common point of reference for a many of its viewers. However, because television news discourse relies on a closed understanding of identity (based on common religion, customs and blood), it excludes those who do not conform to the 'cultural' definition of identity.

Concluding remarks

The findings in this chapter connect with those of other news reception studies. Knowledge is always a matter of class, race and gender positioning, among other things (Morley 1999: 139). The group of apprentices in the Nationwide study was cynical towards the programme while being at the same time 'in line' with the preferred reading of the text and accepting the perspectives offered by and through the programme's presenter (Morley 1992: 115–16). In this context the comprehension-incomprehension distinction is significant. As Morley notes, we need to distinguish between the moments when people fail to make 'dominant' readings of the news because they lack the particular forms of literacy to read the news, or because they lack the resources to develop any coherent alternative perspective on the events reported in the news media (Morley 1999: 140). In these cases an idiosyncratic reading is not something to be celebrated. This finding relates to the decodings made by the least resourceful informants who were critical of the media in a general way expressing a distrust towards their practices, but who could not argue thoroughly their differentiated interpretation (such examples were some of the Greek and Turkish housewives and younger informants).

Another study with which the findings in this chapter connect is Philo's study (1990) on the coverage and reception of the English miners' strike in 1984–85. Philo identified a correspondence between certain recurrent themes in the news' reporting of the strike and the viewers' accounts. Although in this chapter there was no clear correspondence between the themes present in the news and the viewers' interpretations, in the Kosovo retellings people reverted to an 'us and them' frame that was present in the news. Gillespie has made a similar observation (1995). In her ethnography among Punjabi Indians in Southall, she observed that during the first Gulf War the young informants reverted to a binary mode of thinking about their identities when discussing the news. As she notes, her informants, despite the openness that characterised their identity discourses, 'in the face of events which represent a challenge to their sense of identity, became acutely aware of the range of options open to them and trapped in binary thinking themselves' (1995: 206).

Finally, this chapter is in dialogue with some of the top-down works on media and nationalism, and particularly the work of Billig on *Banal Nationalism* (1995). The chapter attempts to integrate two levels of analysis, that of the text and that of its reception. In so doing it challenges the assumption that banal nationalism is reproduced unproblematically, as most interviewees challenged the nationalism in the news and the dominant identity discourses it projected. This contestation, however, has its limits. The concept of cultural intimacy (Herzfeld 1996) was useful in identifying the shifts from dominant to demotic.

CHAPTER 8

CONCLUSIONS

This book started with an image of a televised public event and a question: do the media provide the catalyst for belonging to the nation? Although this question was subsequently abandoned in favour of a more nuanced one, it is still important to address the relationship between media and identity in the light of the empirical data. This is what this chapter will do, together with a summary of the overall argument and implications of the study for the fields of media and nationalism.

This book has proposed a new approach to the media/identity relationship that examines identity as lived and as performed. Theories that have favoured a top-down approach have assumed strong media effects on identity, whereas theories that emphasise a perspective 'from below' have argued for powerful audiences and resilient local cultures. Both approaches, despite their insights, were described as inadequate insofar as they tended to essentialise culture and identity. In Chapter 2 I suggested that, instead of focusing on identity and how it is shaped by the media, I would focus on the ways in which people articulate and perform their identities in different contexts. The book therefore asked whether the media play any role in these articulations and the shifts from openness to closure. In order to answer this question I followed the circulation of discourses about the nation in the media and in people's lives. This study contrasts what was termed in Chapter 2 as the dominant and the demotic discourses on identity (Baumann 1996). Dominant is the discourse that reifies culture and treats community or minority as given categories. Demotic discourse is the one that challenges such reifications and aims to break down the barriers of segregation. Dominant and demotic discourses coexist[1] and the challenge is to examine whether the media play any role in their occurrence. When do people use the dominant discourse and when do people contest it with the demotic? Moreover, drawing on the work of Barth (1969b) and other anthropologists, I investigated whether the media play any role in raising the boundaries for inclusion and exclusion from public life.

Chapter 3 grounded the theoretical framework on identity proposed in Chapter 2, in relation to the case of Greece. Through a historical perspective it emerged that identities were relational and often ambivalent, thereby challenging

---

1   Dominant and demotic should not be seen as synonyms for official/elite and local. Dominant
     discourses are very popular among informants (Chapter 7).

the dominant assumption of a single, homogenous national identity. Chapter 4 argued that the relationship between media and identity should be understood as a process, thus echoing recent developments towards a theory of mediation. Such an approach, drawing on existing work in audience research and the move towards media anthropology, aims to develop a nuanced approach to media power.

In Chapter 5 I mapped the available media used by the informants, exploring how these were integrated in their everyday lives. Moreover, I examined whether media usage and media related experiences affected the ways in which people articulated their identities. Although it was argued that television does not foster identity, for a number of the informants television news provides a common point of reference, while for others it is experienced as a form of exclusion. These points are summarised below.

(1) Rethinking the media and identity relationship

The media/identity relationship is not a causal one. Not only would such an assumption be misleading, but it can also have adverse consequences as it might encourage ethnic segregation. In Chapter 5, watching satellite television from Turkey emerged as an ordinary practice, challenging popular perceptions that Turkish television provides the umbilical cord to the 'national centre' and thus to Turkish nationalism. This finding confirms the arguments by Robins and Aksoy (2001), Milikowski (2000) and Öncü (2000). The Turkish-speaking informants watched both Turkish and Greek television and some mentioned that there were not that many differences between the two national broadcasting systems. Differences were identified in relation to television news, but most informants said that they preferred to watch the news from the country in which they live. Recall that the Turkish minority in Greece is not an immigrant minority, that is, people never left Turkey to come to Greece; rather they are Greek citizens who were born in Greece. Technologies, therefore, do not determine identities. They do, however, enable the moving from one symbolic space to another, a process in which most informants engage. The informants' media use habits are differentiated according to gender, age and education. In this context it is not possible to talk of a homogenous community or minority.

(2) A common point of reference?

Greek television news provides a common point of reference for most of the interviewees. News stories are in constant circulation in people's everyday lives. The Greek informants, in particular, are heavy news viewers, some describing themselves as 'addicted to the news'. In some instances news programmes become an integral part of the informants' lives as they watch themselves on the news and use the news instrumentally in order to make their voices heard (Chapter 5). In this sense, news programmes extend beyond their traditional informational dimension and emerge as a wider socio-cultural phenomenon that mediates the private and public spheres.

(3) News and exclusion

Not all the informants, however, shared this common point of reference. Disenfranchised informants, regardless of their ethnic background, who feel that television news did not reflect their reality, decided to switch off their television sets. Interestingly, this dissatisfaction is often expressed in ethnic terms, although it primarily reflects social exclusion (the reasons for this will be discussed below).

Exclusion is also evident in relation to personal experiences with journalists and the media. This is most obvious in the case of the Turkish informants. Chapter 5 contrasted the ordinariness with which Gaziots used both Turkish and Greek media, to the frustration and sense of injustice that they experienced in their personal contacts with the media and journalists. The Turkish-speaking informants felt that whenever they saw themselves in the media there was distortion and misrepresentation. In turn, the exclusion that the Turkish speakers experienced is in sharp contrast to the largely positive direct experiences of the Greek informants with the media and journalists.

(4) News projects a common identity

The openness of identity discourses described in Chapter 5 (notwithstanding the moments of exclusion) is contrasted with the relatively homogenous identity that the news reports project (Chapter 6). Chapter 6 examined two televised occasions, which were termed the 'airspace incident' and the 'Kosovo conflict'. The former was a relatively routine event that involved Greece and Turkey and indirectly Cyprus, while the latter was an international issue that was nationalised by the Greek media, revealing global, national and local dynamics. From the analysis of the news reports in both case studies it emerged that to a large extent television news reports – especially those of the popular private channels – are based on an 'us and them' binary scheme of thought and project a common identity grounded on primordial attachments rather than citizenship. In the mainstream Greek media, Greek is equated with Orthodox Christian and this tenet goes largely uncontested even though it suggests a retreat to the overtly nationalistic slogans of the Colonels' dictatorship (1967–74): 'Greece belongs to Orthodox Christians.'

(5) Contesting the banal nationalism of the news

Chapter 7 examined the reception of the news reports among the interviewees and contrasted the discourse in the news (Chapter 6) to that generated at a local level. It emerged that most of the interviewees challenged the banal nationalism in the news, based on their personal experiences and histories. This was particularly the case during the 'airspace incident' when almost all the interviewees were critical of the news content and media practices in general, and themselves made analytical and historically informed interpretations of the largely ahistorical news reports. Thus, contextual knowledge and the existence of alternative resources emerged as significant parameters that shape interpretation and allow for a possible contestation of the dominant discourse. Those informants with few media and educational resources, as well as those who lacked personal experiences (mainly because of age) that would provide them with knowledge of the historical context, were less likely to contest the news reports. In this sense context emerges as belonging to the vertical dimension of communication and not just the horizontal, as Livingstone has suggested (1998c: 251).

(6) Cultural intimacy

However, in the Kosovo conflict retellings, many of the interviewees shifted to a more essentialist discourse. In Chapter 7, I drew upon the theory of cultural intimacy (Herzfeld 1996) in order to explain the shifts from relatively open to closed ways of articulating informants' identities and their position in the nation state. I argued that the discursive oscillations are not contingent, but are rather determined by context – in relation to whom and what identities are articulated. Cultural intimacy refers to '... the cultural traits that define insiderhood, but are also felt to be disapproved by powerful outsiders' (Herzfeld 1996). This tension between collective self-knowledge and collective self-representation can explain why Greek informants allowed dissent when discussing an internal issue (the airspace incident). Conversely, they interpreted the Kosovo conflict as an external challenge to which they had to reply by asserting their identity. Thus, some of the national symbols that were challenged in the airspace decodings were embraced in the Kosovo case study. Similarly, the concept of cultural intimacy can partially explain the mass gatherings in the central squares of Athens and Thessaloniki in the early 1990s. The so-called 'Macedonian issue' was largely perceived as an external threat to Greece's sovereignty and identity. The mobilisation was so immense precisely because the threat was perceived as external (exacerbated by the popular feeling that the rest of Europe and the US was unsympathetic to Greece's position). Cultural intimacy was also evident in the context of the 2004 Olympic Games in Athens. During the summer of 2004 what emerged as a major concern in Greece (especially the Greek media) was the country's image and representation abroad. In this context criticisms regarding the preparations for the Games were accepted as long as they were reported within the confines of the nation state. As a Greek living in England, I was frequently asked to comment on how Greece and the Games were reported in the British media during the Olympics.

(7) Exclusion again

Exclusion is also experienced in relation to the text (news content) whenever it projects an essentialist or dominant discourse (Chapter 7). It seems that essentialism produces essentialism. Exclusion is heightened in the Greek news because, instead of being based on an all-embracing notion of citizenship, it presents a primordial model of belonging based on 'national' homogeneity and unity. The strongest effect of the homogenising news seems to be the fact that it is experienced as exclusive by those informants who feel that they do not conform to this identity. Drawing upon Barth's theory (1969a), I argued that in such instances the media contribute to the drawing of boundaries for ethnic categories and also inclusion and exclusion from public life.

When informants reflected on their identities and place in society in their daily interactions there was often openness in their discourses. However, when they were confronted with closure in the media, some adopted a more 'closed' discourse themselves. The far-reaching effect is that such closure can have political and social consequences taking identity politics into a vicious circle. Of course, the media are not the sole forces raising boundaries. They reflect existing material inequalities. Importantly, the informants who seemed more vulnerable to revert to a dominant and essentialist discourse when confronted with closure, were those with fewer resources and weaker confidence. Examples include the Turkish speakers in Gazi, who did not feel confident enough to initiate a dialogue with the media and the journalists. A similar point is made by Arendt, who argued that the only viable strategy when an identity is under attack in times of defamation and persecution is to respond by embracing this very identity (1968: 17).

Another significant observation is that, although the informants make claims to citizenship when they react to news content and their experiences with journalists, they often use ethnic categories instead in order to make this point. The finding that the dominant discourse is often challenged should not mask its pervasiveness at a local level. This is perhaps explained through the dominance of ethnic categories. Baumann observed in his fieldwork in Southall that the dominant discourse '... represents the currency within which people must deal with the political and media establishments on both the national and the local level' (1996: 192). The dominant discourse then becomes 'a hegemonic discourse within which people from minorities must explain themselves and legitimate their claims' (1996: 192).

Thus, the media/identity relationship emerges as a multifaceted process that depends on context. The media provide a common reference for some, while for others those references might be experienced as exclusive. Exclusion can also be circumstantial; the same person can experience inclusion on one occasion and exclusion on another. Inclusion and exclusion from the public communicative space that the media create take place in parallel both in relation to media technologies and in relation to media content. The news is considered to be an internal public sphere in which the 'dirty laundry' of the nation can be exposed, echoing the phrase that television is the private life of the nation state (Ellis 1982: 5). In this study, it emerged that it is within this private sphere that dominant discourses about the nation can be contested. At the same time, however, the news is also the bridge to the outside world. It conveys the representations of Greece abroad and in this sense provides a mirror against which the viewers have to measure themselves. In this sense the media are at the heart of the tensions between collective self-knowledge and collective self-representation that define cultural intimacy (Herzfeld 1996).

From the summary of the main findings it emerges that neither of the two hitherto dominant paradigms (strong media/weak identities and weak media/powerful identities) are adequate to explain the relationship between the media and identity. It is proposed that the relationship between the media and identity is investigated as a process that takes into account both a top-down and a bottom-up perspective. In this context, the theory of mediation emerges as a promising possibility. Different moments of the media and identity relationship were described and analysed in the previous pages, including direct experiences with the media and journalists, consumption of the media as objects, the media as text, reception and context, all of which are parts of the mediation process. The media and identity relationship cannot be exhausted in one moment, but is rather a complex process that contains a number of often contradictory aspects. By examining as many moments as possible it is possible to achieve empirical confirmation across levels and attempt to pinpoint the diffuse power of media.

In this context, this book is an attempt to contribute to the growing interest in theorising mediation (Couldry 2000b; Silverstone 1999). A mediational perspective on the media and identity relationship emerged as pertinent as it can capture the dynamism of identity discourses and the processual nature of the media. To examine the articulation of identities only in relation to news decodings would mean ignoring all the other mediated moments during which identity discourses are articulated and which are inevitably interrelated. Thus, while informants contested banal nationalism in their decodings of the news and made sophisticated and analytical readings, they reverted to an essentialist dominant discourse in certain contexts (personal experiences with journalists, and interpretation of the reporting on Kosovo). The ethnographic perspective adopted allowed for a capturing of the various nuances and contradictions between what people say and do. Chapter 5 argued that such paradoxes or contradictions can be revealing of media power.

This book also argues that representation (through the media text) is still important; we cannot abandon the text when investigating the relationship between the media and identity. It is a combination of the sheer presence of the media and representations that affect discourses about identities. From the analysis of the news interpretations and the integration of the media in people's lives, it emerged that the distinction between media as objects and media as texts is mostly an analytical one, confirming Livingstone's arguments (1998b). Media as objects and media as texts are deeply intertwined and both dimensions should be part of the mediational approach. Moreover, in the analysis the distinction between decoding and context emerged as analytical (cf Livingstone et al: 2001). Similarly, the vertical and the horizontal dimensions of communication cannot be separated easily either. As mentioned previously, context is understood both horizontally (as the surround of the moment of consumption) and vertically, insofar as consumption depends on availability and access to resources and material structures (Livingstone 1998c: 251).

The book argues that the move towards media anthropology can converge with the development of a theory of mediation. Media ethnography can capture the diffuse nature of media power and examine how different moments of the mediation process interrelate. By examining both people's discourses and practices, ethnography can describe the ambivalence and contradictions both in processes of identity and in media consumption. Moreover, ethnography can highlight the affective and intimate dimensions of media consumption, which are not in opposition to the critical and rational aspects, as Chapter 5 (and 7) argued. The increasing convergence of media studies and media anthropology can challenge the assumptions and the expectations of the disciplines themselves. At the risk of oversimplifying, if media studies have often reified identity and culture (the object *par excellence* of anthropological research) as Chapter 2 suggested, anthropologists have sometimes reified media power (the concern of most media studies). This study benefited from the combination of media theories and the anthropological concepts and perspectives on identity.

These findings, confirming those in other studies (for example, see Couldry 2000b), suggest that the development of a mediational perspective might provide a new challenge for audience studies and its theorisation of power. Such a development would also move the research agenda beyond the confines of a research canon, which according to Livingstone can hinder the progress of the field (1998c).

Finally, this study also makes a contribution to the identity and nationalism debates. Although it did not aim to make arguments about identity construction in Greece (at least not in isolation from media processes), the data gathered are inevitably related to this issue. For example, through the observations among the Turkish minority it is possible to contest the myth of the homogenous nation that occupies a 'historic homeland' (Smith 1998: 22). As two Turkish-speaking informants, Ismail and Nazim, put it: 'I was born here, and so were my grandparents, great-grandparents and so on.' Instead, what emerged were the shifting boundaries of the nation, which according to context might include Cyprus and its minorities.

A number of concepts have been key to this study, such as cultural intimacy (Herzfeld 1996), the distinction between dominant and demotic (Baumann 1996) discourses and practices, boundaries (Barth 1969a) and critical *and* affective viewers. In the next few paragraphs I will add three more concepts that have been important in this study: experience, resources and citizenship.

Experience proved a useful term in this study as it added a personal dimension to the collectivity that the concept of identity implies. Similar events are experienced in different ways by different people, who in turn transform their experience into a different set of ideas, perspectives and interpretations. Such an example was Chryssa whose experience of the Cyprus problem, and thus her decodings, were significantly different from those of the other Cypriot informants. The shortcoming of the notion of experience is that it might be reduced to relativism and thus cannot be theorised easily. However, the different ways in which events are experienced is not arbitrary, but depends in turn on material and symbolic structures. In this sense experience is linked to resources.

Resources, the symbolic and material means through which people make sense of the world, are an important parameter in the mediation process. They are related to Bourdieu's concept of capital (1986), although the concept is meant in a broader way. Resources include education and access to media and information. As Chapter 7 showed, decodings depended on contextual and other knowledge, and the resourceful informants were the most critical viewers. To return to the example of Chryssa in the previous paragraph, her differentiated interpretation of the events in Kosovo and Cyprus depended on her experience, which in turn depended on her education and further training in counselling. The concept of resources might also provide a way to link – or explore further – the relationship between the vertical and the horizontal, the micro and the macro, and media and identity.

Finally, the notion of citizenship takes the ideas developed in this book into the spheres of politics and policy. The informants who felt excluded by the dominant media discourse reacted to it by making claims to citizenship. Recall the comments by Nihat and Hasan: 'We were born in this country'; and 'I served in the army here.' However, as mentioned in the previous section, this exclusion is often expressed in ethnic terms ('I become a Turk'). This was interpreted as a result of the prominence of ethnic categories in public life. If this book could make any sort of recommendations at a policy level in terms of media and exclusion, it is that we need to think more in terms of belonging to a community of equal rights and obligations rather than to one defined by primordial attachments and blood relations (which is the perspective advocated by the news in Greece).

Citizenship has been theorised recently as extending beyond the nation state. It has been proposed that the meaning of citizenship is changing and 'a new and more universal concept of citizenship has unfolded in the post-war era, one whose organising and legitimating principles are based on universal personhood rather than national belonging' (Soysal 1994: 1). Soysal urges us to recognise that national citizenship is no longer an adequate concept upon which to base a perceptive narrative of membership. As she notes, 'postnational formations of membership challenge us to refurbish our definitions and theoretical vistas of and about citizenship and the nation-state' (1994: 167). Similarly, Held suggests a broad definition of citizenship 'as the struggle for membership and participation in the community' (Held 1991: 20), which can adapt to a postnational perspective.

In this book I have attempted to add a story to the growing body of work on media and identities. I have tried to follow Said's suggestion of thinking 'contrapuntally' about identities within the nation state (Said 1993: 407–08; see, also, Silverstone in press), that is, to recognise the diversity of traditions and the existence of otherness within what is often considered as homogenous and complete. More work is needed in this field for what could become a wider political project extending beyond the confines of the nation state, while recognising the interconnections and cultural change that are already taking place at a transnational level.

In this Appendix I will give a brief account of the methodology followed. I will discuss the issues relating to the interviews and participant observation as well as the sampling and analysis of data. Different methods were necessary to study the different facets of the communication process, namely the text and its reception and the media and their consumption. Moreover, behind the combination of different methods in the collection and analysis of data lies the methodological principle of triangulation, in which each method complements the shortcomings and limitations of the other so as to achieve broader and better results (Denzin 1989). Participant observation allows for an unobtrusive approach, which is important in the context of identity articulations. To ask people to reflect on their identity in an interview context might unwittingly direct the respondents to think in a particular way. In this context, interviews were coupled with observations of people's actions. The approach followed here echoes Bourdieu's arguments for the development of a reflexive sociology and a soft approach to interviewing (Bourdieu 1999; Bourdieu and Wacquant 1992).

This study is based on participant observation and interviews with seventy-two Greek, Greek Cypriot and Turkish-speaking people living in Athens. A list of all informants, with their names changed, and some contextual information can be found in Appendix II. As in most qualitative work, I cannot make claims for the general population. Yet this was never the intention. As Mead has written:

> Anthropological sampling is not a poor and inadequate version of sociological or sociopsychological sampling, a version where n equals too few cases. It is simply a different kind of sampling, in which the validity of the sample depends not so much upon the number of cases as upon the proper specification of the informant, so that he or she can be accurately placed, in terms of a very large number of variables ... Each informant is studied as a perfect example, an organic representation of his complete cultural experience (Mead 1953: 654–55).

The sample was based on 'purposeful selection' (Lindlof 1995: 126). My basic criteria were to retain a balance in terms of gender, age, social class and education.

Doing ethnography 'at home', or 'indigenous anthropology' (Hastrup 1995), or 'auto-anthropology' (Strathern 1987) as it is also called, is still a contested issue within the anthropological field, although it is now considered as a valid ethnographic approach. Recent anthropological theory, especially after the 'cultural critique' movement (Clifford and Marcus 1986; Marcus and Fischer 1986), considers the concepts of culture, of the 'self' and the 'other', not as fixed entities, but rather as categories of thought (Abu-Lughod 1991; Hastrup 1995). From this it emerges that studying one's own society is a valid enterprise as long as the researcher can embody the distance needed to look for otherness within the familiar (Marcus and Fischer 1986: 111–36). Loizos has noted that in the end what matters is not whether the position of the ethnographer is privileged (or not) in the culture they studies, as this is not measurable anyway, but rather the adequate awareness of their position in the culture studied (1992: 170).

Many ethnographers have written on the advantages and disadvantages of doing anthropology at home. It has been argued that the ethnographer may possibly enjoy a more privileged access to some aspects of the local culture, mainly regarding 'the emotive and other intimate dimensions' (Ohnuki-Tierney 1984). This was relevant in my fieldwork. I remember viewing on television the 'peace' concert in Athens' central square (26 April 1999) during the period of the Kosovo crisis[1], when songs of resistance were sung, evoking memories from the resistance to the junta in the 1960s and 1970s. In this instance I was privileged to be able to be in tune with the public display of emotions; at the same time I was distancing myself in order to understand what was going on. I was singing and at the same time keeping notes in my diary.

Another dimension relating to researching one's own culture is the immediate positioning of the researcher within existing social categories and, more importantly, the larger pressure for conformity to the local norms (Hastrup 1995: 158). People immediately knew where to place me in the Athenian society and were thus projecting their expectations. This might have opened doors in some cases, while in others it created tension.

These debates become meaningful in the context of the concept of cultural intimacy, which was discussed in Chapter 2. Cultural intimacy was defined in previous chapters as the ensemble of cultural traits that define insiderhood, but are also felt to be disapproved of by powerful outsiders (Herzfeld 1996). Consequently, as an insider, I could easily relate to the 'dirty laundry of the nation' to which, as an insider, I was granted access. As an insider, I could expect people to confide in me as a 'family' member. Problems arose, however, about making my intention to make the research public (through the writing of the book) to people who are considered outsiders. This way I was betraying the unwritten rule upon which insiderhood and strangerhood were based. When I told Marianna, a Cypriot woman in her fifties, that I was also doing research in Gazi she told me: 'Be careful what you write about these issues abroad.' Her warning was not so much directed to my interest in what she saw as the 'outsiders' within the nation, but that I would make this information public 'abroad', outside the confines of the 'national family'.

INTERVIEWING

A core method in this study (as part of the ethnographic approach) was that of interviewing. After getting acquainted with most of the informants (through informal chats and visits to their homes and/or neighbourhood) and keeping notes of these observations, I conducted semi-structured individual and group interviews that focused on the decodings and the retellings of the television news. All interviewees were guaranteed anonymity. They took place in the informants'

---

1   This concert is analysed as a media event, as part of the analysis of the news. The image described in the opening paragraph of the book is also taken from this same event.

chosen space, lasted sixty to ninety minutes and were tape-recorded. The data collected were coded into analysable units in a procedure similar to that advanced by the proponents of grounded theory (Glazer and Strauss 1967; Strauss 1987).

Group discussions

Focus groups have been popular in mass communications research (Lunt and Livingstone 1996), especially since Morley's *Nationwide* study (1980), although they were introduced in the 1950s (Merton *et al* 1990 [1956]). The reason they were included in this study is because there is a 'social' dimension to the data produced, as a result of the group dynamics. This is why the 'focus group' has been described as the 'miniature of the thinking society' (Moscovici 1984: 16).

The participants in the group discussions were familiar to each other (either as family members or friends or colleagues). This resembles the approach of Liebes and Katz in their study of the reception of *Dallas*. They were 'less interested in random selections of a sample of each community members than ... in clusters of community members who are in close contact and among whom television programs are likely to be discussed' (1993: 23).

In-depth individual interviews

In-depth interviews were employed as a means of achieving a more intense rapport with the interviewee, so as to enhance self-disclosure. The interviews lasted from sixty to seventy minutes.

Sampling the news

The study is also based on the analysis of television news reports from two different periods; in total I sampled nine news broadcasts for the airspace incident event and thirty-one for the Kosovo conflict (a total of forty news broadcasts). For the airspace study I sampled the broadcasts of the news from the two most popular private channels (MEGA and ANTENNA), as well as from the public service channel (ET-1), for the whole period during which it was reported. For the Kosovo study, I sampled ten news broadcasts from the first month of the conflict from the same three television channels. I also sampled one news broadcast, from SKAI channel, now renamed ALPHA[2].

---

2   SKAI became ALPHA in September 1999. In the months following that date the ownership changed as well. Due to the takeover processes, the SKAI channel changed its policy and did not provide me with the full sample of videotapes as agreed. Nonetheless, one particular broadcast was sampled and analysed as it was representative of a televised public ritual on Greek television.

Analysing the news

The textual analysis of the news aims to identify any thematic and discursive patterns in the reports. The analysis of the news was based on a combination of qualitative and quantitative methods, namely thematic content analysis and interpretive analysis. The two methods are intended to be complementary. Content analysis in the context of this research is used in the broadest sense, as the quantification of the occurrence of selected themes within a sample of news reports. This approach was considered pertinent mainly due to the unwieldy number of the reports. Thematic analysis permitted data reduction, and quantification systematised what would otherwise be impressionistic comments. Moreover, through the statistical analysis of the themes for which each item was coded, a cluster analysis was performed that allowed the identification of discursive patterns in the reports. Interpretive analysis is understood in this context as a hybrid technique drawing on different traditions, namely those of discourse analysis (Billig 1995; van Dijk 1991) and grounded theory (Strauss 1987) in the sense that the coding categories partially emerge from the data. Content analysis offers a methodological rigour to the qualitative analysis, while the qualitative analysis adds more context and depth. It should be noted that these data could also be described as qualitative in the sense that they are dependent on qualitative judgements as they have to be assigned to a specific thematic category (Morley and Brunsdon 1999).

In the thematic content analysis the unit of analysis (henceforth, *item*) was defined as every news story, 'live' or recorded (including its introduction by the presenter), within the news programme. An item could also be a live studio discussion within the context of the programme. Items were of varying duration. Only the items relating to Kosovo were coded. An item was identified as relating to Kosovo if it had a direct or indirect reference to the conflict. This also included items that focused on the reactions toward the NATO strikes and the effects of the conflict in Greece and the region. The intention was to examine the whole range of discourses and issues that this conflict produced. In total, 464 items were coded and analysed.

In order to determine whether the coding was consistent, reliability was checked by inviting another coder to code a section of the sample (three programmes in total out of twenty-seven, that is, fifty-one items out of 464). Reliability was calculated as follows: $r = a/(a+d)$, where a=number of cases of agreement, d=cases of disagreement. The overall reliability was 0.95, a percentage that was considered satisfactory.

Cluster analysis

Cluster analysis identifies relatively homogeneous groups of cases or variables based on selected characteristics. More specifically, a clustering method is a multivariate statistical procedure that starts with a data set containing information about a sample of entities (in this case a sample of variables) and attempts to organise them into homogenous groups (Aldenderfer and Blashfield 1984: 7) The procedure uses an algorithm that starts with each case or variable in a separate cluster and combines clusters until only one is left. For the analysis of the data set, an agglomerative hierarchical method was performed in order to identify clusters of variables. The method used was Ward's method using Squared Euclidean distance as a measure of dissimilarity. The clusters are depicted in the graph (7.1) in the shape of a tree called a dendrogram. The fact that the thematic variables grouped together through cluster analysis were the same as those identified through the qualitative analysis was a confirmation of the research methods.

DESCRIPTION OF INFORMANTS

The list in alphabetical order; all names have been changed.

Aggeliki is a 50-year-old high school teacher in a working class neighbourhood in Athens. She is married and lives with her husband and children.

Alexandros is in his early twenties and was an undergraduate student in London at the time of the interview. He comes from an upper middle class family and lives with his parents when in Greece.

Aliki is a final year high school student from a working class neighbourhood in Western Athens, preparing for her exams to enter university.

Andreas is in his mid thirties and works as a paramedic in the army. He lives with his parents in a working class neighbourhood in Athens.

Anna is a woman in her late twenties. Born in Cyprus, she came to Greece to study and pursue a career as a classical singer. She lives on her own in central Athens.

Ayşe is 53-years-old and works as a cleaner in one of the local government buildings in the centre of Athens. She is married and lives with her husband and children in Gazi.

Bahar is in her late fifties. She used to work as a domestic cleaner; in recent years she only works part-time. She lives in Gazi close to her daughter (Nazli) and Nuriye with whom she exchanges frequent visits.

Christos is an architect in his late twenties. At the time of the interview he had just finished his military service and started work in an architectural firm. He shared a flat with a friend in Athens.

Chryssa is in her fifties and was born in Cyprus. She has been living for most of her life in Athens apart from a period when she studied in London. She is a social worker and lives with her husband and two sons.

Dafne is a 17-year-old high school student from a working class neighbourhood in western Athens, preparing for the final year exams.

Dina was born in Cyprus and lives and works in Athens in a private company.

Elpida was born in Cyprus and is an undergraduate student at Athens University.

Eugenia is in her sixties and used to be a primary school teacher. She has now retired and lives with her husband, Ilias in a working class suburb in Western Athens.

Eva was born in Cyprus and is an undergraduate student at Athens University. She is actively involved in one of the Cypriot-student parties.

Faruk is Süleyman's 16-year-old son. He attends a technical school and is involved with sports.

Fotini is in her early thirties. A law school graduate, she is a junior partner in Tasos' and Michalis' firm. She lives on her own in central Athens.

Fotis is an 18-year-old high school student from a working class neighbourhood in western Athens, preparing for his exams to enter university.

Georgia is a housewife in her fifties. She lives with her husband in a working class neigbourhood in Athens.

Giota is a housewife in her late forties. She has two daughters who now live on their own. Giota lives with her husband in a flat in Athens close to Georgia, with whom she exchanges frequent visits.

Hamdi used to be the head of one of the clubs in Gazi. He is in his late forties and works in a shipyard. He lives with his wife and kids.

Haris is a high school teacher. He is in his forties and is married with two children.

Hasan is Umut's father. An unskilled worker, he was receiving a pension which was the only regular salary in the extended household. In 1974 he fought with the Greek army in Cyprus. He lives in Gazi.

Ilias is in his seventies. He had fought in the Civil War and was subsequently persecuted for being left wing. He spent a large part of his life in 'exile', in the rock islands of the Aegean, as a political prisoner. Later, he also worked in a petrol station, which he co-owned. He lives with his wife Eugenia in a working class suburb in western Athens.

Ioanna was born in Cyprus and has been living in Greece in the past thirty years. She is in her fifties and lives with her husband and children. She is involved in charity work.

Irini is a 17-year-old high school student from a working class neighbourhood in western Athens, preparing for the final year exams.

Ismail is in his late forties. At the time of the interview he was working in a construction site. He lives with his wife and children in Gazi.

Jenny was born in Cyprus, but has lived in Athens most of her life. She works in a research company and lives with her husband. She is in her late thirties.

Katerina is a medical assistant in an army hospital. She is in her early thirties and lives with her parents.

Lena is a high school teacher in her early thirties. She lives on her own in central Athens.

Levent is 17-years-old. He lives with his parents in Gazi and occasionally works in a garage.

Lia is in her early forties; originally born in Cyprus she has lived in Athens most of her life. She studied in London and now works in higher education and is also registered as a part-time PhD student. She is married to Yannos.

Marianna is in her fifties. She was born in Cyprus, but has lived most of her life in Athens. She studied in the US and was a college lecturer in Athens. She has been actively involved in promoting awareness of the Cyprus problem.

Marilena is a high school teacher. She is 45-years-old and lives with her husband and children.

Mehmet was finishing high school at the time of the interview and was preparing for his university exams. He lives in Gazi with his family.

Metin is 38-years-old, lives in Gazi with his wife. He is unemployed.

Michalis is a lawyer working in his father's firm. He is 36-years-old and lives on his own in central Athens.

Mumin is in his forties and lives in Gazi. He was been working in various jobs, with intermittent periods of unemployment. He used to be a sailor for ten years before he came to settle in Athens with his wife.

Murat is a man in his thirties. He is the only graduate in the Gazi neighbourhood. He has a degree in education and wants to work as a teacher, although during my fieldwork he was working in a small factory (*viotehnia*).

Myrto is in her late forties. She was born in Cyprus, but has been living in Athens for almost thirty years. She works in a company in Athens.

Nazim is in his fifties. At the time of the interview he was working on the construction site for the new Athens metro. He has lived in Athens for twenty years and before that he was an immigrant worker in Germany.

Nazli is Nuriye's daughter-in-law and Bahar's daughter.

Nicos was an undergraduate student in London at the time of the interview. He comes from an upper middle class family and lives with his parents when in Greece.

Nihat is in his twenties and works in a garage. He had to give up school after the compulsory nine years of education – despite the fact that he was a good student – in order to work and help his family out.

Nuriye is 55-years-old. She used to work as a domestic cleaner in the past, but at the time of the interview she did not work outside the home. She lives in Gazi with her husband and younger son. Her elder son lives with his wife next door and they all exchange visits frequently.

Orestis was born in Cyprus and is an undergraduate student at Athens University. Before starting university he completed his two year military service in Cyprus. He is 24 years old.

Orhan is in his twenties and works in a small factory in Athens. Born in Thrace, he has lived in Athens for most of his life. Educated in the Greek system, he had to leave school after the nine compulsory years in order to help out his family. He is married.

Rena is 60-years-old. She is a housewife, although she used to work as a seamstress in the past. She lives with her husband in a working class neighbourhood in Athens.

Sergios is in his mid-twenties and works in advertising. During the time of the interview he was completing his compulsory military service and still lived with his parents in central Athens.

Sevgi is in her early twenties and works in her husband's restaurant in Gazi.

Sophia is in her early twenties and was an undergraduate student in London at the time of the interview.

Spyros is in his forties and teaches in a high school in Athens. He is married with children.

Stavros was born in Cyprus. He lives in Athens and works in his own company. He lives with his partner.

Stelios is in his mid-twenties and was completing his military service at the time of the interview. Normally he works as a paramedic.

Süleyman works as a clerk in a bank and also operates a karate school, which was a hangout for a lot of the young men in Gazi. Many of the interviews took place there. In 2000, Süleyman had to close the school due to financial difficulties. He lives with his wife and kids in Gazi.

Tasos is in his late sixties and works as a lawyer in his own firm, together with his son. Although he is not as active as in the past in representing clients, he still goes to the office everyday. He lives with his wife in central Athens.

Tatiana is an 18-year-old high school student from a working class neighbourhood in western Athens. At the time of the interview she was preparing for her exams to enter university.

Thodoris is in his late thirties and works as a taxi driver. He lives in a working class neighbourhood in western Athens with his wife Sevasti and at the time of the interview they were expecting their first baby.

Umut is in his thirties, married to Baris and has one son. Umut, an unskilled worker, was often unemployed during fieldwork. He lives together with his wife, son and both of his parents in a one bedroom flat in Gazi.

Vassilis is a man in his forties. He runs his own business, which allows him to travel a lot and spend time in his holiday home in southern Greece. He is twice divorced, with three children and lives on his own in an Athens suburb. In 1974 he fought in Cyprus.

Yannis is a final-year high school student from a working class neighbourhood in western Athens, preparing for his exams to enter university

Yannos is married to Lia. He was born in Cyprus, in the northern part that is now Northern Cyprus. He studied in the US and Britain and now works at Athens University. In previous years, he had been involved in Greek-Cypriot organisations in Athens. At the time of the interview he and Lia had decided to stop watching television at home.

Yilmaz is in his twenties and works in a small factory in Athens. Born in Komotini, he came to Athens at the age of seven and was educated in a Greek school, which he left after he completed the nine compulsory years. He is married and lives with his wife in Gazi.

Yiorgos is an undergraduate student in his early twenties. He lives with his sister, who has been living permanently in Athens for more than a decade. They were both born in Cyprus.

Zoe is in her late twenties and works as a paramedic at an army hospital. She lives with her parents and brothers in Piraeus.

BIBLIOGRAPHY

Abu-Lughod, L (1995) 'The objects of soap opera: Egyptian television and the cultural politics of modernity', in Miller, D (ed), *Worlds Apart*, London: Routledge, pp 190–210

Abu-Lughod, L (1993) 'Finding a place for Islam: Egyptian television serials and the national interest', *Public Culture* vol 5(3), pp 493–513

Abu-Lughod, L (1991) 'Writing against culture', in Fox, R (ed), *Recapturing Anthropology*, Santa Fe, School of American Research Press, pp 137–61

Abu-Lughod, L (1989) 'Bedouins, cassettes and technologies of public culture' *Middle East Report*, vol 159(4), pp 7–11

AGB Hellas (2000) *TV Yearbook, 1999-2000*, Athens: AGB Hellas

AGB Hellas (1999) *TV Yearbook, 1998-99*, Athens: AGB Hellas

AGB Hellas (1998) *TV Yearbook, 1997-98*, Athens: AGB Hellas

Aggelopoulos, Y (1997) 'From the Greek as person, to the person as Greek', *The Greek Review of Political Science* [*Elliniki Epitheorisi Politikis Epistimis*], 9, pp 42–64 [in Greek]

Aksoy, A and Robins, K (2000) 'Thinking across spaces: transnational television from Turkey', *European Journal of Cultural Studies*, vol 3(3) pp 343–65

Aksoy, A and Robins, K (1997) 'Peripheral vision: cultural industries and cultural identity in Turkey', *Environment and Planning A*, 29 pp 1937–952

Aldenderfer, M and Blashfield R (1984) *Cluster Analysis*. Series: Quantitative Applications in the Social Sciences, Newbury Park, CA: Sage

Allen, T (1999) 'Perceiving contemporary wars', in Allen, T and Seaton, J (eds), *The Media of Conflict: war reporting and representations of ethnic violence*, London and New York: Zed Books, pp 11–42

Altheide, D (1987) 'Ethnographic content analysis' *Qualitative Sociology*, vol 10(1), pp 65–67

Anagnostou, D (1999) 'Oppositional and integrative ethnicities: regional political economy, Turkish Muslim mobilisation and identity transformation in Southeastern Europe', unpublished PhD dissertation, Cornell University, Ithaca: New York

Anderson, B (2001) 'Western nationalism and eastern nationalism: is there a difference that matters?', *New Left Review* II/vol 9 May–June 2001, pp 31–42

Anderson, B (1998) *The Spectre of Comparisons*, London: Verso

Anderson, B (1991 [1983]) *Imagined Communities*, London: Verso

Ang, I (1996) *Living-room Wars: rethinking audiences for a postmodern world*, London: Routledge

Ang, I (1989 [1985]) *Watching Dallas: soap opera and the melodramatic imagination*, London: Routledge

Anthias, F (2001) 'New hybridities, old concepts: the limits of culture' *Ethnic and Racial Studies*, vol 24(4), pp 619–41

Arendt, H (1968) *Men in Dark Times*, New York: Harcourt, Brace and World

Armstrong, J (1982) *Nations before Nationalism*, Chapel Hill: University of North Carolina Press

Askew, K and Wilk, R (eds) (2002) *The Anthropology of Media*, Oxford: Blackwell

Attalides, M (1979) *Cyprus: Nationalism and International Politics*, Edinburgh: Q Press

Avramopoulou, E and Karakatsanis, L (2002) 'Identity trajectories: from Western Thrace to Gazi', *Theseis Quarterly Review* 79, pp 127–61 [in Greek]

Barth, F (ed) (1969a) *Ethnic Groups and Boundaries: the social organisation of culture difference*, London: Allen and Unwin

Barth, F (1969b) 'Introduction', in Barth, F (ed), *Ethnic Groups and Boundaries: the social organisation of culture difference*, London: Allen and Unwin, pp 9–38

Barthes, R (1977) *Roland Barthes*, London: Macmillan

Baumann, G (1997) 'Dominant and demotic discourses of culture: their relevance to multi-ethnic alliances', in Werbner, P and Modood, T (eds), *Debating Cultural Hybridity*, London: Zed Books, pp 209–25

Baumann, G (1996) *Contesting Culture: discourses of identity in multi-ethnic London*, Cambridge: CUP

Bausinger, H (1984) 'Media, technology and daily life', *Media, Culture and Society*, vol 6(4), pp 343–51

Billig, M (1995) *Banal Nationalism*, London: Sage

Blumler, J and Katz, E (1974) *The Uses of Mass Communications: current perspectives on gratifications research*, Beverly Hills: Sage

Blumler, J, Katz, E and Gurevitch, M (1974) 'Utilisation of mass communications by the individual', in Blumler, J and Katz, E (eds), *The Uses of Mass Communications*, Beverly Hills: Sage, pp 249–68

Born, G (2004) *Uncertain Vision: Birt, Dyke and the reinvention of the BBC*, London: Secker & Warburg

Bourdieu, P, *et al* (1999 [1993]) *The Weight of the World: social suffering in contemporary society*, Cambridge: Polity Press

Bourdieu, P (1986 [1979]) *Distinction: A social critique of the judgement of taste*, London: Routledge

Bourdieu, P and Wacquant, L (1992) *Invitation to Reflexive Sociology*, Chicago: University of Chicago Press

Bovill, M and Livingstone, S (2001) 'Bedroom culture and the privatization of media use', in Livingstone, S and Bovill, M (eds), *Children and their Changing Media Environment: a European comparative study*, Mahwah, NJ: Laurence Erlbaum, pp 179–200

Breuilly, J (1996) 'Approaches to nationalism', in Balakrishnan, G (ed), *Mapping the Nation*, London: Verso, pp 146–74

Brunsdon, C (1996) 'Satellite dishes and the landscapes of taste', in Hay, J, Grossberg, L and Wartella, E (eds), *The Audience and its Landscape*, Boulder, CO: Westview Press, pp 343–57

Calhoun, C (1997) *Nationalism*, Buckingham: Open UP

Calhoun, C (ed) (1992) *Habermas and the Public Sphere*, Cambridge, Mass: MIT Press

Carey, J (1989) *Communication as Culture: essays on media and society*, New York: Routledge

Carrithers, M (1992) *Why Humans Have Cultures: explaining anthropology and social diversity*, Oxford: OUP

Clifford, J and Marcus, G (eds) (1986) *Writing Culture: the poetics and politics of ethnography*, Berkeley: University of California Press

Clogg, R (1992) *A Concise History of Modern Greece*, Cambridge: CUP

Comaroff, J (1996) 'Ethnicity, nationalism and the politics of difference in an age of revolution', in Wilmsen, E and McAllister, P (eds), *The Politics of Difference: ethnic premises in a world of power*, Chicago: University of Chicago Press, pp 162–83

Comaroff, J and Stern, P (eds) (1995) *Perspectives on Nationalism and War*, Amsterdam: Gordon and Breach

Corner, J (1996) 'Reappraising reception: aims, concepts and methods', in Curran, J and Gurevitch, M (eds), *Mass Media and Society* (2nd edn), London: Arnold, pp 280–304

Corner, J (1995) *Television Form and Public Address*, London: Arnold

Couldry, N (2000a) *Inside Culture: re-imagining the method of cultural studies*, London: Sage

Couldry, N (2000b) *The Place of Media Power: pilgrims and witnesses in a media age*, London: Routledge

Curran, J (1990) 'The new revisionism in mass communication research', *European Journal of Communication* vol 5(2/3), pp 135–64

Danforth, L (1995) *The Macedonian Conflict: ethnic nationalism in a transnational world*, Princeton: Princeton University Press

Dayan, D and Katz, E (1992) *Media Events: the live broadcasting of history*, Cambridge, Mass: Harvard University Press

Demertzis, N and Armenakis, A (1998) 'National identity and national issues in the media: the case of the intermediate agreement between Greece and FYROM in the Press', *Vima ton Koinonikon Epistimon*, vol 6 no 23, pp 115–38 [in Greek]

Demetriou, Olga (2002) 'Divisive Visions: a study of minority identities among Turkish speakers in Komotini, Northern Greece', unpublished PhD thesis, University of London

Denzin, N (1989) *The Research Act* (3rd edn), Englewood Cliffs, NJ: Prentice Hall

Deutsch, K (1953[1966]) *Nationalism and Social Communication: an inquiry into the foundations of nationalism*, Cambridge, Mass: MIT Press

Divani, L (1995) *Greece and Minorities*, Athens: Nepheli [in Greek]

Domínguez, V (1989) *People as Subject, People as Object: selfhood and peoplehood in contemporary Israel*, Madison, Wis: University of Wisconsin Press

Douglas, M (1966) *Purity and Danger: an analysis of concepts of pollution and taboo*, London: Routledge and Kegan Paul

Eagleton, T (1990) 'Irony and commitment', in Eagleton, T, Jameson, F and Said, E *Nationalism, Colonialism and Literature*, Minneapolis: University of Minnesota, pp 23–39

Eco, U (1985) 'Innovation and repetition: between modern and postmodern aesthetics', *Daedalus* 774, pp 161–84

Eco, U (1979) *The Role of the Reader*, Bloomington: University of Indiana Press

Eisenstein, E (1979) *The Printing Press as an Agent of Change: communications and cultural transformations in early-modern Europe*, Cambridge: CUP

Eley, G and Suny, R (1996) 'Introduction: from the moment of social history to the work of cultural representation', in Eley, G and Suny, R (eds), *Becoming National*, New York: OUP, pp 3–37

Ellis, J (1982) *Visible Fictions*, London: Routledge & Kegan Paul

Eriksen, T H (1993) *Ethnicity and Nationalism: anthropological perspectives*, London: Pluto Press

Eurobarometer (2000) Eurobarometer: Public opinion in the European Union, Report number 53, Brussels: DG10/European Commission

Eurobarometer (2003) Flash Eurobarometer: Internet and the public at large. Brussels: DG10/ European Commission

Feuer, J (1983) 'The concept of live television: ontology as ideology', in Kaplan, E (ed), *Regarding Television*, Los Angeles: The American Film Institute

Fiske, J (1987) *Television Culture*, London: Routledge

Fiske, J and Hartley, J (1989 [1978]) *Reading Television*, London: Routledge

Fraser, N (1992) 'Rethinking the public sphere', in Calhoun, C (ed), *Habermas and the Public Sphere*, Cambridge, Mass: MIT Press, pp 109–42

Gamson, W (1992) *Talking Politics*, Cambridge: CUP

Gans, H (1979) *Deciding What's News*, New York: Vintage Books

Gauntlett, D and Hill, A (1999) *TV Living: television culture and everyday life*, London: Routledge

Geertz, C (1973) *The Interpretation of Cultures: selected essays*, New York: Basic Books

Gellner, E (1996) 'Reply to critics', in Hall, J and Jarvie, I (eds), *The Social Philosophy of Ernest Gellner*, Amsterdam: Rodopi, pp 625–87

Gellner, E (1983) *Nations and Nationalism*, Oxford: Blackwell

Giakoumopoulos, C (1997) 'The minority phenomenon in Greece and the European Convention on human rights', in Tsitselikis, C and Christopoulos, D (eds) *The Minority Phenomenon in Greece*, Athens: Kritiki, pp 23–72 [in Greek]

Giddens, A (1991) *Modernity and Self-Identity: self and society in the late modern age*, Cambridge: Polity Press

Giddens, A (1985) *Nation-State and Violence*, Cambridge: Polity Press

Giddens, A (1984) *The Constitution of Society: outline of the theory of structuration*, Cambridge: Polity Press

Giddens, A (1979) *Central Problems in Sociological Theory*, London: Hutchinson.

Gilbert, N and Mulkay, M (1984) *Opening Pandora's Box: a sociological analysis of scientists discourse*, Cambridge: CUP

Gillespie, M (1995) *Television, Ethnicity and Cultural Change*, London: Routledge

Ginsburg, F, Abu-Lughod, L and Larkin, B (2002) *Media Worlds: anthropology on new terrain*, Berkeley: University of California Press

Glazer, B and Strauss, A (1967) *The Discovery of Grounded Theory*, Chicago: Aldine

Golding, P and Murdock, G (1996) 'Culture, communications and political economy', in Curran, J and Gurevitch, M (eds), *Mass Media and Society* (2nd edn), London: Arnold, pp 11–30

Goldmann, K, Hannerz, U and Westin, C (2000) 'Introduction', in Goldmann, K *et al* (eds), *Nationalism and Internationalism in the Post-Cold War Era*, London: Routledge, pp 1–21

Gray, A (1992) *Video Playtime: the gendering of a leisure technology*, London: Routledge

Gunter, B and Svennevig, M (1987) *Behind and in Front of the Screen*, London: John Libbey

Gupta, A and Ferguson, J (1992) 'Beyond "culture": space, identity and the politics of difference', *Cultural Anthropology*, vol 7(1), pp 6–23

Habermas, J (1989 [1962]) *The Structural Transformation of the Public Sphere*, Cambridge: Polity Press

Hall, J (ed) (1998) *The State of the Nation: Ernest Gellner and the theory of nationalism*, Cambridge: CUP

Hall, S (2000) 'The multicultural question', in Barnor, B (ed), *Unsettled Multiculturalisms: Diasporas, Entanglement, Transruptions*, London, New York: Zed Books, pp 219–255

Hall, S (1996) 'Introduction: who needs identity?', in Hall, S and du Gay, P (eds), *Questions of Cultural Identity*, London: Sage, pp 1–17

Hall, S (1994) 'Reflections upon the encoding-decoding model: an interview with Stuart Hall', in Lewis, J and Cruz, J (eds), *Viewing, Reading, Listening: audiences and cultural interpretation*, Boulder, CO: Westview Press, pp 253–74

Hall, S (1992) 'The question of cultural identity', in Hall, S *et al*, *Modernity and its Futures*, Cambridge: Polity Press, pp 274–325

Hall, S (1990) 'Cultural identity and diaspora', in Rutherford, J (ed), *Identity: community, culture, difference*, London: Lawrence and Wishart, pp 222–37

Hall, S (1980) 'Encoding/Decoding', in Hall, S *et al* (eds), *Culture, Media, Language*, London: Hutchinson, pp 128–38

Hannerz, U (1992) *Cultural Complexity: studies in the social organisation of meaning*, New York: Columbia University Press

Hargreaves, A and Mahjoub, D (1997) 'Satellite television viewing among ethnic minorities in France', *European Journal of Communication* vol 12(4), pp 459–77

Harindranath, R (2000) 'Ethnicity, national culture(s) and the interpretation of television', in Cottle, S (ed), *Ethnic Minorities and the Media*, Buckingham: Open UP, pp 149–63

Hastrup, K (1995) *A Passage to Anthropology: between experience and theory*, London: Routledge

Hechter, M (1975) *Internal Colonialism: the Celtic fringe in British national development, 1536–1966*, London: Routledge and Kegan Paul

Held, D (1991) 'Between state and civil society: citizenship', in Andrews, G (ed) *Citizenship*, London: Lawrence & Wishart, pp 19–25

Heraclides, A (1997) 'Greek minority policy: anachronistic attitude and its causes', *Syghrona Themata*, II: 63, April–June

Herzfeld, M (1996) *Cultural Intimacy: social poetics in the nation-state*, London: Routledge

Herzfeld, M (1991) *A Place in History: social and monumental time in a Cretan town*, Princeton: Princeton University Press

Hirschon, R (1989) *Heirs of the Greek Catastrophe: the social life of Asia Minor refugees in Piraeus*, Oxford: Clarendon Press

Hobsbawm, E (1992 [1990]) *Nations and Nationalism since 1780: programme, myth, reality* (2nd edn), Cambridge: CUP

Hobsbawm, E and Ranger, T (eds) (1983) *The Invention of Tradition*, Cambridge: CUP

Horkheimer, M and Adorno, T (1979) *Dialectic of Enlightenment*, London: Verso

Human Rights Watch Report (1998) *Greece: The Turks of Western Thrace*, New York and London: Human Rights Watch

Huntington, S (1996) *The Clash of Civilisations and the Remaking of the World Order*, New York: Simon and Schuster

Ignatieff, M (2000) *Virtual War: Kosovo and beyond*, New York: Metropolitan Books

Innis, H (1951) *The Bias of Communication*, Oxford: OUP

Iser, W (1978) *The Act of Reading: a theory of aesthetic response*, Baltimore, Md.: Johns Hopkins University Press

Jensen, KB (1998) 'Denmark', in Jensen, KB (ed), *News of the World: world cultures look at television news*, London: Routledge, pp 39–60

Kaplan, R (1994) *Balkan Ghosts: a journey through history*, London: Papermac

Karakasidou, A (1997) *Fields of Wheat, Hills of Blood: passages to nationhood in Greek Macedonia 1870-1990*, Chicago: University of Chicago Press

Karakasidou, A (1995) 'Vestiges of the Ottoman past: Muslims under siege in Greek Thrace', *Cultural Survival Quarterly*, vol 19 (2), pp 71–75

Katz, E (1992) 'The end of journalism: news on watching the war', *Journal of Communication*, vol 42(3), pp 5–13

Katz, E (1980) 'On conceptualizing media effects', *Studies in Communications*, vol 1, pp 119–41

Kedourie, E (1960) *Nationalism*, London: Hutchinson

Kitromilides, P (1993) 'Intentions and questions in the analysis of nationalism: comment on Anthony Smith's paper' *Istor* (6), pp 13–17 [in Greek]

Kitromilides, P (1990) 'Imagined communities and the origins of the national question in the Balkans', in Blinkhorn, M and Veremis, T (eds), *Nationalism and Nationality*, Athens: Sage-Eliamep, pp 23–66

Kitromilides, P (1977) 'From coexistence to confrontation: the dynamics of ethnic conflict in Cyprus', in Attalides, M (ed), *Cyprus Reviewed*, Nicosia: The Jus Cypri Association, pp 35–70

Kitzinger, J (1993) 'Understanding AIDS: researching audience perceptions of the acquired immune deficiency syndrome', in Eldridge, J (ed), *Getting the Message: news, truth and power*, London: Routledge, pp 271–304

Kitzinger, J and Barbour R (1999) 'Introduction: The challenge and promise of focus groups', in Kitzinger, J and Barbour, R (eds), *Developing Focus Group Research: politics, theory, practice*, London: Thousand Oaks: California: Sage, pp 1–20

Kuper, A (1999) *Culture: the anthropologist's account*, Cambridge, Mass: Harvard University Press

Laitin, D (1998) *Identity in Formation: the Russian-speaking populations in the Near Abroad*, Ithaca: Cornell University Press

Lazarsfeld, P and Merton, P (1948) 'Mass communication, popular taste and organised social action', in Bryson, L (ed), *The Communication of Ideas*, New York: Harper

Lekkas, P (1992) *Nationalist ideology: five working hypotheses for historical sociology*, Athens : EMNE Mnimon [in Greek]

Lévi-Strauss, C and Pouillon, J (1961) *Race et Histoire*, Paris: Editions Gonthier

Lewis, J (1994) 'The meaning of things: audiences, ambiguity and power', in Lewis, J and Cruz, J (eds), *Viewing, Reading, Listening: Audiences and Cultural Interpretation*, Boulder, CO: Westview Press, pp 19–32

Lewis, J (1991) *The Ideological Octopus: an exploration of television and its audience*, London: Routledge

Liebes, T (1998) 'Television's disaster marathons: a danger for democratic processes?', in Curran, J and Liebes, T (eds), *Media Ritual and Identity*, London: Routledge, pp 71–84

Liebes, T (1997) *Reporting the Israeli-Arab conflict: how hegemony works*, London: Routledge

Liebes, T (1996) 'Notes on the struggle to define involvement in television viewing', in Hay, J, Grossberg, L and Wartella, E (eds), *The Audience and its Landscape*, Boulder, CO: Westview Press, pp 177–86

Liebes, T and Katz, E (1993 [1990]) *The Export of Meaning: cross-cultural readings of Dallas*, New York: OUP

Liebes, T and Ribak, R (1991) 'A mother's battle against TV news: a case study of political socialisation', *Discourse and Society*, vol 2(2), pp 203–22

Lindlof, T (1995) *Qualitative Communication Methods*, Thousand Oaks, CA: Sage

Livingstone, S (2003) 'Debating Media Literacy', *Media@LSE Electronic Papers*, London: LSE

Livingstone, S (1998a) 'Audience research at the crossroads: the "implied audience" in media and cultural theory', *European Journal of Cultural Studies*, vol 1(2), pp 193–217

Livingstone, S (1998b [1990]) *Making Sense of Television: the psychology of audience interpretation* (2nd edn), London: Routledge

Livingstone, S (1998c) 'Relationships between media and audiences: prospects for audience reception studies', in Curran, J and Liebes, T (eds), *Media Ritual and Identity*, London: Routledge, pp 237–55

Livingstone, S (1991) 'Audience reception: the role of the viewer in retelling romantic drama', in Curran, J and Gurevitch, M (eds), *Mass Media and Society*, London: Arnold, pp 285–306

Livingstone, S and Lunt, P (1994) *Talk on Television*, London: Routledge

Livingstone, S, Allen, J and Reiner, R (2001) 'Audiences for crime media 1946–1991: a historical approach to reception studies', *The Communication Review*, vol 4(2), pp 165–92

Llobera, J (1994) *The God of Modernity: The development of nationalism in Europe*, Oxford: Berg

Loizos, P (1992) 'User friendly ethnography?', in Pina-Cabral, J and Campbell, J (eds), *Europe Observed*, Oxford: Macmillan, pp 167–87

Loizos, P (1976) 'Notes on future anthropological research in Cyprus, in Dimen, M and Friedl, E (eds), *Regional Variation in Modern Greece and Cyprus: Towards a Perspective on the Ethnography of Greece*, Annals of the New York Academy of Sciences, 268, New York: New York Academy of Sciences

Lull, J (1990) *Inside Family Viewing: ethnographic research on television's audience*, London: Routledge

Lull, J (ed) (1988) *World Families Watch Television*, Newbury Park, CA: Sage

Lunt, P and Livingstone, S (1996) 'Rethinking the focus group in media and communication research', *Journal of Communication* 46(2), pp 79–98

Lunt, P and Stenner, P (2005) 'The Jerry Springer Show as an Emotional Public Sphere', *Media, Culture and Society*, vol 27(1), pp 59–81

Lyons, J (1977) *Semantics*, vol 2, Cambridge: CUP

MacCabe, C (1981) 'Realism and the cinema: notes on some Brechtian themes', in Bennet, T *et al* (eds), *Popular Television and Film*, London: BFI, pp 216–35

MacKenzie, D and Wajcman, J (1999) 'Introductory essay', in MacKenzie, D and Wajcman, J (eds), *The Social Shaping of Technology* (2nd edn), Buckingham: Open UP

Malkki, L (1995) *Purity and Exile: violence, memory and national cosmology among Hutu refugees in Tanzania*, Chicago: University of Chicago Press

Mankekar, P (1999) *Screening Culture, Viewing Politics: an ethnography of television, womanhood, and nation in Postcolonial India*, Durham and London: Duke University Press

Mann, M (1993) *The Sources of Social Power, vol 2. The Rise of Classes and Nation States*, Cambridge: CUP

Marcus, GE (ed) (1999) *Paranoia within Reason: a casebook on conspiracy as explanation*, Chicago: University of Chicago Press

Marcus, George (1995) 'Ethnography in/of the world system: the emergence of multi-sited ethnography *Annual Review of Anthropology* 24, pp 95–117

Marcus, GE and Fischer, M (1986) *Anthropology as Cultural Critique: an experimental moment in the human sciences*, Chicago: University of Chicago Press

Martin-Barbero, J (1993 [1987]) *Communication, Culture and Hegemony: from the media to mediations*, translated by Elizabeth Fox and Robert A White, London: Sage

Martin-Barbero, J (1988) 'Communication from culture: the crisis of the nations and the emergence of the popular', *Media, Culture and Society*, vol 10, pp 447–65

Mavratsas, C (2001) 'Greek Cypriot identity and conflicting interpretations of the Cyprus Problem', in Keridis, D and Triandafyllou, D (eds), *Greek Turkish Relations in the era of Globalisation*, Dulles, VA: Brassey's, pp 151–79

Mavratsas, C (1998) *Facets of Greek nationalism in Cyprus: ideological contest and the social construction of Greek Cypriot identity 1974-1996*, Athens: Katarti [in Greek]

McGrew, A (1992) *A Global Society?*, in Hall, S, Held, D and McGrew, T (eds), *Modernity and its Futures*, Cambridge: CUP, pp 61–116

McLuhan, M 1987 [1964] *Understanding Media*, London: Routledge and Kegan Paul

Mead, M (1953) 'National character', in Kroeber, AL (ed), *Anthropology Today*, Chicago: University of Chicago Press, pp 642–67

Merton, R, Fiske, M and Kendall, P (1990 [1956]) *The Focused Interview: a manual of problems and procedures*, New York: The Free Press

Meyrowitz, J (1985) *No Sense of Place*, Oxford: OUP

Milikowski, M (2000) 'Exploring a model of de-ethnicization: the case of Turkish television in the Netherlands', *European Journal of Communication*, vol 15(4), pp 443–68

Miller, D (1998) *Material Cultures: why some things matter*, London: UCL Press

Miller, D (1992) 'The Young and the Restless in Trinidad', in Silverstone, R and Hirsch, E (ed), *Consuming Technologies*, London: Routledge, pp 163–82

Miller, D (1988) *Material Culture and Mass Consumption*, Oxford: Blackwell

Miller, D and Slater, D (2000) *The Internet: an ethnographic approach*, Oxford: Berg

Minority Rights Group (1992) *Minorities in Greece and the Political World*, Athens: MRG [in Greek]

Minority Rights Group (MRG) (1997) *Cyprus: in search of peace*, London: MRG

Morley, D (2000) *Home Territories: media, mobility, identity*, London: Routledge

Morley, D (1999) 'Finding about the world from television news: some difficulties', in Gripsrud, J (ed), *Television and Common Knowledge*, London: Routledge, pp 136–58

Morley, D (1996) 'The geography of television: ethnography, communications and community', in Hay, J, Grossberg, L and Wartella, E (eds), *The Audience and its Landscape*, Boulder, CO: Westview Press, pp 317–42

Morley, D (1995) 'Television: not so much a visual medium, more a visible object', in Jenks, C (ed), *Visual Culture*, London: Routledge

Morley, D (1992) *Television, Audiences and Cultural Studies*, London: Routledge

Morley, D (1986) *Family Television*, London: Comedia

Morley, D (1980) *The Nationwide audience*, London: BFI

Morley, D and Brunsdon, C (1999) *The Nationwide Television Studies*, London: Routledge

Morley, D and Robins, K (1995) *Spaces of Identity: global media, electronic landscapes and cultural boundaries*, London: Routledge

Morley, D and Silverstone, R (1991) 'Communication and context', in Jankowski, N and Jensen, K B (eds), *A Handbook of Qualitative Methodologies for Mass Communication Research*, London: Routledge, pp 149–62

Mosco, V (1996) *The Political Economy of Communication: rethinking and renewal*, London: Sage

Moscovici, S (1984) 'The phenomenon of social representations', in Farr, R and Moscovici, S (eds), *Social Representations*, Cambridge: CUP, pp 3–69

Mouzelis, N (1998) 'Ernest Gellner's theory of nationalism: some definitional and methodological problems', in Hall, J (ed), *The State of the Nation: Ernest Gellner and the theory of nationalism*, Cambridge: CUP, pp 158–65

Mouzelis, N (1994) *Nationalism in Late Development*, Athens: Themelio [in Greek]

Moynihan, D (1993) *Pandaemonium: ethnicity in international politics*, Oxford and New York: OUP

Murdock, G (1989a) 'Critical inquiry and audience activity', in Dervin, B *et al* (eds), *Rethinking Communication*, vol 2, Newbury Park, CA: Sage, pp 226–49

Murdock, G (1989b) 'Cultural studies: missing links' *Critical Studies in Mass Communication*, vol 6(4), pp 436–40

Neuman, R, Just, M and Crigler, A (1992) *Common knowledge: news and the construction of political meaning*, Chicago and London: University of Chicago Press

Neuman, R (1982) 'Television and American culture', *Public Opinion Quarterly* 46: 471–87

Nightingale, V (1993) 'What's ethnographic about ethnographic audience research?', in Turner, G (ed), *Nation, Culture, Text: Australian cultural and media studies*, London: Routledge, pp 164–77

Nohrstedt, S *et al* (2000) 'From the Persian Gulf to Kosovo – war, journalism and propaganda', *European Journal of Communication*, vol 15(3), pp 383–404

Ogan, C (2001) *Communication and Identity in the Diaspora: Turkish migrants and their use of media*, Lanham, Maryland: Lexington Books

Ohnuki-Tierney, E (1984) 'Native anthropologists' *American Ethnologist*, vol 11(3), 584–86

O'Leary, B (1998) 'Ernest Gellner's diagnoses of nationalism: a critical overview or, what is living and what is dead in Ernest Gellner's philosophy of nationalism?', in Hall, J (ed) *The State of the Nation: Ernest Gellner and the theory of nationalism*, Cambridge: CUP, pp 40–88

O'Leary, B (1996) 'On the nature of nationalism: an appraisal of Ernest Gellner's writings on nationalism', in Hall, J and Jarvie, I (eds), *The Social Philosophy of Ernest Gellner*, Amsterdam: Rodopi, pp 71–112

Öncü, A (2000) 'The banal and the subversive: politics of language on Turkish television', *European Journal of Cultural Studies*, vol 3(3), pp 296–318

Ong, W (1967) *The Presence of the Word*, New Haven: Yale University Press

Ozkirimli, U (2000) *Theories of Nationalism: A critical introduction*, London: Macmillan

Panteli, S (1984) *A New History of Cyprus*, London and the Hague: East-West Publications

Papadakis, Y (1998) 'Greek Cypriot narratives of history and collective identity: nationalism as a contested process', *American Ethnologist* 25 (2), pp 149–65

Papathanassopoulos, S (1999) 'The effects of media commercialisation on journalism and politics in Greece' *The Communication Review* vol 3(4), pp 379–402

Papathanassopoulos, S (1990) 'Broadcasting, politics and the state in Socialist Greece' *Media, Culture and Society*, vol 12, pp 387–97

Philo, G (1990) *Seeing and Believing: the influence of television*, London: Routledge

Pinney, C and Dwyer, R eds (2001) *Pleasure and the nation: the history, politics, and consumption of public culture in India*, New York: OUP

Polyviou, P (1980) *Cyprus: conflict and negotiation 1960–1980*, London: Duckworth

Potter, J and Wetherell, M (1987) *Discourse and Social Psychology: beyond attitudes and behaviour*, London: Sage

Poster, M (1995) *The Second Media Age*, Cambridge: Polity Press

Radway, J (1988) 'Reception study', *Cultural Studies*, vol 2(3), pp 359–76

Robins, K (2001) 'Becoming anybody: thinking against the nation and through the city', *City* vol 5(1), pp 77–90

Robins, K (2000) 'Introduction: Turkish (television) culture is ordinary', *European Journal of Cultural Studies*, vol 3(3), pp 291–95

Robins, K and Aksoy, A (2001) 'From spaces of identity to mental spaces: lessons from Turkish-Cypriot cultural experience in Britain', *Journal of Ethnic and Migration Studies*, vol 27(4), pp 685–711

Robins, K and Webster, F (1999) *Times of the Technoculture: information, communication, and the technological order*, London: Routledge

Rozakis, C (1988) 'The international legal status of the Aegean Sea and the Greek Turkish crisis: bilateral and international issues', in Alexandris, A *et al* (eds), *Greek-Turkish Relations 1923-1987*, Athens: Gnossi, pp 269–492 [in Greek]

Said, E (1993) *Culture and Imperialism*, London: Chatto & Windus

Scannell, P (1996) *Radio, Television and Modern Life: a phenomenological approach*, Oxford: Blackwell

Scannell, P (1989) 'Public service broadcasting and modern public life', *Media, Culture and Society*, vol 11, pp 135–66

Scannell, P and Cardiff, D (1991) *A Social History of Broadcasting, vol 1, 1922–1939: serving the nation*, Oxford: Basil Blackwell

Schlesinger, P (2000a) 'The nation and communicative space', in Tumber, H (ed), *Media Power, Professionals and Politics*, London: Routledge, pp 99–115

Schlesinger, P (2000b) 'The sociological scope of "national cinema"', in Hjort, M and MacKenzie, S (eds), *Cinema and Nation*, London: Routledge, pp 19–31

Schlesinger, P (1987) 'On national identity: some conceptions and misconceptions criticised', *Social Science Information* 26(2), pp 219–64

Schudson, M (2000) 'The sociology of news production revisited (again)', in Curran, J and Gurevitch, M (eds), *Mass Media and Society* (3rd edn), London: Edward Arnold, pp 175–200

Seaton, J (1999) 'The new ethnic wars and the media', in Allen, T and Seaton, J (eds), *The Media of Conflict: war reporting and representations of ethnic violence*, London and New York: Zed Books, pp 43–63

Siguan, M (1990) *Linguistic Minorities in the European Economic Community: Spain, Portugal, Greece*, Luxembourg: Office for Official publications of the European Communities

Silverstone, R (in press) 'Mediation and communication', in Calhoun, C, Rojek, C and Turner, B (eds), *International Handbook of Sociology*, London: Sage

Silverstone, R (1999) *Why Study the Media?*, London: Sage

Silverstone R (1996) 'From audiences to consumers: the household and the consumption of communication and information technologies', in Hay, J, Grossberg, L and Wartella, E (eds), *The Audience and its Landscape*, Boulder, CO: Westview Press, pp 281–96

Silverstone, R (1994) *Television and Everyday Life*, London: Routledge

Silverstone, R (1989) 'Television and everyday life: towards an anthropology of the television audience', in Ferguson, M (ed), *Public Communication: the new imperatives: future directions for media research*, London: Sage, pp 173–89

Silverstone, R (1988) 'Television, myth and culture', in Carey, J (ed), *Media, Myths and Narratives*, Newbury Park, CA: Sage, pp 20–47

Silverstone, R and Hirsch, E (eds) (1992) *Consuming Technologies: media and information in domestic spaces*, London: Routledge

Skopetea, E (1988) *The Small Kingdom and the Great Idea*, Athens: Polytypo [in Greek]

Smith, AD (1999) *Myths and Memories of the Nation*, New York: OUP

Smith, AD (1998) *Nationalism and Modernism*, London: Routledge

Smith, AD (1995) *Nations and Nationalism in a Global Era*, Cambridge: Polity Press

Smith, AD (1993) 'Nationalism and national conflicts', *Istor*, vol 6, pp 6–11 [in Greek]

Smith, AD (1991) *National Identity*, London: Penguin

Smith, AD (1986) *The Ethnic Origins of Nations*, Oxford: Basil Blackwell

Soysal, Y (1994) *Limits of Citizenship: Migrants and Postnational Membership in Europe*, Chicago: University of Chicago Press

Sreberny, A (2002) 'Collectivity and connectivity: diaspora and mediated identities', in Tufte, T and Stald, G (eds) *Global Encounters: Media and Cultural Transformation*, Luton: University of Luton Press

Sreberny, A (2000a) 'The global and the local in international communications', in Curran, J and Gurevitch, M (eds), *Mass Media and Society* (3rd edn), London: Arnold, pp 93–119

Sreberny, A (2000b) 'Media and diasporic consciousness: an exploration among Iranians in London', in Cottle, S (ed), *Ethnic Minorities and the Media*, Buckingham: Open UP, pp 179–96

Sreberny-Mohammadi, A and Mohammadi, A (1994) *Small Media, Big Revolution: communication, culture and the Iranian revolution*, Minneapolis: University of Minnesota Press

Strathern, M (1987) 'The limits of auto-anthropology', in Jackson, A (ed), *Anthropology at Home*, London: Tavistock, pp 16–37

Strauss, A (1987) *Qualitative Analysis for Social Scientists*, Cambridge: CUP

Sutton, D (1998) *Memories Cast in Stone: the relevance of the past in everyday life*, Oxford: Berg

Taylor, C (1994) 'The politics of recognition', in Taylor, C and Gutmann, A (eds), *Multiculturalism: examining the politics of recognition*, Princeton, NJ: Princeton University Press, pp 25–74

Thompson, JB (1995) *The Media and Modernity: a social theory of the media*, Cambridge: Polity Press

Thussu, D K (2000) 'Legitimizing "humanitarian intervention"? CNN, NATO and the Kosovo crisis', *European Journal of Communication*, vol 15(3), pp 345–61

Tomlinson, J (1999) *Globalization and Culture*, Chicago: University of Chicago Press

Tomlinson, J (1991) *Cultural Imperialism: a critical introduction*, London: Pinter Publishers

Troumbeta, S (2001) *Constructing Identities among the Muslims of Thrace. The cases of the Pomaks and the Rom*, Athens: Kritiki [in Greek]

Tsagarousianou, R (1997) 'Mass communication and nationalism: the politics of belonging and exclusion in contemporary Greece', *Res Publica*, vol XXXIX, pp 271–79

Tsaliki, L (1997) The role of Greek television in the construction of national identity since broadcasting deregulation, unpublished PhD thesis, University of Sussex

Tsaliki, L (1995) 'Media and the construction of an imagined community: the role of media events on Greek television', *European Journal of Communication*, vol 10(3), pp 345–70

Tsoukalas, K (1977) *Dependence and Reproduction: the social role of the educational mechanisms in Greece (1839–1922)*, Athens: Themelio [in Greek]

Turkle, S (1996) *Life on the Screen: identity in the age of the Internet*, London: Weidenfeld and Nicolson

Turner, V (1967) *The Forest of Symbols: aspects of Ndembu ritual*, Ithaca: Cornell University Press

van Boeschoten, R (2000) 'When difference matters: sociopolitical dimensions of ethnicity in the district of Florina', in Cowan, J (ed), *Macedonia: The politics of identity and difference*, London: Pluto Press

van den Berghe, P (1981) *The Ethnic Phenomenon*, New York: Elsevier

van Dijk, T (1991) *Racism and the Press*, London and New York: Routledge

van Gennep, A (1960) *The Rites of Passage*, London: Routledge and Kegan Paul.

Verdery, K (1994) 'Ethnicity, nationalism and state-making', in Vermeulen, H and Govers, C (eds), *The Anthropology of Ethnicity: beyond ethnic groups and boundaries*, Amsterdam: Het Spinhuis, pp 31–58

Waisbord, S (1998) 'When the cart of media is before the horse of identity: a critique of technology-centred views on globalisation', *Communication Research*, vol 25(4), pp 377–98

Wallman, S (1979) *Ethnicity at Work*, London: Macmillan

Werbner, P (1997) 'Essentialising essentialism, essentialising silence: ambivalence and multiplicity in the constructions of racism and ethnicity', in Werbner, P and Modood, T (eds), *Debating Cultural Hybridity*, London: Zed Books, pp 226–54

Williams, R (1977) *Marxism and Literature*, Oxford: OUP

Wolf, E (1982) *Europe and the People without History*, Berkeley: University of California Press

INDEX